The Civil Service since 1

Making Contemporary Britain Series

General Editor: Anthony Seldon
Consultant Editor: Peter Hennessy

Published

Northern Ireland since 1968
Paul Arthur and Keith Jeffrey

The Prime Minister since 1945
James Barber

British General Elections since 1945
David Butler

The British Economy since 1945
Alec Cairncross

Britain and the Suez Crisis
David Carlton

The End of the British Empire
John Darwin

Religion in Britain since 1945
Grace Davie

British Defence since 1945
Michael Dockrill

British Politics since 1945
Peter Dorey

Britain and the Falklands War*
Lawrence Freedman

Britain and European Integration
since 1945
Stephen George

British Social Policy since 1945
Howard Glennerster

Judicial Politics since 1920:
A Chronicle
John Griffith

Consensus Politics from Attlee to
Major
Dennis Kavanagh and Peter Morris

The Politics of Immigration
Zig Layton-Henry

Women in Britain since 1945
Jane Lewis

Britain and the Korean War*
Callum Macdonald

Culture in Britain since 1945
Arthur Marwick

Crime and Criminal Justice since 1945
Terence Morris

The British Press and Broadcasting
since 1945
Colin Seymour-Ure

Third Party Politics since 1945
John Stevenson

The Trade Union Question in British
Politics
Robert Taylor

The Civil Service since 1945
Kevin Theakston

British Science and Politics since
1945
Thomas Wilkie

British Public Opinion
Robert M. Worcester

Forthcoming

British Industry since 1945
Margaret Ackrill

Foreign Policy since 1945
Anthony Adamthwaite

The Conservative Party since 1945
John Barnes

The British Monarchy
Robert Blackburn

Town Planning in Britain since 1900
Gordon Cherry

Electoral Change since 1945
Ivor Crewe and Pippa Norris

Sport in Britain since 1945
Richard Holt and Tony Mason

Class and Inequality in Britain
Paul Keating

Parliament since 1945
Philip Norton

British Youth Cultures
William Osgerby

The Labour Party since 1945
Eric Shaw

Terrorism since 1945
Paul Wilkinson

Local Government since 1945
Ken Young and Nirmala Rao

*Indicates title now out of print.

The series *Making Contemporary Britain* is essential reading for students, as well as providing masterly overviews for the general reader. Each book in the series puts the central themes and problems of the specific topic into clear focus. The studies are written by leading authorities in their field, who integrate the latest research into the text but at the same time present the material in a clear, ordered fashion which can be read with value by those with no prior knowledge of the subject.

THE INSTITUTE OF CONTEMPORARY BRITISH HISTORY

50 Gordon Square, London WC1H 0PQ

The Civil Service since 1945

Kevin Theakston

BLACKWELL
Oxford UK & Cambridge USA

First published 1995

Blackwell Publishers Ltd
108 Cowley Road
Oxford OX4 1JF

Blackwell Publishers Inc.
238 Main Street
Cambridge, Massachusetts 02142
USA

British Library Cataloguing in Publication Data
A CIP catalogue record for this book is available from the British Library.

Library of Congress Cataloging-in-Publication Data
Theakston, Kevin, 1958–
    The civil service since 1945 / Kevin Theakston.
        p.   cm. — (Making contemporary Britain)
    Includes bibliographical references and index.
    ISBN 0–631–18824–X. — ISBN 0–631–18825–8 (pbk.)
    1. Civil service — Great Britain — History — 20th century.
    2. Government executives — Great Britain. I. Title. II. Series.
JN425.T48   1995   95–14749
331.7′6135441—dc20   CIP

Typeset in 10 on 12pt Ehrhardt
by Grahame & Grahame Editorial, Brighton, East Sussex

Printed in Great Britain by Hartnolls Limited, Bodmin, Cornwall
This book is printed on acid-free paper

Contents

List of Abbreviations   viii

General Editor's Preface   x

Acknowledgements   xii

1   Ministers and the Mandarins   1
2   The Topmost Mandarins   34
3   Business as Usual: The Civil Service in the 1940s
    and 1950s   56
4   Reforming the Machine: Whitehall in the 1960s
    and 1970s   83
5   The Civil Service at the Crossroads: Thatcher,
    Major and Whitehall since 1979   120
6   Whitehall Accountability and Control   164
7   Conclusion   186

Index   197

Abbreviations

AT	Administration Trainee
CAG	Comptroller and Auditor-General
CPRS	Central Policy Review Staff
CSD	Civil Service Department
CSSB	Civil Service Selection Board
DEA	Department of Economic Affairs
DHSS	Department of Health and Social Security
DOE	Department of the Environment
DSS	Department of Social Security
DTI	Department of Trade and Industry
ENA	Ecole Nationale d'Administration
EO	Executive Officer
FDA	First Division Association
FMI	Financial Management Initiative
FoI	Freedom of Information
GOC	Government Organisation Committee
HEO	Higher Executive Officer
HMSO	Her Majesty's Stationery Office
IPCS	Institution of Professional Civil Servants
MAFF	Ministry of Agriculture, Fisheries and Food
MBO	Management by Objectives
MG	Machinery of Government
MINIS	Management Information System for Ministers
MoD	Ministry of Defence

MPO	Management and Personnel Office
NAO	National Audit Office
OMCS	Office of the Minister for the Civil Service
OPSS	Office of Public Service and Science
PAC	Public Accounts Committee
PAR	Programme Analysis and Review
PCA	Parliamentary Commissioner for Administration
PESC	Public Expenditure Survey Committee
PSA	Property Services Agency
SEO	Senior Executive Officer
SPATS	Senior Professional Administrative Training Scheme
TCSC	Treasury and Civil Service Committee
UKREP	UK Permanent Representative to the European Community

General Editor's Preface

The Institute of Contemporary British History's series *Making Contemporary Britain* is aimed directly at students and at others interested in learning more about topics in post-war British history. In the series, authors are less attempting to break new ground than presenting clear and balanced overviews of the state of knowledge on each of the topics.

The ICBH was founded in October 1986 with the objective of promoting the study of British history since 1945 at every level. To that end, it publishes books and a quarterly journal, *Contemporary Record*; it organizes seminars and conferences for school students, undergraduates, researchers and teachers of post-war history; and it runs a number of research programmes and other activities.

A central theme of the ICBH's work is that post-war history is too often neglected in British schools, institutes of higher education and beyond. The ICBH acknowledges the validity of the arguments against the study of recent history, notably the problems of bias, of overly subjective teaching and writing and the difficulties of perspective. But it believes that the values of studying post-war history outweigh the drawbacks, and that the health and future of a liberal democracy require that its citizens know more about the most recent past of their country than the limited knowledge possessed by British citizens, young and old, today. Indeed, the ICBH believes that the dangers of political indoctrination are higher where the young are *not* informed of the recent past.

The size, shape and nature of British government has changed beyond all recognition in the fifty years since 1945. The Civil Service grew rapidly for the first forty years and then began to contract under the policies of Margaret Thatcher and John Major. The Civil Service has been attacked by both left and right, by the former for its alleged antipathy to socialism, by the latter for its alleged liking for big government.

Kevin Theakston pilots the reader skilfully through all the debates around and changes to the Civil Service since 1945. Students of politics will find invaluable material on questions such as relations between ministers and officials, and who runs Britain. Students of history will discover a lucid and most readable account of the processes by which government policy has been delivered since World War Two.

I have always been amazed by those who claim to find the Civil Service a less than stimulating subject. Kevin Theakston's book shows how wrong-headed such people are.

Anthony Seldon

Acknowledgements

Crown-copyright material in the Public Record Office is reproduced by permission of the Controller of Her Majesty's Stationery Office. I am grateful for the advice and assistance I have received from academic colleagues at the University of Leeds and elsewhere. My friend and former colleague Dr Chris Painter very kindly read and commented on several chapters in draft, but of course I alone am responsible for the contents of this book. My greatest debt is to Breda Theakston and my family for their support and encouragement.

1 Ministers and the Mandarins

As Harold Wilson entered Number 10 Downing Street following Labour's victory in the February 1974 general election, the civil service staff and the private secretaries who had been working until a few hours before for the outgoing Conservative Prime Minister Edward Heath lined up in the entrance hall, as is the convention, to politely applaud their new political boss. The scene neatly symbolizes the administrative continuity embodied in and provided by a permanent civil service and the tradition that it serves governments of different political complexions with equal loyalty.

Whitehall has been required to make this transition between the parties on five occasions since 1945: in 1951, 1964, 1970, 1974 and again in 1979. The civil service assiduously studies the electoral portents, but it can still be surprised by the results – it did not expect the Conservatives to win in 1970, for instance. It has developed a smooth routine. During the election period the Cabinet Office prepares two draft Queen's speeches based on the provisions of the competing parties' manifestos; and each department assembles two sets of briefs on the main issues in its area of policy and on how manifesto commitments could be translated into action.

Under rules introduced by Sir Alec Douglas-Home in 1964, the run-up to an election also sees confidential meetings between the Opposition and top officials to discuss possible machinery of government changes and related policy issues (the Labour Opposition did not have meetings with the Permanent Secretaries in 1983 and 1987, but did before the 1992 election).

There are, however, divergent interpretations of what exactly is happening at this critical moment in the life-cycle of British governments, which link to and illustrate a wider debate about the role and power of the civil service in the running of the country. Sir Robin Butler, current Head of the Civil Service, thinks that the preparations undertaken in 1992 'put us [the civil service] in a position where we could have hit the ground running if there'd been a change of government.'[1] In support of this view, Harold Wilson has testified to the speed with which proposals for immediate action on some of Labour's key commitments were presented to ministers in March 1974.

Sir Ian Bancroft (Civil Service Head in the late 1970s) admitted that there could be arguments with the new ministers. Opposition plans had been drawn up 'without the benefit . . . of the advice of the old pros who've been in and around this business for quite some time'. Modifications might have to be suggested, the difficulties of implementing some manifesto pledges pointed out. The civil service did not want to 'get in the way of the wishes of the electorate', said Bancroft, but it did need to be 'faithful to the facts'.[2]

Tony Benn, in contrast, sees a process of nefarious civil service manipulation in pursuit of its own ends:

> The deal that the civil service offers a minister is this: if you do what we want you to do, we will help you publicly pretend that you're implementing the manifesto on which you were elected. And I've seen many ministers, of both parties actually, fall for that one . . . They are always trying to steer incoming governments back to the policy of the outgoing government, minus the mistakes that the civil service thought the outgoing government made.[3]

After four successive Conservative election victories, many observers in the 1990s had become sceptical about the ability of the civil service to switch effortlessly and give loyal and effective service to a government of a different political complexion. Did Whitehall's impartiality depend on the political pendulum swinging regularly?

Some members of the new Labour government in 1964 had been suspicious of the civil service, fearing that official attitudes would have been strongly coloured by thirteen years of Conservative rule, though those concerns turned out to be unfounded. Incoming ministers might have similar doubts about the mandarins when the present long period of Conservative rule is finally ended. Robin Cook, a senior Labour front-bencher, asserted in 1994, for instance, that 'after a decade and a half in power, the Conservatives have surrounded themselves with senior officials who are incapable of distinguishing between their loyalty to the political ambitions of their minister and their duty to the nation to provide a civil service above party politics'.[4] But government ministers, the Head of the Civil Service and the all-party Treasury and Civil Service Committee all insisted in 1994 that Whitehall could and would serve a government of another party with equal commitment. Governments and politicians, they implied, would come and go, but the civil service would go on for ever.

The Experience of Office

Some post-war governments have entered office suspicious of the civil service; others seem to have come in with no doubts about Whitehall's neutrality. In the event, the civil service and government departments have changed course when one party has taken over the reins of power from an other. Successive governments have made major policy changes. This suggests, then, that either civil servants have co-operated fully with ministers or that political will can successfully overcome official resistance or sluggishness.[5]

John Garrett has characterized the position since the Second World War in the following way:

> There have been two very radical governments which came in with very clear and novel agendas, one was the Attlee Government in 1945 and the other was the Thatcher Government in 1979. They . . . implemented those programmes and . . . the Civil Service . . . found itself basically in a position of taking orders or executing decisions which had been taken by a Government. In the intervening period, in the 1950s, 1960s, 1970s, the so-called years of consensus politics, it was essentially the Civil Service machine which was managing a relatively stable political picture and ministers tended to be carried by that machine with their agendas fixed by their departments.

In other words, the picture is of a normal period in which officials played a large role in making policy, and exceptional periods in which new governments have had very clear agendas of their own and forced a change of direction. Garrett's argument is, however, open to the objection that the so-called consensus policies may in fact be just as much the result of conscious political decisions by ministers as the so-called radical policy departures.[6]

Contrary to the predictions of left-wingers like Harold Laski in the 1930s, the Labour government of 1945–51 had no reason to complain of civil service obstruction.[7] Attlee's confidence in the civil service was demonstrated when he returned to the Potsdam peace conference accompanied by the same team of officials that had accompanied his Tory predecessor, Churchill. Out of office in the 1950s, he argued that the fact that the same officials who had worked out the details of Labour's programme were now busy pulling it to pieces for their Conservative masters was proof of the loyalty and impartiality of the civil service. Other leading Labour ministers also praised the Whitehall machine – Herbert Morrison's (1954) book on *Government and Parliament* ending with a 'Tribute to the British Civil Service'. It would be nonsense to claim that officials 'sabotaged' the policies of Dalton and then Cripps at the Treasury, or of Bevan at the Ministry of Health (the fiery left-wing minister established an effective relationship with his officials, unlike Tony Benn thirty years later). And Bevin was certainly not the Foreign Office's poodle (if the government failed to pursue the 'socialist foreign policy' its left-wing critics demanded it was because of the hard facts of Britain's international situation and not Foreign Office machinations).

Labour's ministerial team in 1945 had the twin advantages of a five-year apprenticeship in government in the Churchill coalition and a bureaucracy ready to build upon war-time developments in economic planning and social reconstruction. There were radical impulses at work in the Treasury and elsewhere in the Whitehall machine that chimed with Labour thinking and initiatives. On the other hand, Labour's plans in key areas – economic planning, nationalization, and the welfare state – were fairly vague. Without adequate blueprints, ministers inevitably had to rely upon civil servants to work out detailed schemes, but all the same the government's momentum over its first three years was remarkable. In dealing with the economic and financial crises that it faced, the government was undoubtedly heavily dependent on the official machine for support and advice. But insiders' accounts and detailed studies of particular areas of policy support Hennessy's view that 'by and large, late-forties Whitehall approached the "team model" of ministers and officials pulling together in an atmosphere of mutual respect'.[8]

Returning to office in 1951, the Conservatives were suspicious of the civil service, feeling that it was 'in the pocket of the Labour Party'. There were doubts that 'after twelve years of heavy state controls since 1939, the Civil Service would be reluctant to adapt to the Conservatives' different approach'.[9] Churchill is reported to have remarked that the Number 10 staff were 'drenched with socialism' and he cut back on the number of inter-departmental committees of officials, fearing that their proliferation under Attlee had increased the power of the civil service. All the same, he apparently regarded Sir Edward Bridges and Sir Norman Brook as his two 'chums' among the civil service – 'the "boys" would know', he told Macmillan when sending for them to explain the housing set-up in 1951. Macmillan initially complained in his diary that 'the "Trade Union" of officials is back in power', and that ministers were seen as 'temporary nuisances', but he was able to stamp his will on the Ministry of Housing and Local Government (albeit by-passing his Permanent Secretary and relying on the dynamic and forceful Deputy Secretary, Evelyn Sharp).

The Conservatives were, of course, anything but temporary residents in government office, lasting thirteen years until 1964. Seldon's judgement is that 'Whitehall readily fell in with the government's plans' and that within two years almost all of the earlier suspicions of the mandarins' loyalty had dissolved. Some ministers – for instance, Duncan Sandys – had strained relations with officials, but the reasons were personal rather than policy-related. Sir Norman Brook's very close relationship with Churchill and Macmillan (see chapter 2) raised the question of whether some mandarins actually became too closely identified with the Conservatives during their long hold on power.

Over Suez – '*the* greatest professional trauma experienced by the British Civil Service before or since 1957'[10] – officials seem to have swallowed their doubts, carried out the politicians' instructions and kept tight-lipped. Except for a handful of key advisers, Eden kept the Foreign Office in the dark about his plans. Whitehall was in fact deeply dismayed by the Suez adventure. Brook thought the invasion to be 'folly', the outgoing Treasury Permanent Secretary, Bridges, was denied access to key documents, and his successor, Sir Roger Makins, thought ministers were 'running in blinkers'. A couple of junior diplomats resigned in protest from the FO, but there were no Ponting-style whistle-blowers. 'The soul of our service is the loyalty with which we execute ordained error', Lord Vansittart, head of the Foreign Office in the 1930s, once observed. And the civil service's conduct during Suez surely demonstrated a remarkable discipline and loyalty to ministers (to a degree perhaps difficult to imagine thirty years later).

The Labour left's interpretation of the experience of the 1964–70 and 1974–9 governments is that the civil service baulked ministers rather than smoothed their path.[11] Marcia Williams, Harold Wilson's Downing Street aide, talked of Labour's 'defeats' in the 'battle . . . against the Civil Service' after 1964 and argued it was impossible to accept 'the neutrality argument'. Critical comments on Whitehall personalities, civil service obstruction and the negative power of the Treasury fill the diaries of left-wing ministers in the Wilson and Callaghan Cabinets. Without major reform – to broaden the class base of recruitment, curb secrecy, reinforce ministers with teams of political advisers – the power of the mandarins would remain a formidable obstacle in the way of a Labour government's socialist programme, the left argued. Some figures on the party's centre and right also admitted after 1979 that there could be problems: the civil service 'is a beautifully designed and effective braking mechanism. It produces a hundred well-argued answers against initiative and change', said Shirley Williams; '"the system" can defeat Ministers', argued Joel Barnett. Denis Healey, however, identified the problem as 'the sheer intractability of the process of Government in Britain as it is now conducted' rather than 'bureaucratic sabotage or political prejudice' on the part of officials.

Though a number of incoming ministers in 1964 were distrustful of the civil service, there seems to have been good will in Whitehall towards Labour and its modernizing programme. Harold Wilson himself was something like a permanent secretary *manque*, a war-time 'temporary' who had identified himself with the fashionable 1960s cause of governmental reform, but who had at the same time a great admiration and respect for the civil service machine. His close relationship with Cabinet Secretary Sir Burke Trend became a central axis of the 1964–70 government. A critical view would be that Wilson's political style and his institutional conservatism reinforced each other. Absorbed into the Whitehall ethos, he came to regard the smooth processing of business through the official machine as the equivalent of dealing with real problems.

When it was put forward in the Labour Party's evidence to the Fulton Committee, Wilson scorned the idea that some ministers were tools of their civil servants because of the amount of information kept from them and because of the way in which inter-departmental committees hammered out policies without a ministerial steer. But this was exactly the sort of conspiratorial view of how the system operated against socialist ministers that was held by Crossman and Benn, and which became almost taken for granted on the left in the 1970s and 1980s. The accounts of Crossman and Benn must be treated with care, however. In some ways Crossman was a bull-in-a-china-shop figure who had little idea about how to use the civil service machine properly in order to reach his political goals. An important – but often overlooked – theme of his diaries is how clever and determined ministers (such as Crossman . . .) can in the end triumph over civil service opposition. And in his Godkin Lectures at Harvard in 1970 he was adamant that Labour's mistakes and failures could *not* be blamed on the civil service – the real problem, he said, was that the government did not have a clear enough sense of direction and that its policy planning before taking office had been inadequate.

Tony Benn's experience at the Industry Department in the 1970s suggests that when a Labour Prime Minister and Cabinet are clear about what they want, they do not find the civil service blocking their way, though as in that case, a departmental minister out of step with his political colleagues may well choose to complain about civil service obstruction. Officials at the Industry Department and elsewhere in Whitehall were clearly unhappy about key aspects of the interventionist industrial policy set out in Labour's programme and which Benn was committed to. More importantly, the party leadership was also unhappy about that policy but had been unable to block it in Opposition. If Benn and his policy had had the confidence and the backing of Wilson and the Labour Cabinet the story would have been different. But, as his Permanent Secretary pointed out, and as Benn recognized himself, he was a radical minister in a non-radical government.

Heath in 1970 does not seem to have shared the wariness of Churchill in 1951 on encountering the Whitehall machine after a period of Labour rule.[12] At the time of the Fulton Committee he had rejected the argument that ministers needed the support of *cabinets* and suggested that Labour ministers were too weak or too overwhelmed to get a firm grip on their departments. Heath had a rational and managerial approach to government, as seen in his organizational reforms and in his closeness to the top officials around him (particularly Sir Willam Armstrong – see chapter 2). He merged separate ministerial and official committees, 'a step which weakened the distinction between the "political" and "administrative" aspects of government and probably enhanced the political influence of civil servants', argued Kavanagh.[13]

Heath himself insisted that Whitehall was under firm political control during his premiership. But the failures of his government and its economic policy U-turn fuelled distrust in Conservative circles. Douglas Hurd, an adviser to Heath in Number 10, commented that Whitehall's firm belief in the merits of action by the state worked to the advantage of Labour governments and meant that the civil service was not a natural ally of the Conservatives, particularly if they were trying to cut back the public sector as in 1970–1. Nicholas Ridley, on the right of the party, argued – like the Labour left – that civil service pressure tended to pull ministers back to the policy position that the mandarins preferred: 'To overthrow conventional Civil service wisdom requires a political determination which British Governments rarely possess.'

Mrs Thatcher, of course, was to provide that determined political leadership after 1979. Her experience as a junior minister in the 1960s and a Cabinet minister under Heath had made her distrustful of and aggressive towards the civil service. She rejected the style and the substance of the 'failed' post-war consensus institutionalized by Whitehall and was suspicious that the civil service would be reluctant to implement radical policies. 'No government has been elected whose leader was as deeply seized as this one of the need to overturn the power and presumption of the continuing government of the civil service: to challenge its orthodoxies, cut down its size, reject its assumptions, which were seen as corrosively infected by social democracy, and teach it a lesson in political control', argued Hugo Young. Her attitude towards the mandarin class was described as 'ferocious' and a mixture of 'dislike . . . hatred . . . [and] contempt' by a close observer, but it is noticeable that she struck up close, trusting and even warm relations with the officials around her in Downing Street, some of whom became closer to her than most politicians.[14]

Whitehall was not, it must be said, 'massing in blank hostility', as Hugo Young put it. Some departments, such as Defence (anticipating a higher budget), welcomed the new government for reasons of institutional self-interest. The Treasury approved of the promised tougher approach to public spending and was not the citadel of unreconstructed Keynesianism some Thatcherites supposed. Moreover, the civil service had found the experience of the late 1970s, in which the Labour government lacked a parliamentary majority, debilitating and frustrating. The 1979 election at least had the positive result of producing a government with a clear mandate and firm policies. 'The civil service is quite good at doing what it's told', a senior official said. 'It just hasn't been told anything clearly for years.'

Tony Benn publicly wondered in 1980 how long it would be before civil service pressure drove the Thatcher government to abandon its manifesto and keep to the centre-ground policies favoured by Whitehall, as had been the case, he believed, with successive Labour and Conservative Cabinets. In fact, any civil service resistance or foot-dragging there might have been in the 1980s, with numerous press leaks adding to suspicions of disloyalty, failed to stymie the Thatcher administration. An elected government with radical intentions and clear priorities *was* able to impose its will upon Whitehall.

'The constitutional textbooks are truer now than they have been for some time', Hugo Young observed in 1990.[15] But there was a fierce debate about Mrs Thatcher's alleged 'politicization' of the civil service (see below), and it was suggested that the civil service role was now seen as being to implement ministerial policy without asking questions rather than giving objective advice (government reforms emphasized officials' role as *managers*). The abolition of the CPRS 'think-tank' in 1983 also showed the government was unwilling to listen to advice which did not fit in with its ideological preconceptions. The Whitehall 'grovel count' was higher than it had been under other governments, Lord Bancroft commented, and others detected an increase in what was termed the 'creep' or 'courtier' factor. The classic civil service 'snag-hunting' function of presenting to ministers critical judgements or unpalatable facts which may frustrate their plans seemed to have atrophied, as the poll tax fiasco revealed.[16]

There were also fears that civil service neutrality was being undermined in various ways by the Conservative government. The activities of Bernard Ingham, Mrs Thatcher's long-serving press secretary, were judged by many observers to be incompatible with his ostensible status as a professional civil servant. Whitehall's publicity and advertising budget was massively increased and there were fears that the distinction between the legitimate explanation of government policies and party-political image-building were being blurred. Civil servants were asked to cost the Labour Opposition's policy commitments, something which some of them felt was party-political work.

The issue remained a live one even after Mrs Thatcher's departure from the scene. MPs criticized senior Treasury officials for authorizing the use of public funds to help pay the then-Chancellor Norman Lamont's legal fees in a private case; a Labour MP alleged that DTI officials were ordered to go through company files to see if they could unearth evidence of donations by Robert Maxwell in order to embarrass the Labour Party. John Smith, Labour leader 1992–4, argued that, increasingly, Whitehall's 'impartiality is being compromised' and expressed concern about a 'Conservative mind-set' among officials. Lord Callaghan, the former Labour premier, said that ministers appeared to be regarding the civil service 'as part of their private fiefdom'. He also argued that 'when you have a government like the government we had in the 1980s, which emanates a very strong flavour, the civil service picks up the scent. Some are repelled by it, some are attracted by it, and I think the civil service has become more politicized as a consequence of this.'[17] Pressure mounted for a civil service code of ethics and for protection for officials who sought to resist the identification of a party's interest with the national interest.

A few months before Mrs Thatcher was overthrown, Sir Robin Butler admitted in 1990 that in the early 1980s the relationship between the Thatcher government and Whitehall had been bumpy, but said that it had then settled down. Her successor, John Major, was not in Thatcher's 'anti-system', conviction-politician mould, and appeared to have a more stable relationship with the civil service. Where she looked to outside 'think-tanks' and personal advisers and gurus for policy ideas, he was said to rely more on top civil servants. However, such was the disarray in the conduct and in the policies of his government by mid-1993 that civil servants were reported to be frustrated by ministerial indecision, the lack of a firm lead and by governmental losses of nerve in relation to back-bench protests and external buffeting.[18]

At the same time, observers continued to be concerned that, as William Plowden put it, something was 'going wrong' with the relationship between ministers and civil servants, and that the traditional values and understandings that underpinned that relationship were breaking down. Plowden detected 'a worrying deterioration, in some cases at least, in the working relationship between ministers and officials' due to the reluctance of a growing number of ministers to listen to unfavourable advice and a consequent reluctance by officials to put their heads above the parapet and tell them things they did not want to hear. 'The government knows what it wants and needs no advice', a senior official told him. Civil servants increasingly gave ministers the answers they wanted. There were reports that Home Secretary Michael Howard's relationship with his officials was particularly stormy, with civil servants complaining of abrupt and dismissive treatment, that their advice was consistently ignored and that ministers' approach was overly-ideological (Sir Clive Whitmore, the Home Office Permanent Secretary, retired early but denied any rift with his political boss). What was being lost was what Hugo Young called 'institutionalised scepticism'.[19]

There were also worries about alleged party political interventions by civil servants. Opposition politicians were disturbed by John Major's action in defending Sir Duncan Nichol, the NHS chief executive and a senior civil servant (grade 2) who had publicly and vigorously defended government policy on the NHS and attacked Labour in the run-up to the 1992 election.

That Major won a fourth election victory for the Conservatives in 1992 inevitably left some observers wondering whether civil service neutrality could survive serving the same political masters for seventeen or eighteen years. After such a long period of one-party rule, many Conservative ways of thinking and doing things may have become the Whitehall conventional wisdom or standard practice. Compared to their predecessors of 20–30 years ago, many senior officials have very little or no experience of the changes in approach consequent upon a change of government.

Could the civil service switch in 1996/7 to working on the conventional basis for a government of a different political complexion? The answer would seem to depend partly on Opposition reactions to developments in the civil service, and partly on the actions and attitude of the government: civil service neutrality can be maintained if politicians want to do so and make it possible. The introduction of a new code of conduct for civil servants in January 1995 signalled a concern to underline the values of impartiality and neutrality (see chapter 6). Although some Labour politicians entertained doubts about the consequences of Mrs Thatcher's 'is he one of us?' approach, Neil Kinnock appeared prepared to accept the assurances of the Head of the Civil Service that if he made it to Number 10 he could count on Whitehall's loyalty. John Smith did not doubt that a new government could sweep away the prevailing 'Conservative mind-set'. Some 're-engineering of thought patterns' might be necessary, as Peter Hennessy admitted, but Labour leaders did not seem to be thinking in terms of a massive purge of a 'politicized' mandarinate.

Ministers

Ministers are few in number relative to the size of the civil service. After the 1945 election Attlee's government consisted of twenty Cabinet ministers, eleven departmental ministers not in the Cabinet and thirty-two junior ministers (ministers of state and parliamentary under-secretaries) – a total of sixty-three ministers (excluding whips and law officers). After his 1992 victory John Major had a Cabinet of twenty-two ministers and appointed fifty-nine other ministers to his government – a total of eighty-one ministers. The bulk of the work of government has, inevitably, to be delegated to civil servants: the Vehicle and General inquiry in the 1970s found that less than one per cent of the work of the DTI went before ministers. Ministerial 'control' in this situation is therefore less a matter of issuing orders and more the result of indirect influence – 'climate-setting', officials' anticipations of how ministers will react, and so on.

Ministers in the post-1945 period – like their Victorian predecessors – have remained parliamentary generalists, political 'all-rounders', lacking specialist subject expertise or extra-parliamentary executive experience. Sir John Hoskyns launched scathing attacks in the 1980s on ministerial amateurism and the limited pool of talent provided by Parliament. But most 'outsiders' brought in to government have been judged unsuccessful as ministers; for instance the union leader Frank Cousins in the 1964 Wilson Cabinet, and the businessmen John Davies and Lord Young in the Heath and Thatcher governments, though Ernest Bevin must be *the* outstanding exception to the rule. Headey identified different types of minister in British governments: policy initiators, policy selectors, executive (managerial) types, ambassador ministers, and 'ministerial minimalists', showing that the role-conceptions of Labour and Conservative ministers were very similar. But Simon James argued that ministers in the 1970s and 1980s were more assertive in their departments than their counterparts in earlier decades, reflecting the greater ideological polarization of politics.[20]

Many ministers have the tenure of unsuccessful football club managers, spending on average about two and a half years in each post. This means that they are just starting to get on top of their jobs when they are reshuffled to a different post (or sacked). Though Harold Wilson is frequently portrayed as a particular villain in this respect, ministerial turnover in his administrations was in fact at about the same rate as under other post-war premiers. In addition, there are many pressing demands on ministers' time: only about a third of their working week is spent running their departments, as opposed to *representing* them in Parliament, Whitehall committee rooms, television studios and on other public occasions. The burden on ministers seems to have increased in the post-war period. In the late 1950s, Macmillan was so concerned by the growing load that he ordered a review of the issue, urged greater delegation of work to junior ministers and tried to stop the Cabinet and its committees being clogged-up with business that could be settled at lower levels.[21] Since the 1970s, the European Community/Union has added to the overload (involving meetings in Brussels and other trips). One of the rationales for the Next Steps programme launched in 1988 (see chapter 5) was to try to reduce the pressure on ministers of executive casework, giving more time for long-term strategy, but the treadmill still seemed as oppressive as ever in the early 1990s.

Barbara Castle, a Labour minister in the 1960s and 1970s, once spoke of 'the loneliness of the short-distance runner'. Ministers are relatively isolated in their departments. The number of junior ministers has grown over the post-1945 period and their role in recent decades has become much more significant than in the first twenty years after the war, with more responsibility for departmental and policy work being delegated to them. Until the 1960s most government departments had one ministerial chief and one junior minister; with the move towards 'giant' departments, four or more junior ministers could usually be found working under each Secretary of State. But because they are appointed by Prime Ministers who are often looking to engineer a party balance in their governments, and because of the pressures of career politics in a parliamentary system, ministerial teams in a department do not always work well together. Government documents regulating the conduct of ministers (first circulated by Attlee, added to over the years, and published only in 1992) emphasize that the constitutional convention of ministerial responsibility does not allow junior ministers to take final decisions against civil service advice – officials can and do by-pass junior ministers and appeal to their departmental boss.[22]

Whitehall had seen occasional politically-appointed special advisers before (mostly on the Number 10 staff – for instance, Attlee used Douglas Jay as his personal economic adviser 1945–6, Macmillan brought in John Wyndham as a personal confidant), but it was only with the 1964–70 Wilson government's so-called 'irregulars' (the PM and a number of other ministers bringing in a small number of expert advisers and political aides) that the practice really took off, receiving the backing of the Fulton Committee and prompting many would-be reformers to urge the adoption of a French-style *cabinet* system. The Heath government made less use than did its Labour predecessor of outside, non-civil service, advisers, but the return of a Labour government in 1974 saw the extension and institutionalization of the system of special advisers (who usually numbered around twenty-five or thirty in the late 1970s – a small group working in the Number 10 Policy Unit created by Wilson, the rest spread around the departments). Although in Opposition they had attacked Labour's appointments, the Conservatives after 1979 brought in their own advisers (albeit fewer in number than Labour's) and Mrs Thatcher strengthened the resources of political advice available to her as Prime Minister (retaining the Policy Unit – but, obviously, changing its staff – and appointing additional special advisers in Number 10).

The results of this innovation have been mixed. Special advisers have been too few in number to supplant the mass of career bureaucrats and have had no place in the administrative chain of command implementing decisions. They are thus not a 'counter civil service'. But it would be going too far to dismiss them as a minor cosmetic. Some have been ineffective, marginalized by officials and contributing little to policy-making. Some advisers have, however, contributed impressive subject-expertise (Brian Abel-Smith, Labour's DHSS adviser in the 1960s and 1970s, is a notable example), while others have been general political aides and party linkmen. They have added an extra dimension to the support that officials provide ministers, keeping in touch with the party and generating alternative ideas on policy within a framework of political values shared with the minister. And successive Prime Ministers since 1974 have found their Number 10 Policy Unit (precursors of which were Lloyd George's 'Garden Suburb' in the First World War and Churchill's Statistical Section in the second) an invaluable reinforcement in the battle for influence over policy inside government.

Although Richard Crossman popularized the idea of the party manifesto as the 'battering ram' of change in British politics, only 6 per cent of the ministers interviewed by Headey in the late 1960s and early 1970s defined their role in terms of implementing party policy. Ministers are in fact usually heavily dependent upon the civil service for policy ideas and advice because of the difficulties that parties in Opposition have in preparing clear and well-thought-out plans. The policy research capabilities of British political parties are small and over-stretched. Parties' programmes often contain more wishful thinking than clear and coherent priorities, are often based on inadequate information, and they are rarely properly costed. Few ministers seem to enter office armed with detailed proposals or well-defined objectives. A classic example of this, worthy of *Yes, Minister*, occurred when Manny Shinwell, Attlee's Minister of Fuel and Power, went to the Transport House files for the Labour Party's plan for coal nationalization: all he found were two copies of a pamphlet by James Griffith, one of them a translation into Welsh! Labour's preparations were equally flimsy before 1964. The party had no detailed plans worked out to deal with the sterling crises it encountered immediately on taking office. Almost as soon as he entered the Cabinet in 1964, Richard Crossman was complaining that 'what we lacked was any comprehensive, thoroughly thought-out Government strategy. The policies are being thrown together'. In a secret document in June 1970, the Conservative's Public Sector Research Unit warned Heath about the way in which the lack of precisely-defined goals in key areas of policy, and the absence of information about the scope for cuts and the public expenditure resources available, could go a long way to 'minimise the impact of an incoming administration' – and this was *after* a large-scale exercise in policy-preparation by the Conservative Opposition in the late 1960s.

Civil Service Power

In constitutional theory and orthodox textbook accounts the position is quite straightforward: the civil service has no constitutional personality or responsibility distinct or separate from that of the government of the day; it is a non-political and neutral bureaucracy loyally committed to the aims and interests of that government; the duty of officials is to ensure that ministers are fully apprised of the problems, constraints and options they face, but then it is also their duty to make the best of the policy ministers lay down and to put into effect their decisions, for which ministers are responsible. This is the normative theory of the British constitution as it has been understood throughout the twentieth century and as restated in the 1985 Armstrong Memorandum: that ministers, not civil servants, should have the final power because they carry the final accountability to Parliament and the public.

Participants in government (politicians and senior officials) have frequently said that this is what life in Whitehall is really like; conversely, critics' reform schemes are often intended to close what they claim to be the gap between reality and this model. For both sets of people the model is important – as a description or as a normative standard.

An alternative model of minister-mandarin relations has portrayed them as conflictual, with a constant struggle for power and control over policy going on between elected politicians and permanent bureaucrats, and the civil service actively obstructing and sabotaging ministerial initiatives. 'Whitehall is the ultimate monster to stop governments changing things', complained the Thatcherite ex-minister John Nott. As we have seen, some Labour politicians have suspected officials of being closet Tories, some Conservatives have alleged that they really have socialist sympathies, and others have claimed that the civil service has its own interests and agenda. These critical views gained in popularity from the late 1960s onwards as the frustrations and failures of successive Labour and Conservative governments produced a search for scapegoats and a questioning of the post-war consensus on policy institutionalized by the civil service. Whitehall, it was argued, aimed to maximize continuity and was committed to defending the status quo – whether in the form of narrow departmental interests or, more broadly, the post-war social democratic/Keynesian consensus – against any radical challenges.

Other close observers and former ministers have maintained that things are not so clear cut, however. Sir Edward Boyle, a Conservative minister in the 1950s and early 1960s, dismissed claims that there is 'a sort of ju-jitsu game' or a struggle for power between ministers and mandarins. Civil servants, it has often been argued, actually prefer a 'strong' minister to a cipher because they rely on him or her to fight for the department in Cabinet, to have clear ideas about future policy, to win a proper share of resources for the department's programmes, and to represent it effectively in public. For their part, ministers need officials for advice on the detailed formulation and implementation of policy and to manage their departments efficiently. Ministers and mandarins form a 'Society for Mutual Benefit', as Richard Neustadt shrewdly observed.[23]

The lines of division inside government are complex and fluid. The fact is that Whitehall is not a monolithic entity – departments often disagree with one another on policy issues, there are recurring tensions and battles between the Treasury and spending departments, and officials within each ministry are not necessarily united. Similarly, there are usually deep fissures on the ministerial side of government, caused by ideological and (party) factional differences, personal ambition, and the effects of departmental self-interest as ministers 'fight their corners'.

Ministers take decisions largely on the basis of information about problems and options provided by the Whitehall machine, a dependence which critics interpret in conspiratorial terms but which the mandarins themselves see as the inevitable process of bringing politicians face to face with what one top civil servant once called 'on-going reality'. As Sir Robin Butler put it, the civil service's role is 'to inform government policies, to refine them, to make them practicable'. 'The biggest and most pervasive influence is in setting the framework within which questions of policy are raised', Sir William Armstrong observed. In his time, he recalled, the Treasury's economic policy was framed on neo-Keynesian assumptions. 'We set the questions which we asked ministers to decide arising out of that framework and it would have been enormously difficult for any minister to change the framework, so to that extent we had great power.' Ministers, said Armstrong, did not question the framework, they just operated within it.[24] As the economic policy consensus crumbled in the 1970s, however, it became clear that inside the Treasury there was no longer a coherent policy framework, but instead deep divisions between neo-Keynesians, monetarists and pragmatists existed at official level. And by the end of the Thatcher period, it could be argued that the dominant framework within which Whitehall evolved policy reflected the Conservatives' principles and philosophy.

Many observers have testified to the existence of well-established 'departmental views' which shape the advice ministers receive and which affect the implementation of policy. Sir Edward Bridges interpreted this benignly: 'it is the duty of a Civil Servant to give his Minister the fullest benefit of the storehouse of departmental experience; and to let the waves of the practical philosophy wash against the ideas put forward by his Ministerial master'. Shirley Williams argued that because each department had its own ethos and outlook, usually reflecting its last major achievement or reform, it was wrong to describe the civil service as a collectivity as being either pro-Labour or pro-Conservative. Thus the former DHSS – champion of the National Health Service – 'has a tendency to seem to defend Labour Government achievements rather than Conservative Government achievements', she said, while the Home Office, with a pronounced law-and-order perspective, tended to be a 'Conservative department' when it came to major changes. (It should be noted, however, that the Home Office is reported to have welcomed Conservative plans for the police in 1979 but to have opposed the 'short, sharp shock' proposals for young offenders; and ministers' plans for tighter immigration controls are said by Simon James to have offended its 'basically liberal instincts'.)[25] 'The Ministry of Agriculture looks after farmers, the Foreign Office looks after foreigners', quipped Norman Tebbit, a reminder that these 'departmental philosophies' can reflect close (even incestuous) links with outside 'client' groups (the National Farmers' Union in the case of Agriculture).

A belief in the need for wages restraint and an incomes policy seems to have been held by the Treasury for much of the post-war period, with plans being brought out, dusted down and presented to ministers at moments of economic crisis from the 1940s onwards. The Board of Trade was well-known over a long period for its free-trade outlook but officials in the Ministry of Technology in the 1960s had a more interventionist approach to industry; when Heath merged the two into the Department of Trade and Industry in 1970 the continuance of different traditions exacerbated problems of internal co-ordination in the 'giant' ministry. Taking over the Industry Department in 1979, the new Conservative minister, Sir Keith Joseph, handed over a reading list so that officials could educate themselves in the new thinking about markets and frame policy advice accordingly. For a while there were continuities with the pre-1979 policies (as seen in continuing massive state aid to British Leyland, for instance), but over the 1980s DTI spending was to plummet and the idea of an industrial policy was abandoned by the government – ministers successfully imposed *their* policies. 'There is probably no domestic department left that retains a "departmental view" that would be at odds with Thatcherism' concluded a study of Mrs Thatcher's impact on the civil service, testimony to the success with which her government was able to dominate the 'Whitehall village' and overturn departments' traditional ideas on policy.[26]

The Foreign Office has often been suspected of pursuing its own policies irrespective of the wishes of the government of the day. Churchill mistrusted the diplomats in the 1950s (he once called them 'a cowardly lot of scuffling shufflers'), as did Thatcher in the 1980s. During the Falklands War she reputedly said that she was having to fight the Foreign Office as well as the Argentines, and she believed the department was too 'wet' and too interested in good relations with other countries, and in particular did not stand up strongly enough for British interests in Europe.

In the 1950s, the Foreign Office had been sceptical about the EEC and it was Sir Frank Lee, head of the Treasury, who was the key official involved in persuading the Macmillan government to apply for membership. But by the early 1960s, the Foreign Office was converted to a zealously pro-European line. EEC membership was in the national interest, the Foreign Office believed; it was also in the Foreign Office's own interest, critics pointed out, as that department claimed a right to be involved in policy-formulation over a wide range of 'European' issues (agriculture, energy, economic policy, etc). Hennessy suggests that if a Labour government had been elected in the 1980s which had tried to take Britain out of the European Community and adopt a non-nuclear defence policy, it could have faced major resistance from Whitehall – commitment to departmental views (and the foreign and defence policy consensus) on these issues being stronger, in effect, than the ethos of a neutral civil service capable of loyally serving any democratically-elected government.[27]

As Shirley Williams suggested, however, it is doubtful if the civil service as a whole can be defined as having a conscious political position of its own to defend. Whitehall's attitude was 'one apart from Party', Sir Edward Bridges said in 1946: 'there were things in the programmes of both the major Parties which we disliked and others equally which we liked'.[28] The general outlook of the bulk of the higher civil service in the inter-war period – a period of Conservative political dominance – had actually been 'Left Centre' according to one 'insider'. In the post-war period the 'Butskellite' label could fairly be applied: 'you tended to be within a narrow line either side of the centre', recalled Sir William Armstrong. 'Most [officials] would like a government with Heath as Prime Minister and [Roy] Jenkins as Chancellor', he said in the 1970s. 'The Civil Service always hopes that it's influencing Ministers towards the common ground', another top mandarin, Sir Antony Part, said in 1980. A survey conducted in 1966 found that Labour voters outnumbered Conservatives by two to one among a sample of youngish 'high-flyers', although when their political attitudes were probed, many of these officials claimed to be floating voters. Roy Jenkins reports how a speech he made in 1979 urging governments to spare us too many 'queasy rides on the ideological big dipper' went down well with the Permanent Secretaries in his audience. Not surprisingly, there were suggestions in the 1980s that a majority of senior officials sympathized with the Alliance parties' approach, being attracted by their attacks on 'manifestoitis'.

The Power of the Treasury

The massive power of the Treasury is often seen as one of the great 'constants' of Whitehall. In one department are combined key functions often separated in other countries: a central role in economic policy-making, control over public spending (giving it a say in all the major decisions in every corner of government), and (except for the 1968–81 period) civil service management responsibilities (since 1981, shared with the Cabinet Office). It is disliked and even feared by other departments, criticized by industrialists and trade unionists for the damage it is alleged to have done to the economy, usually regarded with a wary respect by politicians in office, and often denounced as obstructive by politicians out of office.

The Treasury had claims to be 'the supreme department of state' for much of the inter-war period, but it had been 'under a cloud and not very powerful' during the Second World War when financial considerations were downgraded as a factor in policy-making.[29] After 1945 it moved rapidly back to occupy a central position and has since then seen off challengers such as the Department of Economic Affairs (DEA) in the 1960s, though it has had to accept the growing power of the Cabinet Office as a co-ordinator of the government machine.

Successive post-war governments have had some bruising encounters with the Treasury and it is worth looking at their experience when trying to assess the Treasury's role and power inside Whitehall.

Labour left-wingers (with 1931 constantly in mind) regularly attacked the Treasury as a bastion of Tory values during the late 1940s. Attlee's ministers usually rejected these charges, but battling with the sterling and foreign reserves crisis during mid-1949 were suddenly not so sure. Officials were asked to leave the room at one meeting of the Cabinet's Economic Policy Committee, and Cripps, the Chancellor, burst out, 'One of my difficulties is that my official advisers are all "liberals" and I cannot really rely on them to carry through a "socialist" policy.' Douglas Jay, a Treasury junior minister, believed that officials were half expecting Labour to lose the next election and were beginning to think in terms of a Conservative government and Conservative policies; and Hugh Dalton shared his doubts. Hugh Gaitskell was suspicious of the Treasury's motives too and complained about the manoeuvres of 'the underground Civil Service'. Even Attlee was apparently concerned about the advice he was getting from the Treasury and the Bank of England on the need for public expenditure cuts. It is clear that there were divisions of opinion at both ministerial and official levels over how to react to the currency crisis. Cripps was strongly opposed to devaluation of the pound. Some Treasury officials, including Bridges, along with the Governor of the Bank of England, were advising against devaluation and in favour of large cuts in public spending to 'restore confidence'. Other key Whitehall economic advisers, however, had for some time wanted devaluation and – given vital political backing by the younger economics ministers, particularly Gaitskell – their arguments finally prevailed. The lesson seems to be that ministers in the end took their own decisions though along the way there were some tough battles with deflationist Treasury mandarins.[30]

Churchill's evident suspicion of the Treasury in 1951 was based in part on his belief that as Chancellor in the 1920s he had made a mistake in returning to the Gold Standard, and he blamed officials for giving him bad advice on that issue. The ministerial advisory committee he set up to watch over his Chancellor, Butler, and as a check on Treasury advice, soon disappeared. Butler, for his part, formed an effective alliance with the Treasury mandarins. The Treasury was not united, as the infighting over the 'Robot' scheme for making sterling convertible showed, setting leading officials in the Overseas Finance Division and in the Bank of England against other Treasury staff, particularly the government's Economic Adviser (Hall) and the Chief Planner (Plowden), with ministers also divided. In fact, throughout the 1950s internal divisions at official level meant that Conservative ministers made their own decisions and were not prisoners of a monolithic Treasury 'departmental view'.[31]

Macmillan in the late 1950s apparently operated with a firm belief that 'the Treasury was Up To No Good', as Jock Bruce-Gardyne put it, and was permanently suspicious that it would plunge the country into a slump, provoking officials to keep a tally of the number of times he mentioned Stockton-on-Tees (his old constituency, devastated by unemployment between the wars) in any one week. He was convinced that reforming the Treasury would be 'like trying to reform the Kremlin or the Vatican', and in a calculated insult he twice refused to appoint a career Treasury man to the vacant Permanent Secretaryship, bringing in first a career diplomat (Makins) and then the top official from the Board of Trade (Lee). In the early 1950s Churchill had backed Macmillan against Treasury opposition to the scale of resources going to his housing programme; in the late 1950s and early 1960s Macmillan (from Number 10) consistently pressed for expansionary policies against Treasury orthodoxy. The growth of public spending at that time was a sign of the limits to the Treasury's power.

Harold Wilson is said by Hennessy to have had 'a career-long animus against the Treasury'. In 1964 he set up the DEA with the hope that it would be a champion of industrial modernization and a rival to the Treasury. But his attempt at introducing 'creative tension' into Whitehall failed to break the Treasury's predominance over economic policy. The DEA was handicapped by an ill-thought-out division of functions between it and the Treasury, and by a lack of direct executive powers on key issues. What finally sunk it were political decisions giving priority to the defence of the exchange rate which meant the Treasury would inevitably come out on top in the inter-departmental struggle. Whitehall 'welcome[d] restoration of fiscal and monetary orthodoxy after the end of 1967', as Middlemas noted, but it was the inescapable facts of Britain's economic situation rather than bureaucratic fiat that dictated policy. Roy Jenkins, Chancellor 1967–70, seemed to see eye-to-eye with his senior officials but he was certainly not their stooge.[32]

Heath was apparently critical of the Treasury for its gloomy economic forecasts and for not being fully behind him in its view of the economic consequences of EEC membership. He relied upon the Head of the Civil Service, Sir William Armstrong, rather than the Treasury, to mastermind his economic policy U-turn and his prices and incomes policy. To the Treasury's chagrin, large increases in public expenditure were pushed through. Significantly, in 1977 Heath backed the idea then being floated to split the Treasury, taking away its public spending responsibilities and leaving it as a Ministry of Finance, acknowledging that one aim would be to give the Prime Minister a bigger role as an economic policy arbiter.

On key economic policy issues, the 1974–9 Labour government took its own decisions rather than rubber-stamping the Treasury's. There are accusations that the Treasury tried to 'bounce' ministers into introducing a compulsory pay policy in 1975, but this pressure was resisted by Downing Street political advisers and the Chancellor, Denis Healey, eventually abandoned his own officials' proposals, the result being that Labour's pay policy was a voluntary rather than a statutory one. During the 1976 IMF loan crisis, there were claims that some Treasury officials were secretly briefing the US government and the IMF in order to increase pressure on the government for large expenditure cuts. It was also suggested that public sector borrowing figures were inflated to create a crisis atmosphere and panic ministers into cutting spending (though Healey does not blame the Treasury for this). In fact the Treasury was divided: there was a minority of 'hawks' who backed the IMF line and wanted savage cuts, but other officials opposed cuts or came round finally to accept them but not on the scale the IMF wanted (the course the Labour Cabinet adopted). It is worth noting that the introduction of cash limits in 1976, which led to massive under-spending against targets (at times on a scale matching the Cabinet's planned cuts), received strong political support from Labour's Treasury ministers and actually faced some opposition from within the Treasury itself.[33]

As Prime Minister after 1976, Callaghan was suspicious of Treasury thinking and showed the department no deference.[34] He set up a top-secret 'Economic Seminar' – a small group of senior ministers, officials and Number 10 advisers – to tighten his political grip on the key economic discussions and decisions. There was no monolithic 'Treasury line' constraining Labour ministers – there was at official level a spectrum of opinion about the management of the economy, from Keynesians through to monetarists. The Treasury was of course influential between 1974 and 1979, but its was not a decisive voice.

Mrs Thatcher's years in Downing Street were marked by suspicions of, and periodic clashes with, the Treasury – particularly on exchange rate policy and the European ERM issue. She took steps to build up her own economic advisory capability, the activities of her personal economic adviser, Alan Walters, eventually provoking Nigel Lawson's resignation as Chancellor in 1989. She also took care to appoint officials committed to her policies to the Treasury's top jobs. Sir Douglas Wass, Permanent Secretary when the Conservatives entered office in 1979 and known to hold Keynesian views, was effectively by-passed; Terry Burns, a monetarist economist, was brought in from the London Business School to be the new Chief Economic Adviser (he became Permanent Secretary in 1991); and Wass's successor in 1983, Peter Middleton, was chosen because he had views and a style that fitted in with the government's approach. The Conservatives' free-market, anti-inflation, anti-public spending thinking represented, of course, something like a re-invention of the traditional 'Treasury view'. And the Treasury had a central role in the government's privatization programme. The result was that by the 1990s it could justly be claimed that Treasury 'pre-eminence in the machinery of government has rarely been more marked . . . it is unlikely whether the Treasury's grip on government has ever been tighter'. Keith Middlemas argued that 'a Treasury regime' had developed since the late 1970s, characterized by 'the pervasive influence of "Treasury values" throughout British public policy discussion'. But he admitted that this system depended crucially on 'heavy, continuing support from Number 10'.[35]

The conclusion must be that of course the Treasury has been a powerful core department in the British government machine, but its internal divisions and the attitude of the Prime Minister of the day have meant that it has not necessarily been an all-powerful department over the period since 1945. When premier, Chancellor and departmental Treasury are united, they are irresistible. It is, in a sense, always 'open season' on the Treasury. But the blame for the country's post-war economic record has to be placed ultimately on political shoulders.

Whitehall and Europe

Whitehall's 'hidden arm' was how Young and Sloman described the civil service operation linking British government with the institutions of the European Community (now Union) across in Brussels. The European dimension has steadily increased in importance since Britain joined the EEC in the early 1970s. Large numbers of senior civil servants make frequent (weekly or monthly) trips to Brussels to attend meetings of the multitude of Euro-working groups and committees. In 1982 the Permanent Secretary at the Ministry of Agriculture (MAFF) estimated that 200 of his staff went to Brussels every month (the Common Agricultural Policy looming large on the European agenda). In the 1970s only a handful of Whitehall departments were actively involved in EC business on a regular basis – the Foreign Office, MAFF, Trade and Industry, the Treasury, Customs and Excise. The number had doubled by the 1990s, with over a dozen ministries brought into play on aspects of the Single Market programme. And there is now a European angle to the work of even apparently domestically-oriented departments like the Home Office and the Department of Health on particular issues.[36]

The complex and protracted process of negotiation with other member states and European institutions involved in the development and administration of policy inevitably poses problems of ministerial control and direction. Tony Benn accused officials of agreeing to compromises and package deals that could not be unpicked in London.[37] But officials do report back and consult with their departments and ministers as negotiations proceed, and usually operate with instructions and guidelines put together through the very elaborate system of co-ordination in Whitehall.

It would be wrong to suppose that officials were in some sense 'off the leash' in Brussels.

The Whitehall balance of power was certainly affected by entry to the EEC. A department like MAFF, for instance, moved from the periphery to nearer centre stage. The Foreign Office, as noted earlier, became a new power centre on a range of hitherto 'domestic' policy questions. Benn asserted that the Foreign Office had transferred its allegiance from Britain to Brussels, a view shared by the diplomats' right-wing critics too.

Europe is a dominating presence for the Foreign Office, but it has brought threats as well as opportunities. In the early 1970s there was a Whitehall battle fought over how far the Foreign Office would be the lead department on European business. The decision was taken that European policy would be co-ordinated in the Cabinet Office, where a European Unit – now the European Secretariat – was set up. Because the Foreign Office has and may wish to argue a particular departmental point of view on European issues, it could not at the same time 'hold the ring' inside Whitehall. The Foreign Office is responsible for day-to-day operational co-ordination and remains the formal channel of communication between London and UKREP, the Brussels-based link with the European institutions (whose staff includes high-flyers seconded from the main departments as well as Foreign Office regulars).

The growing involvement of other departments with Europe (increasingly they have established EC co-ordinating divisions of their own), allied to their in-depth expertise in their particular fields of policy, means that the Foreign Office may not be able to convincingly claim that it alone has the expertise needed to negotiate with 'foreigners'. In the longer term, the result might be to blur the distinctions and break down the barriers between the Home Civil Service and the Diplomatic Service.[38]

The British have a (deserved) reputation for having the most effective arrangements for co-ordinating European policy of any member state. The Cabinet Office–Foreign Office–UKREP nexus is the vital mechanism: 'acting together they can exert strong influence on the overall Whitehall view' admits a senior Cabinet Office insider. The Cabinet Office chairs around 200 meetings a year on European issues and circulates over 300 papers. Its European Secretariat plays a very pro-active role in banging out inter-departmental agreements and co-ordinating tactics: it provides 'a neutral but purposive Chair for official level discussions; recording conclusions authoritatively and bludgeoning only rarely.'[39]

The Whitehall machinery and processes developed to handle European business represent in many ways, as Spence suggests, 'a traditional British response to new administrative challenges'. It is a streamlined operation, a tightly-managed structure. Its strengths and weaknesses mirror those of Whitehall generally. There is a premium on co-ordination and the reconciliation of competing departmental interests and viewpoints. But the central role given to a small number of officials means that the focus is very much on day-to-day co-ordination, reacting to events ('fire-fighting') and damage-limitation, rather than on long-term strategic thinking and planning.[40]

Politicization of the Civil Service?

One in seven Permanent Secretaries in the first two decades of this century were brought straight in to the civil service at that rank from outside Whitehall, often at the direct instigation of ministers. It was only under Sir Warren Fisher, inter-war Head of the Civil Service, that the higher civil service fully became a self-managing career service, with politicians largely excluded from top-level promotion decisions. Even then, an interventionist Prime Minister with strong views could have a decisive impact – Neville Chamberlain, for instance, removing Vansittart as head of the Foreign Office in 1938 and installing his *éminence grise* Horace Wilson as Head of the Civil Service and Permanent Secretary to the Treasury in 1939.[41]

In the post-1945 period the pattern was for discreet consultations to be made to ensure that ministers did not strongly object to top-level postings in their departments on grounds of personal incompatibility, but there was no systematic political influence over the filling of Whitehall's top jobs. One reason for this was the widespread acceptance of the civil service ethos of neutrality and chameleon-like adaptability; a second was that Permanent Secretaries typically served longer than particular ministers and so there was a need to consider the long-term interests of the service as a whole when making appointments (Sir William

Armstrong actually planned his dispositions for several years ahead on a sort of chessboard). Successive Prime Ministers (who, since 1919, formally made appointments to Whitehall's top two ranks) generally just rubber-stamped the recommendations of the Head of the Civil Service (Churchill, for instance, is reported as never rejecting a Bridges' recommendation between 1951 and 1955).

Ministers' hands could be seen in some Whitehall moves. When 'Rab' Butler took over the Home Office in 1957 he quickly eased out the formidable and long-serving Permanent Secretary Sir Frank Newsam; this was interpreted as a sign that he meant to be master of his own department, but the move was made easier by Newsam being well past the normal civil service retirement age of sixty. Another signal for 'Whitehall watchers' was Heath's choice in 1970 of Sir Antony Part from the 'free trade' Board of Trade rather than Sir Richard ('Otto') Clarke, a committed interventionist at the Ministry of Technology, to head the new DTI. In 1992 William Waldegrave sacked his Permanent Secretary at the Office of Public Service and Science, Sir Peter Kemp, with personality rather than party-political factors apparently providing the motive (see chapter 5). There was speculation that the resignation of Sir Geoffrey Holland, the Permanent Secretary at the Education Department, in late 1993 after less than a year in the post, was because he had fallen out with his minister, John Patten. If the mandarins dug in, though, ministers could not dislodge them. When Barbara Castle tried to move her Permanent Secretary at the Ministry of Transport in 1966, there were outraged leaks to the press and she failed. Mrs Thatcher wanted to remove her Permanent Secretary at the Ministry of Education in the early 1970s, but was stopped by Heath and William Armstrong.

The attitudes and actions of the Thatcher government after 1979 opened up this previously mainly low-key and 'behind-closed-doors' business and made the alleged 'politicization' of the higher civil service into a politically-controversial subject. It soon became clear that Mrs Thatcher took a much closer personal interest in top-level appointments than did her predecessors in Number 10, using the powers that had long belonged to the PM in a much more active way than before. She did not want just a single recommendation from the Head of the Civil Service but a short-list of candidates for Permanent Secretary positions. She would then choose. The appointment process became more personalized: 'catching the eye' of the PM at meetings, and evincing a dynamic 'can do' managerial style brought favour. She did not, however, apply a partisan litmus test, but preferred a decisive and energetic approach – she wanted action-oriented problem-solvers 'not urbane sceptics who find problems to every solution'.[42] Particularly controversial were the appointments of Sir Peter Middleton to head the Treasury (promoted over the heads of more senior Treasury officials and reportedly chosen against the advice of Sir Robert Armstrong and Sir Douglas Wass) and Sir Clive Whitmore, sent from her private office to run the Ministry of Defence. The retirement of large numbers of senior men in the early 1980s – the generation of Permanent Secretaries who had entered Whitehall after the Second World War – and her long tenure as Prime Minister meant that she had a tremendous cumulative impact on the civil service elite. By the end of her premiership she had appointed every one of the Permanent Secretaries heading the major departments of state.

Some of her supporters felt that she did not go far enough. Sir John Hoskyns, a former Thatcher adviser at Number 10, attacking what he saw as a fossilized and defeatist mandarinate, argued that only a large-scale influx of fresh blood, in the shape of several hundred politically-committed business outsiders, could ensure the radical changes needed to save the country. He criticized Whitehall's 'passionless detachment' – 'as if the process [officials] were engaged in were happening in a faraway country which they service only on a retainer basis'. 'How can you have a radical government without radically-minded officials?' he asked. Sceptics queried whether British businesses really had talent to spare on the Hoskyns scale. And the mandarins fought back: 'conviction politicians, certainly: conviction civil servants, no', declared Lord Bancroft. Sir Douglas Wass argued that ministers needed career officials to expertly operate a complex governmental machine, provide a long-term perspective, and advise them frankly on the obstacles, pitfalls and resource-implications of their proposals: it is 'the strength of the politically uncommitted civil service that it can evaluate all these factors with the objectivity that sometimes escapes the political enthusiast'.[43]

In the event, an army of Hoskyns-style outsiders did not invade Whitehall in the 1980s. The chiefs of the civil service were anxious, however, to reassure the Opposition that the civil service could serve, on the traditional basis, a Labour government. Though some Labour figures had their doubts, Kinnock seemed prepared to accept these pledges. The most an incoming Labour government would have been likely to do in

1987 or 1992 would have been to reshuffle the civil service top brass, not massacre it. The shrewder Labour politicians realized that the new breed of top officials in the 1980s was much more adapted to decisively pushing through ministerial policy than the old. 'If a government of the radical right can pursue its policies,' said Bryan Gould, 'there is no reason why a reforming Labour government should not realise its goals . . . If a British government can introduce anything as barmy, impractical and ill thought out as the poll tax, any government can introduce anything it likes as long as it believes sufficiently in it.'[44]

Whitehall, then, escaped 'politicization' in the ways that it is experienced in other systems. From a comparative perspective, the British civil service remained a special case in the 1990s. There is nothing like the 3,000 political appointees found at the top of the United States federal bureaucracy, or the German 'political officials' who carry party cards and are reshuffled on a change of government, or the French system of ministerial *cabinets* (though the special adviser system could perhaps develop in that direction).

One consequence of the Next Steps management changes and of the moves heralded in the 1994 White Paper to public advertisement and increased outside competition for top jobs (see chapter 5), however, is the possibility that the scope for political influence over senior Whitehall appointments may increase. Ministers appoint agency chief executives, but there has also been speculation that the division between management and 'political administration' in terms of functions and staff, could permit ministers to start applying tests of personal confidence and trust to their senior policy advisers in the Whitehall 'core'.[45] This could be presented as but a formalization of an already accepted convention, but equally it could appear to critics as an open 'politicization' of the civil service. It seems likely, therefore, that the 'politicization' issue will not go away this side of a change of governing party at an election.

Notes

1 Peter Hennessy and Simon Coates, *Bluehall SW1?* (Strathclyde Analysis Papers, no. 11, Glasgow, 1992), p. 5.
2 Hugo Young and Anne Sloman, *No, Minister* (BBC, London, 1982), p. 22; Peter Hennessy, *Whitehall* (Secker and Warburg, London, 1989), p. 509.

3 Young and Sloman, *No, Minister*, pp. 19–20.

4 *Tribune*, 21 January 1994.

5 Peter Kellner and Lord Crowther-Hunt, *The Civil Servants* (Macdonald, London, 1980), pp. 234–5.

6 Treasury and Civil Service Committee, *The Role of the Civil Service: Interim report*, HC 390, 1992–93, qs. 286–7.

7 Kevin Theakston, *The Labour Party and Whitehall* (Routledge, London, 1992), pp. 25–31.

8 Hennessy, *Whitehall*, p. 137.

9 Anthony Seldon, *Churchill's Indian Summer: the Conservative Government 1951–55* (Hodder and Stoughton, London, 1981), p. 114; Anthony Seldon, 'The Churchill Administration 1951–1955', in Peter Hennessy and Anthony Seldon (eds), *Ruling Performance: British Governments from Attlee to Thatcher* (Basil Blackwell, Oxford, 1987), p. 79.

10 Hennessy, *Whitehall*, p. 168.

11 Theakston, *The Labour Party and Whitehall*, pp. 32–45.

12 Kevin Theakston, 'The Heath Government, Whitehall and the Civil Service', in Stuart Ball and Anthony Seldon (eds), *The Heath Government 1970–74: A Reappraisal* (Longman, Harlow, 1996).

13 Dennis Kavanagh, 'The Heath Government 1970–1974', in Peter Hennessy and Anthony Seldon (eds), *Ruling Performance: British Governments from Attlee to Thatcher* (Basil Blackwell, Oxford, 1987), p. 220.

14 Hugo Young, *One Of Us*, paperback edn (Pan, London, 1990), p. 153; Hennessy, *Whitehall*, p. 591.

15 *FDA News*, May 1990.

16 David Butler, Andrew Adonis and Tony Travers, *Failure in British Government: The Politics of the Poll Tax* (Oxford University Press, Oxford, 1994), ch. 9.

17 Hennessy and Coates, *Bluehall SW1?*, p. 10; Treasury and Civil Service Committee, *The Role of the Civil Service: Interim Report*, HC 390, 1992–93, q. 586.

18 *Independent*, 27 August 1990; *Economist*, 1 December 1990; *Financial Times*, 11 June 1993.

19 William Plowden, *Ministers and Mandarins* (Institute for Public Policy Research, London, 1994), pp. 88, 102–9.

20 Bruce Headey, *British Cabinet Ministers* (Allen and Unwin, London, 1974); Simon James, *British Cabinet Government* (Routledge, London, 1992), p. 13.

21 PRO CAB 129/86, CAB 129/90.

22 Kevin Theakston, *Junior Ministers in British Government* (Basil Blackwell, Oxford, 1987).

23 Richard Neustadt, 'White House and Whitehall', in Anthony King (ed.), *The British Prime Minister* (Macmillan, London, 1969), p. 134.

24 *Contemporary record*, April 1990, p. 20; *The Times*, 15 November 1976.

25 Sir Edward Bridges, *Portrait of a Profession* (Cambridge University Press, Cambridge, 1950), p. 19; Shirley Williams, 'The Decision Makers', in *Policy and Practice: the experience of government* (Royal Institute of Public Administration, London, 1980); James, *British Cabinet Government*, p. 45.

26 Graham K. Wilson, 'Prospects for the public service in Britain: Major to the rescue?', *International Review of Administrative Sciences*, 57 (1991), p. 333.

27 Hennessy, *Whitehall*, pp. 402–3.

28 Theakston, *The Labour Party and Whitehall*, p. 29.

29 Keith Middlemas, *Power, Competition and the State*, vol. 3 *The End of the Postwar Era: Britain Since 1974* (Macmillan, London, 1991), p. 455; D. N. Chester, 'The Central Machinery for Economic Policy', in D. N. Chester (ed.), *Lessons of the British War Economy* (Cambridge University Press, Cambridge, 1951), p. 17.

30 Theakston, *The Labour Party and Whitehall*, pp. 28–30.

31 Seldon, *Churchill's Indian Summer*, pp. 171–3; Keith Middlemas, *Power, Competition and the State*, vol. 1 *Britain in Search of Balance 1940–61* (Macmillan, London, 1986), pp. 199–204, 266–8.

32 Hennessy, *Whitehall*, p. 180; Theakston, *The Labour Party and Whitehall*, p. 42.

33 Theakston, *The Labour Party and Whitehall*, pp. 42–4.

34 Bernard Donoughue, *Prime Minister: The Conduct of Policy Under Harold Wilson & James Callaghan* (Cape, London, 1987).

35 *Guardian*, 26 August 1992; Middlemas, *Power, Competition and the State* vol. 3 *The End of the Postwar Era*, pp. 455–9.

36 Young and Sloman, *No, Minister*, p. 73; B. G. Bender, 'Whitehall, Central Government and 1992', *Public Policy and Administration*, 6 (1991), p. 14.

37 Young and Sloman, *No, Minister*, p. 74.

38 Geoffrey Edwards, 'Central Government', in Stephen George (ed.), *Britain and the European Community: the Politics of Semi-Detachment* (Oxford University Press, Oxford, 1992), pp. 74, 78; David Spence, 'The Role of the National Civil Service in European Lobbying: The British Case', in Sonia Mazey and Jeremy Richardson (eds), *Lobbying in the European Community* (Oxford University Press, Oxford, 1993), p. 61.

39 Bender, 'Whitehall, Central Government and 1992', pp. 16, 18.

40 Spence, 'The Role of the National Civil Service in European lobbying', pp. 68–70.

41 Kevin Theakston and Geoffrey Fry, 'Britain's Administrative Elite: Permanent Secretaries 1900–1986', *Public Administration*, 67 (1989), p. 138; *Top Jobs in Whitehall: Appointments and Promotions in the Senior Civil Service* (Royal Institute of Public Administration, London, 1987), p. 17.

42 *Contemporary Record*, Autumn 1987, p. 10. See generally the RIPA report *Top Jobs in Whitehall*.

43 Sir John Hoskyns, 'Whitehall and Westminster: An Outsider's View', *Parliamentary Affairs*, 36 (1983); Sir Douglas Wass, 'The Public Service in Modern Society', *Public Administration*, 61 (1983).

44 *FDA News*, December 1991, p. 3.

45 Nevil Johnson, 'Change in the civil service: retrospect and prospects', *Public Administration*, 63 (1985), p. 431.

2 The Topmost Mandarins

On Whitehall's highest office the social and cultural changes of the half century since the Second World War might seem, on the surface at least, to have made little mark. In 1945 the post of Head of the Civil Service was held by Sir Edward Bridges: educated at Eton, holder of a first-class degree in classics ('Greats') from Oxford, and for twenty years a Treasury high-flyer before being appointed Secretary to the Cabinet in 1938 and then Permanent Secretary to the Treasury and Head of the Civil Service in 1945. The top bureaucratic job in the early 1990s was held by Sir Robin Butler, who was appointed Secretary to the Cabinet and Head of the Home Civil Service in 1988. He had been educated at Harrow and had achieved a first in classics at Oxford (and a rugby blue) before joining the Treasury and gliding to the top via spells in the CPRS think-tank and the Number 10 private office. The comparison would seem to provide wonderful ammunition for critics of elitist, out of touch and amateur mandarins. At the pinnacle of administrative power, the old stereotypes still apparently prevailed, the *Who's Who* entries of the top men in crucial respects interchangeable.

On the whole, even for the politically well-informed, the top civil servants are shadowy figures. They are names in the reference books, the subjects of respectful obituaries, their biographical data aggregated and argued over by sociologists, their contributions and influence often overlooked by historians. Some of them prefer it that way. Sir Douglas Wass, Permanent Secretary to the Treasury 1974–83, once said that he was happy to remain in the background and saw himself as the anonymous 'second violinist at Covent Garden'. Sir Robert Armstrong, Mrs Thatcher's Cabinet Secretary and Civil Service Head 1980–87, confessed that he was 'happier . . . in a kind of backroom'. Writing the first edition of his *Anatomy of Britain*, Anthony Sampson commented that 'with many senior civil servants anonymity is a passion as gripping as fame is for their masters: as they hear a politician proudly produce a phrase that they invented, they feel a thrill of non-recognition'. 'Their comings and goings may revolutionise departments, but they are unproclaimed', wrote Sampson. 'The names of the permanent secretaries . . . are rarely heard outside Whitehall.'[1]

In many ways, though, senior officials have become less anonymous and more 'visible' in the 1980s and 1990s compared to earlier decades. There have always been individual top civil servants who have had a public profile or aroused controversy: for example, Sir Robert Vansittart and Sir Horace Wilson in the 1930s, and Dame Evelyn Sharp (the first woman to become a permanent secretary – in 1955 – and a legendary figure in the Whitehall pantheon). But – whether they like it or not – the spotlight has increasingly been turned on the higher mandarins. They frequently appear as witnesses before the House of Commons departmental select committees established in 1979 (which are now televised). In the 1960s Anthony Howard was 'seen off' as Fleet Steet's first would-be 'Whitehall correspondent', but the quality press now reports major civil service appointments and promotions, and occasionally carries interviews with or 'profiles' of the leading officials (with Peter Hennessy emerging as the media's leading 'Whitehall-watcher' in the 1970s and 1980s). Serving civil servants have discussed their work on radio and television programmes (Sir William Armstrong being the first Head of the Civil Service to give a long interview on television). Ex-ministers' published diaries and memoirs sometimes give frank (if one-sided) accounts of their officials' personalities and views (perhaps most notoriously, the Crossman *Diaries*).

'Thirty years ago few even among the quality papers' readership would have had more than the sketchiest notion of who Sir Norman Brook was', Peter Hennessy has suggested, 'and yet no history of the Attlee, Churchill, Eden or Macmillan administrations would be complete without a detailed treatment of Brook, his character and his considerable and sustained influence as Cabinet Secretary 1947–62'. The contrast with Sir Robert Armstrong – 'the most public public servant since Cardinal Wolsey' – is marked. Armstrong in the 1980s achieved a great and unwanted notoriety as a result of his role in the GCHQ, Ponting, Westland and *Spycatcher* affairs – his Australian courtroom appearances defending the banning of Peter Wright's book made him 'a household name, his face a nightly feature on the television screen' says Hennessy.[2]

Will the Real Sir Humphrey Please Stand Up?

'The Civil Service is run by a small group of people who grew up together', a Treasury official told the authors of a now classic study of Whitehall.[3] Critics of the civil service often seize on evidence about senior officials' class origins and educational backgrounds to argue that their political sympathies must be skewed to the right. As Harold Laski put it in 1942: 'The major assumptions of the important officials are roughly those of the ruling class' – a view still found in left-wing circles. But to 'read off' senior civil servants' political values and administrative behaviour from data on their class backgrounds and public school/Oxbridge education is bad sociology. Senior officials do 'grow up' together but, arguably, more emphasis should be placed on their post-entry socialization into the culture of Whitehall than on pre-entry (family and educational) socialization.

Although it has its limitations as a methodology, analysing basic biographical data (from *Who's Who* and other sources) for groups of Permanent Secretaries at different times over the post-war period tells us something about the character of Britain's administrative elite (table 2.1).[4]

The first point to note about the 111 individual Permanent Secretaries featured in this table (one is counted in two columns – Sir James Dunnett, who was successively the chief official at the Ministry of Transport 1959–62, Ministry of Labour 1962–66, and Ministry of Defence 1966–74) is that only three women are included: Dame Evelyn Sharp (Permanent Secretary at the Ministry of Housing and Local Government 1955–66), Dame Mary Smieton (Permanent Secretary at the Ministry of Education 1959–63), and Valerie Strachan (appointed as head of Customs and Excise in 1993). Only two of the total of 304

Table 2.1   Permanent Secretaries and their experience

	1945	1960	1970	1980	1993
Oxbridge	22 78.6%	19 73.1%	15 88.2%	14 66.6%	14 70.0%
Average age	55.9	55	56.2	56.4	55
Average prior Whitehall service	28.5 years	31.6 years	29.6 years	30.8 years	29.1 years
Private Office experience	18 64.3%	12 46.1%	10 58.8%	16 76.2%	15 75.0%
Treasury experience	9 32.1%	10 38.7%	8 47.1%	7 33.3%	9 45.0%
Cabinet Office (inc. CPRS) experience	0	4 15.4%	6 35.3%	10 47.6%	9 45.0%
Stint in Number 10 Office	1 3.6%	1 3.8%	0	4 19.0%	3 15.0%
Total	28	26	17	21	20

Notes:
1. The table refers to Permanent Secretaries heading the major Whitehall departments in the year featured and does not include data on Second Permanent Secretaries or their earlier equivalents or other Permanent Secretary-ranking posts.
2. 1970 data refers to the situation after Heath's departmental reorganization.
3. Age and prior Whitehall service calculated for the year in question, not for the year in which first appointed Permanent Secretary (if earlier).

Permanent Secretaries serving in the 1900–86 period were women, and only a small number have made it to Second Permanent Secretary rank. Under John Major there are now three women among the 48 senior officials ranked at Permanent Secretary level: the heads of Customs and Excise and MI5, and the Director of Public Prosecutions.

The Oxbridge dominance among the Whitehall 'top brass' has remained pronounced in the post-1945 period. Oxford and Cambridge actually increased their representation at Permanent Secretary level over the century, from 62.7 per cent of all Permanent Secretaries in the 1900–19 period to 75 per cent in the 1965–86 period. However, changes in the background of open competition graduate entrants to the cadet grade of the higher civil service since the 1960s may well mean that more Permanent Secretaries in the twenty-first century come from non-Oxbridge universities.

Although a Harrovian (Sir Robin Butler) succeeded an Etonian (Sir Robert Armstrong) as Head of the Civil Service in 1988, most Permanent Secretaries are nowadays the products of state grammar schools or minor public schools (since 1900 three in every five Permanent Secretaries have attended public schools). The 1945 group included five old Etonians and four others from elite 'Clarendon' schools, with only four educated in the state sector. The 1993 group has only one from Eton and four from state schools. Comparing the post- and pre-1945 data, the proportion within the public school category coming from the most exclusive 'Clarendon' schools has fallen by more than half, while the numbers coming from the direct grant, aided and maintained (day and mainly day) schools has risen to half the total. Permanent Secretaries, the evidence suggests, are largely the offspring of the middle classes, with an increasing proportion coming from lower-middle and even working-class backgrounds and a reduced upper-class contingent. As Kellner and Crowther-Hunt put it, 'Today's mandarins tend to come from families of great diligence and a little prosperity, rather than great prosperity and a little diligence.'[5]

Turning to their career experience, it can be noted that the over-whelming majority of Permanent Secretaries after 1945 entered the civil service straight from university as Assistant Principals in the cadet grade of the old Administrative Class. A small number had initially entered lower grades in the service but were promoted into and then moved up the main administrative hierarchy. Included in table 2.1 are: Sir John Lang, Permanent Secretary at the Admiralty 1947–61, who had joined that department in 1914 as a Second Division Clerk aged 18 and was promoted to the Assistant Principal rank in 1930; Sir Richard Way (Permanent Secretary at the War Office 1960–3 and at Aviation 1963–6), who had joined the civil service as a 19-year-old Executive Officer, Sir Donald Vandepeer (Permanent Secretary at Agriculture 1945–52) who had entered Whitehall at age 18, and Sir John Garlick (Permanent Secretary at Environment 1978–81) who had joined the civil service at age 16. A neat contrast is provided by the case of Sir Terence Heiser (Permanent Secretary DOE 1985–92), who had been born on a council estate in Dagenham and joined the civil service as a clerical officer aged 16 in 1949, studying for a degree in the evening at Birkbeck College and passing the 'limited opportunity' exam to enter the Administrative Class in 1960, and his successor, Richard Wilson, who had gone to an independent boarding school (Radley) and Cambridge (in 1994 he moved across to head the Home Office).

The heads of the Lord Chancellor's Department have invariably been lawyers but hardly any other specialists have travelled along the post-Fulton 'open road to the top' in the main departments of state. Sir James Hamilton, Permanent Secretary at the Department of Education and Science 1976–83, had spent the bulk of his career in aircraft research and experimental establishments (including work on the Concorde project) before being appointed a DTI Deputy Secretary in 1971 and then being picked to head the Cabinet Office's economic secretariat (1973–6). Sir Trevor Hughes, Permanent Secretary at the Welsh Office 1980–5, had joined the Ministry of Transport from municipal engineering at the age of 36, climbing his specialist ladder before taking on senior administrative jobs in the Open Structure in the 1970s.

As the figures indicate, Permanent Secretaries in the post-war period continue to be civil service 'lifers', with on average three decades of Whitehall experience under their belts. Whereas nearly three-quarters of Permanent Secretaries in the 1945–86 period had spent more than twenty-five years in Whitehall before appointment to their positions, only 28.1 per cent had done so in the 1900–19 period (when 32 per cent had served ten years or less), illustrating the way in which the civil service became much more of a lifetime career profession over the course of the century. In other professions (including politics), outstanding men and women can reach very senior positions in their early forties or even their thirties – but not so in Whitehall. In the 1900–19 period, 28 per cent of Permanent Secretaries were appointed before the age of 45 and almost half before the age of 50. But in the 1965–86 period, no Permanent Secretaries at all were appointed to that position before the age of 45, and only one in seven before the age of 50. Thirteen (46.4 per cent) of the 1945 group of Permanent Secretaries in table 2.1 were appointed before the age of 50 compared to six (30 per cent) of the 1993 group. Not since 1945, when Sir John Maud, a war-time 'temporary', was appointed head of the Education Ministry aged 39, has a Permanent Secretary been appointed under the age of 40. Mrs Thatcher and John Major, in their top-level appointments and promotions, on occasion plumped for the (slightly) younger man in his late forties (examples including Sir Terence Burns appointed as Permanent Secretary to the Treasury in 1991 aged 47 and Sir Clive Whitmore sent to head the MoD in 1983 aged 48). Highly critical of what he says is a fossilized Whitehall culture, Sir John Hoskyns (a former Thatcher adviser) said that, given the chance to remodel the civil service, he would pension-off all officials over the age of 50: it can be seen that this would mean virtually decapitating the higher civil service as it is presently structured.

Whitehall opened up a great deal during the Second World War and three of the 1945 group included in table 2.1 had been brought in to government as 'outsiders' at that time: Sir George Gater (Permanent Secretary at the Colonial Office 1939–47) had had a local government career, culminating in the position of Clerk to the London County Council (1933–9); Oliver (later Lord) Franks had been a professor of philosophy before joing the Ministry of Supply as a war-time 'temporary' in 1939, rising swiftly to head the department 1945–6; and Sir John Maud also entered Whitehall from academic life, finishing as Permanent Secretary at Education (1945–52) and then at Fuel and Power (1952–9). Sir Laurence Helsby, Permanent Secretary at the Ministry of Labour 1959–62 and Head of the Civil Service 1963–8, was another don turned war-time civil servant (in the Treasury), who was marked out for high office after serving as Attlee's Principal Private Secretary in Number 10, 1947–50.

Three of the 1993 group of Permanent Secretaries have, by civil service standards, unconventional career backgrounds. Sir Terence Burns (Treasury) had been a London Business School academic (educated at a state grammar school and Manchester University) before being recruited as the government's Chief Economic Adviser in 1980, succeeding Sir Peter Middleton as Permanent Secretary in 1991. Sir David Gillmore (Foreign Office) joined the diplomatic service aged 36, after having worked for Reuters and as a teacher in London. And Sir Patrick Brown (Transport) had worked as a management consultant in the UK and abroad before joining the civil service in his early thirties.

The route to the top for Permanent Secretaries in the post-1945 period has been a familiar one involving a series of classic 'policy-mongering jobs' (in the words of Sir Ian Bancroft, Head of the Civil Service

1978–81). The inter-war Head of the Civil Service, Sir Warren Fisher, consciously made top-level appointments on what he called the 'musical chairs' principle, switching the senior men between departments on the grounds that they had to be 'general managers' not 'experts'. Only a quarter of Permanent Secretaries in the 1900–19 period had worked in more than one department before reaching the top civil service rank; the practice then was to climb the hierarchy in a single ministry. In contrast, the figure was two-thirds in the 1945–64 period and three-quarters in the 1965–86 period (when a third had experience of four or more departments before making it to Permanent Secretary level). The 'amateur' tradition of the Whitehall generalist means that a high (though falling) proportion of Permanent Secretaries are parachuted in to head departments they have no previous experience of during their careers: this was the case with 42.9 per cent of 1945's Permanent Secretaries and 30 per cent of 1993's.

The high flyers are picked out by Whitehall's talent spotters for private office service (Bernard's job in television's *Yes Minister*) and many have experience of the powerful central departments of government, as table 2.1 shows. Working as private secretary to a minister (or, less frequently, to a high official), in a key position at the hub of the departmental and Whitehall machine, affords 'inside knowledge of the way decisions are taken and policies made'. In the view of a former insider, private office postings 'are designed to show the young administrator life at the top of Whitehall so that the accepted ways of operating are passed on and the right values are learned at an early stage'.[6] Under one in five of the pre-1945 Permanent Secretaries had had some Treasury experience – the figure is two in five for those featured in table 2.1. Only after 1970 had a large number of Permanent Secretaries any experience of the Cabinet Office, reflecting the dramatic growth of staff of that department in the 1960s and 1970s (apart from the Cabinet Secretary himself, the staff of the Cabinet Office are typically seconded from their departments for a two-to-three year stint). Three of the 1993 Permanent Secretaries had been members of the Central Policy Review Staff earlier in their careers. The trend is clear: increasingly, Permanent Secretaries have at some time in their careers served in agencies concerned with central co-ordination and planning, reinforcing the generalist's identity with the greater civil service society and perhaps also imparting a 'centre' perspective. These criss-crossing career paths probably do more to shape Whitehall's culture and methods than the earlier associations of class and education. 'You must be clubbable. It's a team game', as one insider told Kellner and Crowther-Hunt.

It is worth pointing out that the Permanent Secretaries appointed by Mrs Thatcher after 1979 (by 1990, as her predecessors' appointees retired, she had appointed *all* of the official heads of the major departments) were in background and career experience identikit mandarins of the type who have long found their way to the top of the civil service. The reason why she did not break the mould at the top of Whitehall was because she continued to choose her Permanent Secretaries from the ranks of the career higher civil service and did not bring in 'outsiders' (though a small number came in to key posts at senior levels, for instance Sir Peter Levene at Defence Procurement). Having only a limited pool of choice, it is not surprising that her appointees' career profiles fitted the established pattern. One important development, though, was that the Number 10 private office emerged in the Thatcher years as an increasingly important promotion route. Sir Robert Armstrong had headed it in the 1970s under Heath and Wilson, and two of the 1993 group of Permanent Secretaries (Butler and Whitmore) had actually been Mrs Thatcher's Principal Private Secretary in the 1980s.

The extent of continuity at this senior level – the backgrounds and career-patterns of the heads of the major Whitehall departments – stands out. Indeed, there were tetchy exchanges between Sir Robin Butler and MPs on the Treasury and Civil Service Committee in its 1993–4 hearings on just this question.[7] Over time, the social composition of the Whitehall elite seems likely to broaden in terms of school and university attendance and gender, though progress may be slow and uneven. The greater emphasis now put on responsibility for the management of resources and programmes, and the introduction of executive agencies, may produce a different sort of Whitehall apprenticeship in the future, but it is too soon to tell. 'Your best chance of reaching the very top will still be to stick to the pure, 100% traditional mainline jobs in the Treasury', commented one insider.[8] Nor will opening-up some Permanent Secretary and other senior posts to external competition (the top job at the Employment Department being publicly advertised in December 1994) necessarily lead to major changes in the character of this elite group. Sir Robin Butler has made it clear that he expects that most of the top jobs

Table 2.2 Whitehall's key officials since 1945

Head of the Civil Service	Permanent Secretary to the Treasury	Cabinet Secretary
Sir Edward Bridges (1945–56)	Sir Edward Bridges (1945–56)	Sir Edward Bridges (1938–46)
Sir Norman Brook (1956–62)	Sir Norman Brook (1956–62)	Sir Norman Brook (1947–62)
	Sir Roger Makins (1956–9)	
	Sir Frank Lee (1960–2)	
Sir Laurence Helsby (1963–8)	Sir Laurence Helsby (1963–8)	Sir Burke Trend (1963–73)
	Sir William Armstrong (1963–8)	
Sir William Armstrong (1968–74)	Sir Douglas Allen (1968–74)	
Sir Douglas Allen (1974–7)	Sir Douglas Wass (1974–83)	Sir John Hunt (1973–9)
Sir Ian Bancroft (1978–81)		Sir Robert Armstrong (1979–88)
Sir Robert Armstrong Sir Douglas Wass (1981–3)		
Sir Robert Armstrong (1983–8)	Sir Peter Middleton (1983–91)	
Sir Robin Butler (1988–)		Sir Robin Butler (1988–)
	Sir Terence Burns (1991–)	

will still be filled from within the civil service rather than by imported businessmen and managers.

Whitehall's Powers That Be

The influence and the personal impact on policy of the most senior officials can be greater and more consistent than that of many of the politicians and ministers whose activities attract public and media attention. The bookshelves are loaded with political biographies, memoirs and diaries, but there are very few in-depth studies of the top mandarins, their personalities and careers. Some of the leading figures of post-war

Whitehall can be briefly sketched here, however. At the very top of the civil service ladder (paid at a higher rate than their colleagues in the club of Permanent Secretaries) are a number of 'super permanent secretaries',[9] the mandarins' mandarins: the holders of the posts of Head of the Civil Service, Secretary to the Cabinet and Permanent Secretary to the Treasury. Since 1945, these jobs have been held in different combinations as the pattern of top-level responsibilities has been periodically reshuffled (see table 2.2).

In 1919 the Permanent Secretary to the Treasury was first formally designated 'Head of the Civil Service' and those titles and duties were still combined in 1945, with the job of Cabinet Secretary (which dates from 1916) a separate one on the organization charts, but in fact all three posts were held by the same person 1945–6 – Edward Bridges (though with Norman Brook in place in the specially created post of Additional Secretary to the Cabinet, Bridges concentrated on his Treasury and Civil Service Headship responsibilities). In 1956 the set-up was changed: the Treasury Permanent Secretary remained answerable to the Chancellor of the Exchequer for the Treasury's economic business, and the Cabinet Secretary took on the job of Head of the Civil Service and doubled up as an additional Permanent Secretary to the Treasury, in charge of its Establishments work. A further reorganization in 1962 meant that the Cabinet Secretary ceased to be Head of the Civil Service and moved out of the Treasury, and inside the Treasury there were two Joint Permanent Secretaries, one responsible for financial and economic policy and the other running the 'pay and management side' of the Treasury as Head of the Civil Service. Following the Fulton Report in 1968, with the newly-formed Civil Service Department taking over the Treasury's responsibilities for the civil service, the CSD's Permanent Secretary became the Head of the Civil Service. When Mrs Thatcher abolished the CSD in 1981, the Cabinet Secretary and the Treasury's Permanent Secretary were designated Joint Heads of the Civil Service, the Cabinet Secretary continuing as sole Head of the Civil Service after 1983 (on the retirement of Sir Douglas Wass from the Treasury).

These top-level dispositions have from time to time aroused controversy. In the inter-war period, Sir Warren Fisher's activities as Head of the Civil Service had attracted a great deal of flak. Whitehall's critics in the late 1950s and 1960s tended to decry the concentration of power in the Treasury produced by vesting in its chief, as Head of the Civil

Service, the power to recommend top-level civil service appointments and promotions to the Prime Minister. For Thomas Balogh, 'the power of the Headships of the Treasury and the Civil Service has grown to menace the future of the country', and the job of Head of the Civil Service, he said, should be put into commission to avoid the danger of an 'over-mighty subject'.[10] In some eyes, Sir William Armstrong emerged as just such an 'over-mighty' civil servant as Head of the Civil Service during the Heath government, though the low-key role played by his successors at the CSD after 1974 (when the Head of the Civil Service was certainly less powerful than the Cabinet Secretary) did not forestall speculation about the reshaping of central departments and functions. And there were criticisms in the mid-1980s of the combination of the posts of Cabinet Secretary and Head of the Civil Service, particularly following the Westland affair, on the grounds of the workload involved and the possibility of conflicts of interest (e.g. between acting as the agent of the Cabinet and the PM in the first capacity, and representing the interests of the civil service as an institution in the second), MPs on the Treasury and Civil Service Committee recommending in 1986 that they be separated, but this idea was rejected by the holder of the two jobs (Sir Robert Armstrong) and by the government. (In its 1994 report the TCSC changed its mind and could see no reason why the two posts should not be combined.)

The two leading Whitehall figures – the 'higher divinities' – in the 1940s and 1950s were Sir Edward Bridges (1892–1969) and Sir Norman Brook (1902–67). Bridges was in many ways 'the last great figure of the old school', according to Sam Brittan. As Hennessy puts it, he was 'the finest flowering of the Victorian public servant – high minded, politically neutral, a gifted all-rounder who believed that government was best served by crowding the higher Civil Service with latter-day Rennaissance men'. For Richard Chapman, he was simply 'a great civil servant – possibly the greatest British civil servant of this century'.[11] He played a crucial role at the Treasury in the rearmament process in the late 1930s and, as Churchill's Cabinet Secretary and chief civilian official adviser, was the indispensable head of the bureaucratic nerve centre of the war effort, having to adapt to the Prime Minister's habit of holding meetings in the small hours and his demands for all policy submissions to be put in to him on one side of A4. As head of the Treasury after 1945 he made no claims to be an expert economist – as Burke Trend, in his *DNB* obituary of Bridges, commented, his approach was based instead on an 'irresistible common sense best exemplified by the question which was, for him, the acid test of any decision – "Have you a better alternative?"'

Bridges had a profound influence on the development of the Whitehall machine. As Chapman says: 'His was the most significant influence on the British civil service in the mid-twentieth century; more than anyone else he set a particular stamp on its character and moulded its ethos and traditions.' He had well-developed views on the reform of the machinery of government, preferring a pragmatic rather than a 'theoretical' approach and succeeding in keeping the issue firmly in the grip of the insiders, ensuring only limited change in the process (see chapter 3). He was also a great champion of the generalist tradition of the intelligent layman, his 1950 lecture *Portrait of a Profession* providing 'an inexhaustible quarry of quotations for radical critics', as Brittan put it.

In the 1980s, Whitehall's senior jobs were filled after elaborate 'succession planning' exercises and meetings of the top-level Senior Appointments Selection Committee (SASC). Bridges described his approach like this:

> . . . the job of giving advice to the Prime Minister in these cases is not a matter of forming an order of merit of the candidates for a particular post, nor indeed of forming orders of merit of the candidates for a succession of several posts. The task is much more complicated. It is much more like that of placing the members of a cricket eleven in the field in the way which will give the strongest result for the team as a whole. It is no good settling that a particular man is the best slip fielder in the eleven if you find that you have got to ask him to keep wicket.

Behind the cricketing metaphors, however, was a formidable and skilled operator of the Whitehall machine, who spent nearly twenty years at the very centre of government, worked closely with four Prime Ministers, and who took for granted that officials had to be concerned with what he called 'the continued well-being of the State'.[12]

His style was informal – transacting important business over cups of tea, sitting on the battered sofa in his office; and he apparently had a great sense of fun. In the 1980s, Bridges could seem like a figure from some lost golden age of the civil service. The managerial emphasis, the appeal to private advantage represented by performance-related pay, and the 'Is he one of us?' syndrome of Mrs Thatcher's Whitehall would all have been anathema to him. At the same time, a more critical vew of Bridges would stress that his personal moral code and high standards could sometimes appear like a form of 'ruthless righteousness', as Chapman put it. Himself privy to many secrets, he was a firm believer in 'closed' rather than 'open' government. Outsiders were to be kept on the outside – the 'mysteries' of government kept secret. He was an 'Establishment' man through and through, very much the product of his class and generation, typifying and epitomizing a narrow, self-confident and self-contained ruling class.

'Norman has the most wonderful judgement. He is always right. Pure inborn judgement, because, as I expect you know, he had no background' Harold Macmillan once remarked about Norman Brook. Macmillan – like Bridges – had been to Eton, Brook, the son of an assessor of taxes, to Wolverhampton Grammar School (a direct grant school) and Oxford. His rise in the civil service had been rapid. Sir John Anderson had been Permanent Secretary to the Home Office when Brook joined that department in 1925, and when – unusually for a civil servant – he entered parliament and became a war-time minister, he took Brook with him as his private secretary and personal assistant in a succession of ministries. Aged 40, Brook was drawn into the heart of the Whitehall machine as Deputy Secretary to the Cabinet (1942) and Permanent Secretary of the Ministry of Reconstruction (1943–5). For eighteen months after the war he was formally under Bridges as Additional Secretary to the Cabinet (an arrangement devised to avoid a conflict of status with Ismay, war-time head of the Military section of the Cabinet Secretariat), succeeding to the Cabinet Secretaryship in 1947 and holding the post for the next sixteen years, taking over as Head of the Civil Service in 1956 (see table 2.2). His influence was unrivalled. 'No one in Whitehall, politican or civil servant, knows as much as Brook', wrote Anthony Sampson in the early 1960s. 'Since 1947, under Attlee, Churchill, Eden and Macmillan, he has attended all cabinet meetings and he has been the confidant of all four prime ministers.' He was 'the central cog in the British government machine'.[13]

Brook was indeed a superb 'machine man'. 'Infinitely unobtrusive . . . impenetrably . . . discreet', as Sampson noted, 'He was a master of minutes, with one of those well-tempered minds which can digest a succession of confused arguments, and present them – in his small, neat hand-writing – in perfect order.' 'The need for good order in public affairs' obsessed him.[14] Looking back on Brook's career, his successor as Cabinet Secretary, Burke Trend, felt that his role was, in the classic Whitehall mould, 'essentially regulatory, rather than innovative, in character' and involved 'the reconciliation of multiple and differing views rather than the pursuit of a single, undivided, purpose' (*DNB* entry). 'His natural disposition was that of the co-ordinator', says Trend, searching for agreement and ironing out inter-departmental differences. Brook was in fact one of the chief architects of the post-1945 extended system of Cabinet committees, institutionalizing the striving for consensus inside government.

Austere and formal (compared to Bridges), Brook was also highly politically attuned. He advised his Prime Ministers on the conduct of Cabinet business through the system of 'steering briefs' which he invented in the late 1940s. His close relationship with Churchill (who relied on Brook more than on any other official or minister) and with Macmillan (who called him 'a tower of strength' in his diary) made him the most powerful mandarin of his day – he accompanied them on overseas tours and gave political and not just policy advice to his chiefs, including suggestions about ministerial appointments. As Hennessy has commented, 'Had the extent of Brook's influence over such wholly political matters become known at the time it would have placed him in the unfortunate category [of 'politicized' officials] occupied by Horace Wilson before him and William Armstrong after him.' Bridges had been consulted by Attlee on Cabinet changes, but he had managed to avoid over-identification with the government of the day as Head of the Civil Service; traditionalists, however, would say that Brook came close to falling into this trap.[15] The relations between these two top officials were not in fact altogether close or easy in the 1950s – Brook was an intimate of Churchill whereas Bridges saw little of him, differences of view arose on machinery of government reform, and the Prime Minister increasingly consulted Brook on matters within Bridge's domain (e.g. senior promotions).

Whitehall in the 1960s and early 1970s was dominated by Sir Burke Trend (1914–87) and Sir William Armstrong (1915–80). Trend worked for Macmillan, Home, Wilson and Heath as Secretary to the Cabinet, 1963–73. He had joined what was then called the Board of Education in 1936 with the inevitable first in classics from Oxford, soon switching to the Treasury where he was in the hot seat as the Chancellor's

Principal Private Secretary under Dalton and Cripps in the post-war Labour government, later working closely with Rab Butler as his chief of staff in the office of the Lord Privy Seal 1955–6. A spell as deputy to Norman Brook in the Cabinet Secretariat (1956–9) was followed by senior Treasury jobs before Trend succeeded to the top Cabinet Office job at the start of 1963.

Trend became Harold Wilson's indispensable adviser and aide during the 1964–70 Labour administration. 'In the many crises of the late 1960s, Wilson relied increasingly on Trend, who seemed to encapsulate the best of mandarin virtues. Trend provided him with briefs on everything, advised him on security matters, and was consulted on Cabinet changes', according to Wilson's biographer. Wilson told Barbara Castle that Trend was 'the best civil servant I've known'. But the Cabinet Secretary was 'the anti-hero of the Crossman Diaries': Crossman feeling that Trend helped to water down Wilson's radicalism and alleging that he cooked the Cabinet minutes. Trend's role in the government's defence and nuclear decisions, and his links with the American authorities and with the intelligence services, also aroused suspicions in left-wing circles.[16]

His relationship was Heath was at times more strained. Trend had a clear view of the civil servant's role in advising ministers which was to indicate, in his careful words, 'both the range of possible decisions open to ministers and the probable consequences of adopting any one of these rather than any other'. As Hennessy puts it: 'Trend preferred the Socratic approach in his steering briefs for the Prime Minister – a series of questions from which, in Trend's view, the political chief could be expected to draw his own, and hopefully correct, conclusion. This could infuriate Heath.' Heath wanted a definite view on what should be done, not an analysis of options with their pros and cons.[17] Trend's successor, Sir John Hunt, was perhaps more in the mould of dynamic and active fixer-doers favoured by Heath. 'Trend belonged to the traditional don-manqué civil service . . . Hunt represented a new, executive breed', says Pimlott. A Whitehall insider compared the two in this way: 'Trend was a very rarefied thinker, for whom the distillation of policy and thought into absolutely the right words was his primary function, while Hunt was pre-eminently a manager who was good at the determination of policy and influencing the action that followed.'[18] The Cabinet Office under Hunt in the 1970s was a power house, increasing its policy influence and making the Cabinet Secretary 'the single most powerful official in Whitehall or indeed in the country', in the words of Bernard Donoughue, head of Wilson's and Callaghan's Number 10 Policy Unit.

William Armstrong had an altogether higher public profile than Burke Trend, particularly as Head of the Civil Service after 1968. Like Trend, he had achieved a first in classics at Oxford and had entered the higher civil service in the late 1930s – an extraordinary achievement given his working-class background and a childhood spent travelling round the country with his parents, who became officers in the Salvation Army. He was always near or at Whitehall's centres of power: private secretary to Edward Bridges in the war-time Cabinet Secretariat; Principal Private Secretary to three successive Chancellors of the Exchequer, 1949–53 (Cripps, Gaitskell, and Butler); and he was dramatically promoted over the heads of his superiors from being a Treasury Third Secretary to become the department's Joint Permanent Secretary on the economic policy side in 1962, at the relatively young age of 47.

Sam Brittan's judgement was that Armstrong had 'a better grasp of the then prevailing framework of . . . economic policy than any previous Permanent Secretary'. His approach was more 'forward' than Trend's: 'I tried always never to make a specific recommendation but always to say here are the various options. This is what I think would be the consequences of acting on any of them', Armstrong once recalled. 'And only if, as often happened, the Chancellor said "yes, well, which would you choose" then I would say which I would choose but never without having paraded them all in advance.' Armstrong was influential and successful not because he was a scheming and manipulative Sir Humphrey figure but because of the superior quality of his advice.[19]

In 1968 he took over as Head of the Civil Service, in charge of the newly-created Civil Service Department. He was a publicly-committed reformer – appearing on television, giving speeches and lectures about civil service reform – but was criticized by the apostles of the Fulton Committee for blocking some of its key proposals; in fact, there were many other obstacles in the way of Fulton (see chapter 4).

But Armstrong's name and reputation is inextricably associated with that of Edward Heath because of the controversial role he played during the economic crises of the Conservative government from 1972 onwards. Following his government's 'U-turn' (Armstrong had been in charge of the secret Whitehall committee that had prepared the new strategy),

Heath came increasingly to rely on Armstrong, rather than the Treasury or even his Cabinet colleagues, for advice on economic policy and in the running of his statutory incomes policy. Armstrong became, in fact, Heath's closest political adviser. Union leaders called him the 'Deputy Prime Minister' after he had appeared sitting alongside the premier at Heath's presidential-style televised press conferences. He accompanied Heath at a meeting with the miners' union leadership which was kept secret from the Cabinet. And in the winter of 1973–4, as the government and the NUM clashed, Armstrong urged a tough line and also gave advice on the highly party-political matter of election timing – something which even he later recognized was crossing the boundary between a civil service and a political role. Armstrong, in the Heath years, clearly became a political official, 'not so much in the ideological sense as in his ambitious desire to embrace a policy without the civil servant's ultimate detachment', as Phillip Whitehead put it.[20] He cracked under the strain, a nervous breakdown removing him from the scene in February 1974 at the denouement of the crisis. His early retirement in March 1974 – leaving to become Chairman of the Midland Bank – prevented any awkwardness with the incoming Labour government which had won the election he had advised Heath against calling and with whom he was persona non grata. It was indeed a tragic end to an outstanding career, with William Armstrong entering the textbooks as a model to avoid – another Horace Wilson.

Just as William Armstrong's name is now synonymous with the Heath years, so that of Sir Robert Armstrong is with the Thatcher decade. The fact that he was the only Cabinet Secretary since the post was created earlier this century to have served only one Prime Minister, together with his unprecedentedly high public profile in that role as a sort of prime ministerial fire-fighter during the Ponting, Westland and *Spycatcher* affairs (the latter involving his damaging admission about being 'economical with the truth'), meant that in some quarters he was perceived as too much a creature of the government – 'damaged goods' in the words of the leaders of the SDP/Liberal Alliance in 1986. But in fact, Armstrong can be seen to have upheld the traditional values of a neutral and permanent civil service, loyally and efficiently serving the governments thrown up by the ballot box.

Robert Armstrong's ascent to the Cabinet Secretaryship and the Headship of the Civil Service has the air of inevitability about it. 'He had never in his career been more than a memo's shove from power', said Peter Jenkins. Joining the Treasury in 1950, he showed his 'great skill was as a manager of great men . . . rather than as a manager of great enterprises', in Hennessy's words.[21] He was secretary to the Radcliffe Committee on the monetary system (1957–9), Private Secretary to Roy Jenkins when he was Chancellor of the Exchequer, and Principal Private Secretary to Heath and to Wilson in Downing Street 1970–5, taking over from John Hunt as Cabinet Secretary in 1979 after a spell as Permanent Secretary to the Home Office in the late 1970s. He was, as Bernard Donoughue says, 'a Rolls Royce in Whitehall'.

When Mrs Thatcher abolished the CSD at the end of 1981, Armstrong added to his responsibilities those of the Head of the Civil Service (in tandem with Sir Douglas Wass, head of the Treasury, until 1983). His role as Secretary to the Cabinet and chief official adviser to the Prime Minister, together with responsibility for senior appointments and the management of the civil service, represented a concentration of Whitehall power not seen since the days of Norman Brook in the 1956–62 period.

Armstrong was right at the very centre of the machine in the Thatcher administration: 'talking each day to the PM, sitting by her side in Cabinet and committees, counselling the PM and other senior ministers as to policy options and on the timing and form in which decisions should be taken'.[22] His relationship with Mrs Thatcher was not an intimate one – he was not as close to her as some Cabinet Secretaries have been to their political chiefs (e.g. Norman Brook). And he could by no stretch of the imagination be called a Thatcherite – he was not 'one of us', his private views apparently being of the 'one nation'/small 'c' conservative type. But as one insider said, 'She trusts Robert's judgement, trusts him to get a solution, to smooth out problems.' 'She needs people (like Robert) who can fix things and make things happen', noted another inside observer.[23] Unlike John Hunt, however, he did not conceive of the Cabinet Office as an activist policy initiator: 'he is not an earth-mover like Hunt, nor is he a reformer or a policy entrepreneur' is how Hennessy compared them. 'Armstrong was always more in the faithful servant mould, who provided a rescue kit for Mrs Thatcher when occasion demanded', comments Seldon. It is known that his advice was overridden on the GCHQ union ban in 1984, when he had preferred a 'no-strike' agreement; he also opposed the abolition of the CPRS by Mrs Thatcher. But he is said to have been a key figure in the negotiation of the 1985 Anglo-Irish agreement. Seldon concludes that Armstrong was probably not the most powerful Whitehall official in the 1980s, suggesting that Sir Peter Middleton (Permanent Secretary to the Treasury) had more influence over the direction of policy.

The selection of Sir Robin Butler to take over as Cabinet Secretary and Civil Service Head at the beginning of 1988 showed that the public service values of the likes of Robert Armstrong and Edward Bridges would continue to be upheld and displayed at the top of Whitehall beyond the political lifetime of Mrs Thatcher and into the late 1990s (Butler being only 50 on appointment). Given Butler's background, his years in the Treasury (which he entered in 1961), and his time in the Number 10 private office under Heath, Wilson and Thatcher (her Principal Private Secretary 1982–5), it is easy to see why Hennessy could talk of a 'natural apostolic succession' when he slipped into Robert Armstrong's seat. Butler was a classic Northcote-Trevelyan high flyer – 'a Renaissance prince', in Hennessy's words, with the personal style of 'an enthusiastic public school head boy' (riding a bicycle to work even as a Permanent Secretary). Like Armstrong, his forte was the traditional mandarin one of policy, not management, in the judgement of an insider, though he had been the Treasury's Principal Establishment Officer (1980–2) and had lead the team which set up the Whitehall computer system for monitoring and controlling public spending in the 1970s.[24]

With civil service morale low in the late 1980s and early 1990s, Butler chose to give his Head of the Civil Service duties a higher priority than Armstrong had done, visiting civil service offices around the country and treading the boards in lecture halls to set out his views on the continuing importance of the civil service as 'part of the infrastructure of a democratic society', as he called it. He admitted to a traditionalist view of the system of government and the role of the civil service, speaking on one occasion of its 'traditional strengths [and] duties – the requirements of equity, accountability, impartiality and a wide view of the public interest'.[25]

Butler was concerned to ensure that the Next Steps changes were seen as a politically-neutral development and anxious to emphasize that the civil service was, after a decade of Thatcherism and successive Conservative election victories, still able to play its textbook role as the efficient and impartial instrument of the government of the day, whatever its political complexion, meeting Neil Kinnock in the run-up to the 1992 election to offer reassurances and discuss Labour's plans in the event of a change of government. Nevertheless, Butler was himself in danger of being drawn into political controversy in the autumn of 1994 when, in investigating allegations of ministerial 'sleaze', some commentators argued that he was providing political cover for the Conservative government. His assertion to the Scott inquiry into arms to Iraq that 'half the picture can be true' also made him look like an apologist for dubious ministerial actions. Questions were raised about whether he would be acceptable to the Opposition in the event of a change of government, though he is due to retire in 1998 anyway and there was press speculation that he may go earlier.[26] But in terms of the traditional mandarin values for which he stands, and not only because of his background, the comparison with Edward Bridges, holder of his post in 1945, which was drawn at the start of this chapter, still seems rather fitting.

Notes

1   Anthony Sampson, *Anatomy of Britain* (Hodder and Stoughton, London, 1962), pp. 236–7.
2   Peter Hennessy in *Contemporary Record*, Winter 1988, pp. 28–31.
3   Hugh Heclo and Aaron Wildavsky, *The Private Government of Public Money*, 2nd edn (Macmillan, London, 1981), p. 76.
4   Kevin Theakston and Geoffrey Fry, 'Britain's Administrative Elite: Permanent Secretaries 1900–1986', *Public Administration*, 67 (1989), pp. 129–47.
5   Peter Kellner and Lord Crowther-Hunt, *The Civil Servants* (Macdonald, London, 1980), p. 193.
6   Kellner and Crowther-Hunt, *The Civil Servants*, p. 153; Clive Ponting, *Whitehall: Tragedy and Farce* (Hamish Hamilton, London, 1986), p. 79.
7   Treasury and Civil Service Committee, *The Role of the Civil Service*, HC 27, 1993–4, qs. 1371–90, 2175–77.
8   Quoted in: Grant Jordan, *The British Administrative System: Principles versus Practice* (Routledge, London, 1994), p. 157.
9   Gavin Drewry and Tony Bucher, *The Civil Service Today*, 2nd edn (Basil Blackwell, Oxford, 1991), p. 92.
10 Thomas Balogh, 'The Apotheosis of the Dilettante: The Establishment of Mandarins', in Hugh Thomas (ed.), *The Establishment* (Anthony Blond, London, 1959), p. 121.

11 Samuel Brittan, *Steering the Economy* (Penguin, Harmondsworth, 1971), p. 69; Peter Hennessy, *Cabinet* (Basil Blackwell, Oxford, 1986), pp. 17–18; Richard Chapman, *Ethics in the British Civil Service* (Routledge, London, 1988).

12 *Top Jobs In Whitehall* (Royal Institute of Public Administration, London, 1987), p. 19; Sir Edward Bridges, *Portrait of a Profession* (Cambridge University Press, Cambridge, 1950), p. 27.

13 Sampson, *Anatomy of Britain*, pp. 244–5.

14 Peter Hennessy, *Whitehall* (Secker and Warburg, London, 1989), p. 146.

15 Hennessy, *Whitehall*, p. 148; Anthony Seldon, *Churchill's Indian Summer: the Conservative Government 1951–55* (Hodder and Stoughton, 1981), p. 108.

16 Ben Pimlott, *Harold Wilson* (Harper Collins, London, 1992), p. 347; Hennessy, *Whitehall*, p. 217; *The Times*, 22 July 1987.

17 Brittan, *Steering the Economy*, p. 52; Hennessy, *Whitehall*, pp. 237–8.

18 Pimlott, *Wilson*, pp. 622–3.

19 Brittan, *Steering the Economy*, p. 71; *The Times*, 15 November 1976; David Dillman, 'The Paradox of Administrative Power: John Macy and William Armstrong', *Public Policy and Administration*, 5 (1990), pp. 5–18.

20 *The Times*, 15 November 1976; Hennessy, *Whitehall*, p. 239.

21 Peter Jenkins, *Mrs Thatcher's Revolution*, paperback edn (Pan, London, 1989), p. 196; Hennessy, *Whitehall*, pp. 659–70.

22 Anthony Seldon, 'The Cabinet Office and Coordination 1979–87', *Public Administration*, 68 (1990), p. 118.

23 Hennessy, *Cabinet*, p. 22; Hennessy, *Whitehall*, p. 663.

24 Hennessy, *Whitehall*, pp. 670–5.

25 *Contemporary Record*, April 1990, pp. 20–1.

26 *Independent on Sunday*, 30 October 1994 and 6 November 1994; *The Economist*, 26 November 1994.

3 Business as Usual: The Civil Service in the 1940s and 1950s

Whitehall and the Second World War

'Wars have always been great watersheds of administrative history', Gavin Drewry has observed, 'bringing in new people . . . breaking down old rigidities . . . and changing the culture.' 'One expects there always to be a ratchet effect – in the sense that things never quite revert to their pre-war state', he says, 'but in the case of the post-1945 civil service, that ratchet did not work very effectively.'[1]

Victory in the Second World War boosted the prestige of Britain's governing institutions and strengthened the country's institutional conservatism. In the mid-1950s it was for Sir Edward Bridges, Head of the Civil Service, a matter of pride that 'much of the character of the Civil Service of today derives to no inconsiderable extent from the Northcote–Trevelyan Report [of 1854]'.[2] Bridges and other senior officials strongly resisted any suggestion of a fundamental overhaul of the civil service and the Whitehall machine in the post-war period. They got away with this because there was no powerful political impetus behind a programme of administrative modernization.

The war had had an immense impact on the civil service. The volume of administrative work and the tempo of business increased enormously as government took on functions of economic control and direction. Existing departments were expanded and new ones sprang up

(Supply, Food, Fuel and Power, Aircraft Production, Information, etc). Civil service numbers expanded dramatically: from 347,000 in 1939 to over 1.1 million in 1945. (Figures quoted in this book on the size of the civil service follow the convention of excluding staff of the Post Office, which became a public corporation in 1969. See *Civil Service Statistics – 1994* (HM Treasury, 1994), p. 41.) There was wholesale evacuation and dispersal of staff from London to the provinces and seaside towns. Recruitment by competitive entry was suspended as many younger officials went into uniform and thousands of 'temporaries' poured into the service. At the very top of the machine, Churchill injected a new sense of urgency – the senior mandarins had been dismayed by his accession to the premiership in May 1940 but within days could actually be seen running along the corridors.

The war's impact can be measured not just in the immediate upheaval it caused but also in the way it influenced and shaped developments over subsequent decades. 'In many respects the period from 1945 to the mid-1960s can be interpreted in terms of [the] working through or practical evolution of reforms which had been largely set in motion during the war years', argue Chapman and Greenaway.[3] Similarly, key themes in the post-war debates about Whitehall reform can be traced back to the experiences, lessons and controversies of 1939–45 (in many cases having roots which go back even earlier).

War-time Whitehall was 'a world-beating bureaucracy', in Peter Hennessy's words. He suggests (tongue-in-cheek) that Adolf Hitler was the last person truly to reform Whitehall because the war forced the British government to find new men and to improvise new methods almost overnight, but with impressive results. The civil service was a crucial instrument in producing the most effective mobilization of national resources of any of the combatant powers. Yet, Hennessy argues, 'the reform Hitler forced on Whitehall was undone by the peace because neither the politicans nor the senior Civil Service tried or cared to devise its peace-time equivalent'. This represented, he claims, 'probably *the* greatest lost opportunity in the history of British public administration'.[4]

Although the pre-war civil service had often be lauded as 'the best in the world' (a claim regularly made in the late 1940s and 1950s too), it had had plenty of critics in the 1930s, particularly from the centre-left supporters of more state intervention and planning. The mandarins were often depicted as cautious, negative, out-of-touch and obstructive, when the problems of the 'positive state' required a more constructive, expert and innovative civil service.

What made the difference during the war was the mix of 'career regulars' and 'outside irregulars', says Hennessy. By April 1945, 71.7 per cent of the non-industrial civil service were 'temporaries'. Many were low-level clerks, but in the more senior grades there was a vital injection of 'enthusiasm . . . expertise . . . [and] administrative vision'. The 'temporaries' brought a fresh outlook and their approach to policy-making has been described as 'wider, less orthodox and less concerned with the practical difficulties involved'. 'Can it be doubted that this new blood would have benefited the service even had there been no war?', asked Norman Chester, an academic turned war-time 'irregular'.[5]

There had also been important institutional innovations at the centre of the war-time machine. The creation of the Central Statistical Office (CSO) 'revolutionized government statistics' and provided a better-coordinated quantitative basis for Whitehall decision-taking. Academic economists were brought in to staff the small Economic Section of the War Cabinet which became a key source of economic advice and intelligence, and which was the most important group responsible for the introduction of Keynesian economics into Whitehall. The Prime Minister's Statistical Section (headed by Professor Lindemann [Lord Cherwell]) functioned as something like Churchill's personal think-tank.[6]

'By the end of the war a new administrative order was rapidly coming into existence', Paul Addison has observed. 'New peace-time departments were in place, new administrative procedures were at an advanced stage of preparation and new mentalities were engrained in officials.' Senior officials accepted that certain features of the administrative landscape had been irrevocably changed by the war. From 1942, at least, they were planning on the assumption that the post-war bureaucracy would be considerably larger than the pre-war. The role of government would be expanded in the provision of social services and in the field of trade and industry, they believed, whichever party would be in power in peace-time. 'After the war the demands made upon the Civil Service will increase rather than decrease', warned the Crookshank committee in 1943, '[and] the need for an efficient Civil Service will be greater than ever'.[7]

On the questions of what that civil service should look like and how it should be organized, outside critics were not short of ideas. The military setbacks up to the end of 1942 had stimulated extensive criticism of the government machine and the civil service over the organization of the war effort, and the looming problems of post-war reconstruction provoked concern across the political spectrum about the administrative capabilities of the British system of government. The press carried articles about the need to overhaul the machinery of government. The Select Committee on National Expenditure suggested in 1942 the reorganization of the Treasury, the creation of a specialist select committee to monitor the civil service, and a civil service training college. A Liberal Party committee drew up a reform plan and a PEP broadsheet arguing the case for a central planning staff and better-trained and more expert officials was a particularly influential contribution to the public debate. The *New Statesman* and the prominent Labour Party intellectual Harold Laski contributed from the left to the pressure for change.

Inside Whitehall there was a debate about how far the civil service would need to change its role and character. In July 1942 Sir Donald Fergusson (Permanent Secretary at Agriculture) argued at the first meeting of the Crookshank committee that 'new types of Civil Servant' would be needed as the role of government grew, who should be more in the nature of 'experts'. A few months later Percival Waterfield, First Civil Service Commissioner, wondered if the committee should consider

> the possibility of eliminating or at any rate restricting the tendency of Civil Servants to play for safety with a view to saving their Ministers from troublesome Parliamentary criticism . . . Ultimately, no doubt, success would depend upon the personality of the Ministers themselves, for the risk of criticism must always remain, and unless Civil Servants know that their Minister is prepared to encourage the man who does things at the risk of being wrong . . . a fundamental change of outlook can scarcely be hoped for.

The question was a fundamental one, he argued, because it affected the type of official recruited. It was no use looking for the 'executive-managerial' type unless 'there is a real prospect of his being given a chance to show his paces'. Another Permanent Secretary, Sir Thomas Gardiner, maintained that 'the Service is suffering from in-breeding on both the administrative and executive levels' and criticized 'the unwisdom of a caste system'. He believed that there was a growing need for 'men of managerial capacity'.[8]

It is clear, however, that the senior mandarins tended to see their task as the cautious adaptation of the institutions of government to the likely post-war conditions rather than the preparation of an ambitious and radical redesign. They did not doubt that the basic conventions of parliamentary and Cabinet government would be restored after the war was over. Insiders believed that their approach was more realistic and that outsiders were over-theoretical. They were often preoccupied more with avoiding what were seen as the mistakes of the last post-war period (e.g. the recruitment arrangements after 1918) than with drawing out the positive lessons of the Second World War on questions like business efficiency in departments.[9]

There was, from the middle of the war, a considerable amount of behind-the-scenes activity. In June 1942 a committee of senior civil servants was set up under the then-Financial Secretary to the Treasury to consider the problems of the civil service after the war (the Crookshank committee). From October 1942 a top-level review of the machinery of government was underway with the appointment of the Anderson committee (a Cabinet committee chaired by Sir John Anderson, Lord President of the Council, supported by a parallel civil service group). Sir Alan Barlow of the Treasury chaired committees on government's scientific staff (1942–3) and on the legal departments (1943–4). In 1943 a committee on the training of civil servants was set up (the Assheton committee). The Civil Service Commission had started working on post-war recruitment problems from 1941 onwards. Treasury officials became involved in extensive negotiations with the staff side unions on post-war recuitment and reorganization issues. Following a report submitted in 1941, a White Paper was published in 1943 creating a new combined Foreign Service separate from the home civil service. It is not surprising that the piecemeal development of plans for the post-war civil service meant that even the top officials found it difficult to keep in touch with what was happening and to form a clear picture of how the pieces of the jigsaw fitted together.[10]

As Michael Lee has observed about the war-time 'MG' work, 'the creation of the administrative apparatus of the "Welfare State" . . . was neither a systematic attempt to break with the past nor an elaborate plan for the future'. There was no over-arching administrative vision. The civil service unions were (naturally enough) principally interested in changes of classification, grading and pay-rates. The Anderson committee exercise took care to 'avoid undue radicalism and to incorporate the main interest groups in Whitehall', as Keith Middlemas noted. 'Theoreticians' were excluded and in practice the Treasury dominated the debate and 'argued a "constitutional" case, based on a classical interpretation that had varied little since before 1914'. Unlike the Haldane committee's wide-ranging inquiry in 1918, first principles were eschewed and the status quo of 1939 accepted - analysis of alternative methods of government was ruled out.[11]

The insiders' intention to keep firm control was seen particularly in the case of the Anderson MG review. Stafford Cripps, a firm believer in Fabian scientific administration, had pushed for 'another Haldane' from the summer of 1942. Churchill was unenthusiastic about an inquiry, pooh-poohing 'mere speculation' about the government apparatus and the desire to achieve 'unnatural symmetry' in the pattern of Cabinet and departmental organization. Senior mandarins were determined on an 'inside job' and opposed to a Haldane-style inquiry dominated by outsiders. What was started was a process of internal machinery of government review that lasted, in one form or another, for ten years (1942–52) but, crucially, one with a practitioners' focus on the immediate and practical, eschewing reflections of a constitutional nature or anything like root-and-branch change.[12]

Although they accepted that government would take on a new, wider role after the war, senior mandarins were much more ambivalent about talk of a new role for the civil service itself and a new type of civil servant. The Crookshank committee, for instance, made some radical noises. 'We would appear to be on the eve of changes in the Civil Service even more far-reaching than those which took place after the last war', it suggested in its incisive report in February 1943. 'It will be necessary to contemplate a Civil Service and Civil Servants differing in certain fundamental respects from what we have hitherto known', the argument continued. 'There will certainly be a more clamant demand than hitherto for the quick thinker and the quick mover ready, at a moment's notice, either to advise his Minister or to take executive action and to see a job through to its completion with the minimum of fuss and the minimum of minute-writing.' But the committee was careful to state its view that 'changes in government . . . after the war will be evolutionary rather than revolutionary.'

Waterfield used the committee to push forward with his ideas about new methods of selection and interview for administrators, adapting the psychological tests of the War Office Selection Board for civil service recruitment. The committee supported the proposal for a civil service college (though a year later the Assheton committee came out against this idea). It wanted a less exclusive administrative class, more open to promotions from below and to interchange with the professional, technical and specialist classes – it should become 'a field as open to the best brains from the rest of the Service as to the recruit from outside'. The future efficiency of the civil service, the committee warned, required a change of attitude and approach in two crucial areas. Departmental Permanent Secretaries would need to give a higher priority to their managerial as opposed to their policy role. And the Treasury would have to play a more flexible, constructive, forward-thinking and imaginative role in relation to its establishment work and its responsibilities for civil service management.[13]

The idea of a 'one class' civil service was aired within Whitehall around this time, receiving support from within the Ministry of Labour. Abolishing the distinctions between the administrative, executive and clerical classes, this would have replaced the existing three ladders of promotion with a common ladder – although there would be entry on different rungs, the theory was that the best individuals would climb the fastest. But the Treasury was strongly opposed to this idea, and a conference of Permanent Secretaries considering the Crookshank report in July 1943 turned it down. Instead, the emphasis was put on the 'wider use' of the executive class. Faced with what Crookshank called 'the growing volume of semi-administrative, semi-executive work', an expanded executive class could take on the work generated by increased regulation and controls, could 'underpin' and support the administrative class, and could provide (the Treasury hoped) better-quality promotees for the administrative ranks.[14] Crucially, however, this expedient avoided a major rethink of the structure, role and character of the elite administrative class which dominated the civil service.

The Second World War (like the first) saw a massive increase in the number of scientists and other specialists working for the government (the number of specialists increasing from 8,000 to 9,000 in 1939 to

70,000 to 80,000 in 1945). In the 1930s specialists had been disgruntled because of their inferior salaries and conditions, compared to administrators, the problems caused by the chaotic grading and structures on the specialist side and their subordinate role in policy-making. The influx of 'temporaries' during the war exacerbated these tensions, and the Barlow committee and Treasury dicussions with the IPCS specialists' union addressed the issues of pay and conditions and the post-war reorganization of the specialists' class structure (proposals emerging in a White Paper in September 1945), but this was essentially a 'tidying-up' operation and did not involve a major transformation of the role of the expert inside government.

During the war the Treasury's position as the controlling department in Whitehall was attacked both by outside critics and from within the civil service itself. Always a politically unpopular department, its record in managing the civil service in the 1919–39 period was strongly criticized by the Select Committee on National Expenditure (1941–2). Inside Whitehall there was sniping at its restrictive approach to establishments work and its tendency to give priority to economy rather than efficiency (e.g. skimping on training). Inevitably, as the main instruments of economic policy were direct controls rather than finance, it lost its pre-war primacy. But the Treasury still co-ordinated inter-departmental organization and 'retained a power in the interstices of bureaucracy', on official committees and working parties.[15]

The appointment of Sir Richard Hopkins as Permanent Secretary in 1942 helped restore the standing of the Treasury and the position of Head of the Civil Service, both of which had suffered because of the association of Sir Horace Wilson (1939–42) with Chamberlain's appeasement policies. And the Treasury strongly fought its corner during the machinery of government review, an official committee report of June 1945 ruling out any substantial change in the functions or organization of the central nucleus of the machine – Treasury, Cabinet Secretariat and Number 10 – endorsing the position of the Permanent Secretary to the Treasury as Official Head of the Civil Service, and recommending continued Treasury control of the civil service. The proposals that it should take over responsibility for the machinery of government, and that it should take the lead in coordination at the official level, were designed to further strengthen its position inside post-war Whitehall.[16]

Harold Laski had argued in 1941 that the post-war situation would call for administrative reform on the Northcote–Trevelyan scale to equip the Whitehall machine to deal with the new functions of government and the needs of the 'positive state'. He believed that civil service reform might be a precondition of meaningful social and economic advice after the war and warned the leaders of the Labour Party 'to remember that every great impetus to administrative reform has, in the past, come from outside the Service'. The mandarins had opted for cautious, piecemeal and pragmatic adjustments to the civil service. Would the Labour Party's unexpected and massive election victory in 1945 challenge the Whitehall Establishment and result in a civil service of a new kind?

The Attlee Labour Government and the Civil Service, 1945–51

The dominance of a centralist and statist approach in the Labour Party's traditional socialist thinking gives a vital role to the civil service and the Whitehall machine in the transformation of society. 'The gentleman in Whitehall knows best', one socialist thinker had declared in the 1930s. Yet, outside a small Fabian circle and apart from spasmodic left-wing attacks, Labour has generally not paid much serious or sustained attention to the problems of civil service organization and efficiency. *Let Us Face the Future*, the party's 1945 manifesto, had promised 'the better organization of Government departments and the Civil Service', but made no specific commitments. There had in fact been no proper attempt to work out a reorganization blueprint for Whitehall as part of the preparations in the 1930s and early 1940s for a future Labour government. The party leadership's experience in the war-time Churchill coalition served mostly to reinforce ministers cautious and pragmatic 'insiders' attitude. As Peter Hennessy noted, 'Attlee and his ministers, despite being a radically intentioned government, did not embark on a reform of the Civil Service because they knew the war-time machine personally and liked what they saw. They had seen the recent administrative past and it had worked.'[17]

In the 1930s Attlee had held Haldane-type views on administrative questions, musing over schemes for the reorganization of the Cabinet and the government machine from first principles and criticizing the absence of a 'general staff' in Whitehall, but he dropped these ideas as

Prime Minister. During the war he had put some moderately reformist proposals to the Cabinet's machinery of government committee, backing a civil service staff college, greater interchange with other public organizations and outside business, and splitting the Treasury to put establishments and personnel directly under the Prime Minister. Senior officials could not hide their relief when, in November 1945, he conceded that these ideas needed 'reconsideration in the light of experience'.[18]

Left-wingers may have bemoaned the 1945 government's conservative attitude towards the constitutional framework and its uncritical reliance on Whitehall, but as far as ministers were concerned, they had experienced none of the bureaucratic resistance or sabotage that Laski and others had predicted and that might have spurred a major programme of reform. They rebuffed outside critics, confident that the machine could work in the way they wanted and did not need fundamental reorganization.

At the top of the civil service itself 'it would not have occurred to [Sir Edward] Bridges or [Sir Norman] Brook that there was anything fundamentally wrong with the service over which they provided', Hennessy has written of post-war Whitehall's 'higher divinities'. Bridges had become Head of the Civil Service and Permanent Secretary to the Treasury in February 1945, and neither wished nor saw the need for a major reshaping of the bureaucracy. Bridges towered over post-war Whitehall and was an outstanding Head of the Civil Service but, it is clear, was not an innovator. His 1950 lecture entitled 'Portrait of a Profession' is marked by a sense of 'unquestioning assurance and self-confidence', and even complacency, about the traditions of the civil service, as a later Head of the Civil Service admitted. He did not conceive of Treasury MG work in terms of putting together a 'programme of action', but as dealing *ad hoc* with tricky organizational disputes and problems. He 'played his cards close to his chest' and appeared preoccupied with questions of timing and tactics when handling these matters. Evelyn Sharp – then one of Whitehall's rising stars – complained in 1947 that the distribution of functions between departments was shaped more by guesswork and personalities than by analysis and judgement, and called for a powerful commission on the machinery of government, but Bridges disagreed, wanting to keep insiders firmly in control.[19]

Whenever outsiders attempted to put civil service reform on the agenda during these years, Whitehall's reaction was defensive and blocking. Parliamentary critics, like Labour MP Geoffrey Cooper agitating for greater 'business efficiency', were dismissed as meddlesome and ill-informed. The Treasury responded in its best patronizing manner to a Fabian group's report on *The Reform of the Higher Civil Service* in 1947: their ideas were all very interesting, but there was little in the report that had not already been thought of inside the service.[20]

Cooper had written to Attlee in February 1946 calling for an independent inquiry into government efficiency and a fundamental reorganization to equip the civil service for its new tasks, given that Parliament was now passing legislation that constituted 'a complete change of policy'.[21] To be fair to them, some senior civil servants believed that Cooper's argument could not be ignored. Sir Percival Robinson, head of the Ministry of Works, told Bridges that he thought 'that it will be necessary in certain branches of the Service to train a Civil Servant to do what the industrialist does, namely, look straight at his objective and brush aside all ancillary considerations instead of, as the Civil Servant is normally trained to do, look all round his problem in order to see the snags'. Oliver Franks, a war-time 'temporary' who had risen meteorically to lead the Ministry of Supply, argued that 'The real difficulty was that in recent years the functions of the Civil Service had changed from being purely regulative (functions for which the education and the training of the civil servant were ideally suited) and had become more and more those of management. Instead of analysing the problems of others, the Civil Servant now had to tackle those problems himself.'

Bridges admitted to his fellow Permanent Secretaries that he had been 'working on the general expectation that Civil Service problems would in a year or so resume more or less the same general pattern which they took before the war'. He convened a meeting of Whitehall's top hamper on 2 March 1946 to discuss the issue and the minutes of the Permanent Secretaries' discussion record that the traditionalists carried the day:

> . . . it was possible to exaggerate the extent to which the Civil Service was 'going into management' . . .
>
> Under the present system the civil servant was first and foremost the servant of·his Minister, and so long as that was so his whole training and outlook would be coloured by that fact . . .
>
> . . . the outlook of the civil servant was inevitably influenced by the Public Accounts Committee and by the fact that what he did today

would be the subject of an enquiry in two years' time. The qualities required for business management coud not possibly develop under such conditions . . .

'There were problems of organization and training to be faced', Bridges smoothly summed up, 'but . . . reform should be undertaken by the Civil Service itself rather than imposed from outside as the result of an enquiry . . . On balance the Civil Service would be more likely to get relief by ad hoc adjustments, on a practical basis, than by deliberately raising the very wide issues involved in a way which necessitated a formal full-dress enquiry.'

'You cannot solve the problems of the Civil Service simply by applying business techniques', he then minuted ministers, proposing an internal review by officials 'who, after all, can tell better than any outsider where the shoe pinches without any long process of collecting evidence'. He got his way and a handful of top-level official working parties on civil service organization were set up, covering accommodation, recruitment, training and business efficiency in departments, which reported between October 1946 and July 1947.[22] 'Precious little of substance emerged', as Hennessy comments. The group on business efficiency was adamant that there was no single or simple means of promoting greater efficiency in government; there were many defects and problems with the existing machinery, but there was no single cure available which was universally applicable throughout Whitehall.

'The perils of allowing the British Civil Service to conduct itself as a self-regulating organization' could hardly be more clear, argues Peter Hennessy. His judgement is damning: Bridges 'had carried off *the* classic manoeuvre of professional self-preservation when, for once, the odds seemed stacked in favour of significant and lasting reform'. It must be doubted, though, whether the odds *were* stacked in favour of radical reform. There can be no suggestion that devious mandarins were thwarting reform-minded ministers. As Hennessy acknowledges, 'the key to understanding the lack of result is not timidity . . . but self-confidence'. Ministers, just as much as senior civil servants, felt that the system worked well enough and that sweeping reorganization would be an unnecessary distraction. Without a firm lead from the top politicians there could be little more than limited adjustments and tinkering with the machine.

This pattern was confirmed a year later when, in August 1947, the Commons Estimates Committee issued a report on Organisation and Methods in government departments and also called for a major reorganization of the administrative machine. These questions, the MPs argued, 'should be attacked scientifically and not as a series of piecemeal adjustments'. O and M techniques should be upgraded and directed at 'planning the structure and machinery of government' rather than merely 'attending to its plumbing and maintenance'. 'It is clear that insufficient thought has been given to adapting the machinery of government to its new tasks', the committee continued. 'Little is to be gained by tinkering with a problem of such fundamental importance', it warned.[23]

The committee got nowhere. Whitehall's commitment to a process of internal review and adaptation was too deeply entrenched. The Treasury ignored the recommendation that the recently-established Government Organisation Committee (GOC) of Permanent Secretaries, dealing with machinery of government and efficiency questions, should be strengthened by outside experts on administration. And the Cabinet's MG committee agreed with the Treasury in rejecting the MPs' idea of a complete overhaul of the whole administrative system to be drawn up by a high-powered external inquiry.[24]

Close observers were arguing as early as 1948 that Whitehall had been seriously weakened by the exodus of war-time 'temporaries' returning to their former occupations – perhaps 200 to 300 being lost from senior policy jobs in the first year or two after the war. The fact that nearly all the economists in government service had left Whitehall at the end of the war was a particularly serious problem. In 1944 the Treasury's economists included Keynes, Hubert Henderson and Dennis Robertson, with Lionel Robbins on hand in the Economic Section; but by 1947 the Treasury had no professional economist on its staff. The number of economists/economic advisers found in other departments was very small, and remained so until after 1964 in fact. The dozen or so staff of the Economic Section (which remained in the Cabinet Office until 1953, when it moved to the Treasury) was the most significant group of economists in Whitehall and exercised a great influence on economic policy in the 1940s and 1950s.[25]

For all the (admittedly vague) talk of an 'Economic General Staff', including outside experts, in the 1930s, and despite the importance of 'planning' in the Labour Party's thinking, no central planning staff was created in 1945, resort being had instead to the standard Whitehall device of an inter-departmental ministerial committee and a 'steering committee' of Permanent Secretaries. This machinery failed to work effectively and the appearance of the Central Economic Planning Staff in 1947, combining insiders, outsiders and economists, was a step forward, but this was soon absorbed into the Treasury (when Cripps became Chancellor in November 1947 and the short-lived Ministry of Economic Affairs amalgamated with the Treasury), and it never developed into a proper long-term planning unit as opposed to dealing with short-term *ad hoc* problems. The sort of bureaucratic innovations – of machinery and of personnel – needed to break the grip of the Treasury and bring outside expertise into Whitehall were simply not seriously considered by Labour ministers. Consequently, the Treasury's primacy in economic policy-making had been re-established by the end of 1947.

Continued Treasury control of the civil service had been agreed by the Cabinet's machinery of government committee in October 1945. The stream of Treasury instructions to departments on civil service matters became more continuous than it had been before the war. Conditions of service were more standardized and co-ordinated, and the detailed rules and regulations governing the civil service were set out in the voluminous *Estacode* – the establishment officer's Bible, started in 1944, and regularly updated with amendments sent out from the Treasury. The tendency to greater centralization was also encouraged by the growing size and influence of the main civil service unions, operating through the staff side organization of the National Whitley Council.[26]

In one crucial respect, though, the Treasury pulled back from close, detailed control of the civil service and decentralized its powers, allowing a measure of self-government to departments in terms of control of establishments.[27] Up until 1939 a nineteenth-century approach had been maintained: 'Not one additional clerk or cleaner was to be engaged by a Department without Their Lordship's authority.' The war had, of course, overwhelmed this centralized and restrictive system and the Treasury had been compelled to delegate and give more freedom over staffing to departments.

The lost ground was not clawed back after 1945. The Treasury recognized that it was now physically impossible, owing to the size and complexity of the service, to require departments to justify in advance each single appointment or variation in complements. A circular in July 1949 set out the new ground rules, the Treasury giving up day-to-day control and authorizing departments to vary complements within their approved staff ceilings in respect of posts up to and including the Principal and Chief Executive Officer grades. Unable to control everything in detail the Treasury had opted for more indirect controls (auditing departments' own control mechanisms and their systems of staff inspection), though the difficulties in reducing the size of the civil service in the 1950s, and its expansion from the end of that decade, perhaps indicated the drawbacks of relying on departmental self-restraint in this field.

The delegation to departments did not extend to varying pay and conditions of service, or to creating new classes and grades of post, without reference to the Treasury. Nevertheless, the 1949 decision was a significant move. It marked, as one contemporary commentator saw, 'the high-water mark of centralized control of civil service affairs; after nearly a century of flood tide, the ebb has begun'.[28]

The Attlee government itself cut the size of the civil service substantially, numbers falling from 1.1 million in April 1945 to 740,000 in April 1951 (excluding the Post Office), a reduction of 33 per cent; though the biggest cuts were in the industrial civil service (down by 300,000) rather than the white-collar, non-industrial staff (a reduction of 74,000).

The issue of the size of the civil service was troublesome for Labour ministers because although the government recognized that some of its policies would increase the number of officials, it was also sensitive to parliamentary, press and Conservative Party accusations about a bloated bureaucracy, and it was concerned to reduce the manpower demands associated with rationing, controls and other functions hanging over from the war. Attlee established a Cabinet committee on civil service manpower in November 1946 which reported (in April 1947) that there was little scope for substantial savings of staff through administrative economies; numbers were not inflated in relation to the tasks falling on the service. Any arbitrary cut in the size of the civil service would depend upon policy decisions. Bridges had favoured taking a firm line with ministers: 'if we are to do with fewer people, we can do fewer things', he told colleagues.[29]

The crises of 1947 – first coal and then sterling convertibility – led the Treasury to emphasize even more strongly the need for manpower economy and to keeping within departmental manpower ceilings, though total numbers actually rose 1948–9 (up by 23,000). In November 1948 the ministerial and official committees on civil service manpower were wound up, and the Treasury resumed full responsibility for controlling the size of the civil service. The pressure for economies was kept up after the 1949 devaluation of the pound and in June 1950 Cripps was able to report to the Cabinet a 26,000 net fall in the non-industrial civil service over the eighteen months to April 1950, a large share coming from the relaxation and abolition of various controls. He anticipated, however, that in the absence of major policy changes, staff levels would remain more or less static or decline at a much slower rate. There was limited scope for squeezing out further administrative slack, he thought: 'most of the obvious economies have already been made'. The government was not in an axe-wielding mood. Treasury officials noted in February 1951 that the new Chancellor, Gaitskell, 'seemed to have no great hankerings after an arbitrary cut', and from mid-1951 civil service numbers were rising again.[30]

Just as after the First World War, when the main administrative hierarchy of the service had been reorganized, with the creation of the administrative, executive and clerical classes in 1920–1, there was another bout of reorganization after 1945 (in line with plans drawn up in war-time). The structure of the administrative class was tinkered with: the old grade of Principal Assistant Secretary being abolished and a new Under Secretrary grade appearing, with the Assistant Principal grade being designated as exclusively a training grade. The traditions of the administrative class were not disturbed, however, such as the preference for empirical, 'on the job' training. Although the Treasury set up a Training and Education Division in 1945, only a two-week course was laid on for APs – a far cry from the lengthy and intensive training provided at the elite training college of the French civil service, the *Ecole Nationale d'Administration*, established also in 1945. Innovation in recruitment methods also did not challenge the administrative ideal of the 'all-rounder'. The Civil Service Commission's war-time work bore fruit in the shape of the residential Civil Service Selection Board (CSSB) 'house party' system, used in the post-war 'reconstruction' recruitment exercise. The system of aptitude tests and extended interviews was continued, alongside the established examination route, when normal administrative recruitment was resumed in 1948 (though after 1950,

CSSB or Method II, as it was known, was no longer held at a country house, but in central London).[31]

The war-time plans for the 'wider use of the executive class' led, in 1947, to the simplification and merger of the clerical and executive hierarchies, and to the introduction of the executive class into departments where it had not been used before and the deployment of its members on a much wider range of work than had been the case before the war. Crucially, however, the administrative and executive classes remained separate, helping to perpetuate the administrative class's perception of its role as chiefly a policy rather than a managerial one.

The biggest changes in structure were those affecting the scientific, technical and professional classes. Within a few years of the end of the war, civil service specialists had largely been reorganized into a small number of new groupings and classes, centrally recruited and with common salary scales. The Scientific Civil Service, the Works Group of Professional Classes and the Legal Class were reconstructed in 1946; the Medical Officer Class was also reorganized in 1946, with a second dose of change after 1951; the Statistician Class was created in 1946 and the Information Officer and Librarian Classes established in 1949. Specialists' salary scales were improved, but even so they still lagged behind their administrative and executive equivalents in terms of status, remuneration and career opportunities. Hankey, the former Cabinet Secretary (1916–38), who had been involved in the creation of the Scientific Civil Service, was unimpressed in 1949 with the progress on improving scientists' and technologists' numbers and standing in Whitehall.[32]

The structure of the post-war civil service was also starting to change in a wider, geographical and social sense. Instead of being concentrated in London, its staff were increasingly spread over the country, partly as a result of the growth of the giant 'clerical factories' of the new welfare departments (such as the Ministry of National Insurance's outstation at Newcastle) and partly as a result of government dispersal policies. In 1931, 72 per cent of civil servants had been based in London, but by the late 1950s only about a third of all non-industrial civil servants were based in the capital (and the proportion had fallen to 26 per cent in 1977 and 20 per cent by 1994). The first dispersal agreement was negotiated with the civil service unions in 1948, and by 1963 25,000 jobs had been moved out of London (with more following in later years). A 'two nations civil service' was developing, with many more younger and female staff in the lower grades, and with the unions representing those staff growing in size and strength.[33]

The Civil Service under the Conservatives in the 1950s

There was a certain amount of apprehension in Whitehall about the Conservative's 1951 manifesto plans to 'simplify the administrative machine' and reduce 'waste and extravagance' in government. The allegedly excessive size of the civil service had ben an obvious target for Conservative attacks in the late 1940s, with Churchill depicting the country as 'one vast Wormwood Scrubbery', shackled by controls and bureaucracy. 'In Opposition many of us concluded that the country was suffering under a weight of government which was excessive both of money and of effort', noted one Conservative minister (Lord Woolton), 'and we looked forward to a freer society which relied less on either direction or support from Government Departments'. But the remark that 'the nation requires its best men in the civil service', made in the (1946) report of a Conservative study group on the constitution, contrasts with the more abrasive Thatcherite line in the 1980s that if officials were any good, they would be making money in the City and not working in government.[34]

Conventional 'reformist' ideas had been aired in Conservative circles after 1945: the better use of scientists and other expert advisers; improved recruitment and training practices; ending Treasury control of the civil service (some Tories blamed the Treasury for holding down defence spending in the 1930s, others criticized the patronage powers of the Head of the Civil Service). After 1951, however, there was no political weight put behind these proposals. Lord Woolton complained in 1954 that the Cabinet had never discussed the reform of the machinery of government. Leading ministers took little interest in the issue. Churchill had his own ideas, wanting to reduce the power of the Treasury and cutback the inter-departmental committee system. But after spending some time with Sir Norman Brook early on in the government, discussing MG issues, he soon lost his enthusiasm for reform. His 'overlords' experiment – appointing political trustees as co-ordinating ministers in the Lords – was opposed by senior ministers and civil servants as well as by the Labour Opposition, and was abandoned after two years.[35]

The leading Permanent Secretaries in the early 1950s were, for the most part, departmentally-minded and little interested in broad MG questions. The GOC was by now reported to be 'practically moribund' and was finally wound up in 1953. Inside the Treasury, MG work was downgraded. Bridges was still committed to the process of internal reform started in the 1940s, and was particularly concerned to rejig the government's economic organization. But Brook was more sceptical about the likely benefits of pressing on with this work and was closer in outlook to the new government. 'If those of us who have lived all our lives in Whitehall and have studied the Whitehall organization give up as hopeless all attempt to reform it from inside, then what hope is there of any reform in our time?' Bridges asked Brook in March 1952.[36]

The restricted terms of reference given to the Royal Commission on the Civil Service that was announced in July 1953 (the Priestley Commission) illustrated the unwillingness to open up a wide-ranging debate about civil service and machinery of government reform. Only a narrow inquiry into pay and conditions of service was instituted, with the Commission itself complaining of the limitations imposed by the narrow scope of its remit as compared to the previous Tomlin Commission (1929–31). The Treasury had been clear from the start about what would be out of bounds to the Commission. 'Should [it] have wide scope, like Tomlin, to examine all Civil Service questions? We think not . . . there is a lot to be said for limiting the Commission's work as far as possible', said a Treasury briefing paper for Bridges. A meeting of Permanent Secretaries in May 1953 agreed that issues of structure and organization would be excluded from the Commission's terms of reference, Bridges minuting the Chancellor, 'I don't think that they would make much contribution' (an earlier draft of the memo said, more bluntly, 'somewhat smugly, we doubt whether there is much practicable in the way of reform in these directions').[37]

The civil service unions reacted lukewarmly to the appointment of the Royal Commission, concerned that it would serve the Treasury's interests rather than theirs. It was in fact becoming increasingly clear in the early 1950s that the existing civil service pay system was not working well, with frequent disagreements arising between the two sides in the Whitley machinery and more frequent resort to arbitration. Treasury officials believed that an outside inquiry might be the way to defuse pressure for increased pay and overhaul the whole salary structure. Butler (the Chancellor) said that the government wanted guidance on the principles to inform future civil service pay changes and a more coherent overall structure. 'Piecemeal settlement of claims is unsatisfactory and expensive', he told Churchill.

Priestley's report, published in November 1955, made little public impact – it was never debated in Parliament and had a poor press. It was mocked as 'unreadable and unread' by one commentator, who called for another Royal Commission to explore the big issues it had left untouched. However, many of its detailed recommendations were quietly implemented over the next few years, such as the introduction of a five-day week (which 'ended the ritual of arriving for work on Saturday morning equipped with golf clubs and country suits', recalled a then-junior administrator). The most important recommendation was that the primary principle governing civil service pay should be 'fair comparison with the current remuneration of outside staffs employed on broadly comparable work', and it proposed the establishment of an independent fact-finding body (what became the Pay Research Unit). Priestley aimed to prevent civil service pay from becoming a matter of political controversy, but can be criticized for assuming that the money would always be available for governments to meet the bill – something that seemed much less reasonable twenty years later, in a different economic climate and with governments more concerned to limit public spending.[38]

The Commission was debarred from addressing the question of what sort of civil service was really needed for the 'positive state' and how it should be organized – Fulton's agenda a decade later. It recognized, for instance, that specialists were now a more numerous and important part of the bureaucracy than before the war (totalling 25 per cent of the non-industrial civil service by 1955), but could deal only with issues of pay and relativities, though its proposal to treat higher officials of all classes as a single group for pay purposes foreshadowed later moves to unified grading. Treasury officials might still extol the generalist's 'wider viewpoints' and 'greater versatility', and claim that 'the average AP [Assistant Principal] entrant is a superior article to the average SO

[Scientific Officer] entrant', but concern about the specialist's place in Whitehall continued to build up, and the issue was to become much more controversial in the 1960s. Similarly, leading civil servants in the 1950s continued to display a rather patronising attitude towards the executive class and the managerial aspects of government work. Keeping the machine running was a job for the NCOs, they implied, while the officer corps concentrated on policy – but critics rightly argued that this distinction was becoming increasingly unrealistic and damaging with the expansion of public services.[39]

The need for a fresh look at problems of recruitment and structure was argued by some outside commentators. More and more young people who, before 1939, would have entered for the Clerical Officer competitions now stayed on at school after 16. The percentage of the relevant age group entering university doubled between 1938 and 1955 (and grew even faster in the 1960s). Full employment made civil service job security, pay and pensions less attractive than in the 1930s, and significant shortfalls in recruitment were emerging. To some extent, the gaps could be filled by relying more on internal promotions and other expedients (60 per cent of executive class vacancies were filled this way in the 1950s, and the proportion of the administrative class who were promotees from below had doubled to about two-fifths by the mid-1950s compared to the 1930s). But a proper consideration of recruitment policy, the development of talent within the service, and the relations between the classes on the administrative side would have to be undertaken sooner or later.[40]

Equal pay for women in the civil service was finally achieved in 1955, thirty-five years after the House of Commons had first passed resolutions (in 1920 and 1921, and on several subsequent occasions) in favour of equality of opportunity and equal pay in government service. In the late 1930s it had been decided that on recruitment women would be paid the same as men, but that their maximum salary would be 80 per cent of the men's in each grade. The influx of women into the civil service in wartime (by 1944 the number of women in the non-industrial civil service was almost equal to the number of men) galvanized the unions' campaign, the Royal Commission on Equal Pay (1944–6) reporting that over a big field, men and women in the civil service were doing identical jobs equally well, but on unequal pay.[41]

In October 1946 the Labour government had abolished the marriage bar (under which women civil servants who married had to resign), a change reflecting a shift in public attitudes towards working wives (in 1931 only one wife in ten worked, in 1951 more than one in five, and in the 1980s more than one in two) and the widespread employment of married women during the war, when the bar had been suspended. Labour Chancellors had said that the government was committed to equal pay in principle but had repeatedly refused to introduce it, claiming that it would be costly and could fuel inflationary pressures in the economy.[42]

Matters came to a head in the early 1950s. The Conservative manifesto committed them to introduce equal pay, finances permitting, but Butler ruled out any action in 1952. The unions stepped up the pressure, presenting petitions with 680,000 signatures in 1954 and employing a public relations firm to help organise their campaign. In February 1954 John Boyd-Carpenter, the Financial Secretary, minuted Butler that the financial argument against equal pay now looked less convincing, suggested its phased introduction, and warned that to delay the start might make it appear as just 'a last minute electoral bribe'. Although there was opposition inside the Treasury, negotiations began in May 1954 and in February 1955 the two sides of the Whitley Council reached agreement on the introduction of equal pay by stages, over six years from 1 January 1955.

(This agreement did not apply to women in the industrial civil service, however, who had to wait until 1970, on the grounds that the government could not take the lead over other industrial employers. Following the 1970 Equal Pay Act, steps were taken to introduce equal pay in this sector too.[43])

The Conservatives struggled throughout the 1950s to cut the size of the civil service, which stood at 740,000 in April 1951. Bridges had had papers on this subject prepared inside the Treasury during the 1951 election campaign.[44] 'There is undoubtedly still some slack in the Civil Service' minuted Douglas Wass (then a Principal, later the Treasury's Permanent Secretary). 'But really drastic reduction could only be achieved by the deliberate curtailment of existing services or by the sacrifice of a good deal of efficiency.' Another official argued that 'many frills could be cut off, if Ministers were in a mood, *which existing [i.e. Labour] Ministers never have been* in, to effect economies' (emphasis in original), and identified the Ministries of Supply, Education and Labour as examples of 'extravagant manning'.

Butler wrote to ministers in November 1951 proposing revised manpower limits and 'a general pruning of existing staffs', but the immediate impact was limited. Total civil service numbers were actually rising as the Conservatives took office (increasing to 762,000 in April 1952), mainly on the industrial side. Only in 1955 was the total head-count (719,000) brought below the 1951 figure. Between 1951 and 1955 the non-industrial civil service was cut by 39,000 (from 425,000 to 386,000), the industrial civil service growing by 31,000 1951–4 (to 347,000 – the post-war peak). Freeing the economy and the progressive abolition of controls and rationing were responsible for the main savings in staff (with the Ministries of Food and Fuel and Power, and the Board of Trade, experiencing substantial reductions).[45]

The government experienced rather more success in cutting the number of government cars, which fell from 722 to 444 by February 1953 (a 38 per cent cut).[46]

Although the industrial civil service was steadily cutback in the second half of the decade (falling to 263,000 in 1960 – a 24 per cent cut since 1954), the attempts to reduce the size of the non-industrial office staffs stalled. The absence of sustained and determined political pressure from the top of the government seems to have been a critical factor. Prime Ministerial interest in this issue was episodic, and the follow-through usually half-hearted.[47]

Churchill, prompted by Lord Cherwell, was roused to query the enlarged size of the Admiralty – 33,500 in 1953 compared to 13,000 in 1939 – asking why there was one civil servant to every ten sailors in 1939, but one to every four-and-a-half now, but in 1956 Eden and Macmillan were still badgering the department for big cuts, with only limited success (though its staff had fallen to 30,000 by 1960).

Sir Norman Brook warned Churchill in April 1953 that attempts to cut numbers would not yield spectacular results:

No determined effort was made in 1945 to cut back drastically the wartime growth of Government staffs. On the contrary, the Socialist Government had their own reasons for maintaining a large bureaucracy. As a result, too many people have come to accept as normal a degree of administration which, though inevitable in war, would previously have been regarded as quite intolerable in peace. It is now too late for the

Geddes axe, which ought to have been allowed to swing freely through
Whitehall immediately after the end of the war.

His advice was that it was better to concentrate on trying to achieve
an arbitrary percentage cut across the board, rather than concentrating
on particular departments, otherwise there was always plenty of scope
for departments to defend themselves with prolonged arguments about
their special problems.

Eden announced in January 1956 that he had asked his Chancellor,
Macmillan, to review civil service numbers and make more savings.
'We intend to go on cutting', he declared, setting a target of a 10,000
to 15,000 reduction. However, Treasury officials estimated in 1959 that
this exercise had in fact achieved a cut of only around 6,000 over a period
of two-and-a-half years.

In 1958 Macmillan and Brook explored the idea of appointing a special
committee of former senior civil servants and outsiders to tackle the
issues of civil service numbers and the efficiency of the machine.
Given the remit of reducing the administrative costs of government
departments, the group would examine each ministry in turn, making
recommendations on staff economies and the reduction or elimination of
services. The idea was dropped after a suitable chairman proved difficult
to find, and instead Macmillan issued a directive on 'Administrative
Economies' in September 1958, asking ministers to report to the Chancellor on what administrative activities they could curtail or eliminate.
Six months later, a Treasury official noted that 'It was common ground
that the last effort to cut out superfluous activities had been a complete
failure and that a broad slash was only possible at rare intervals and
against the background of crisis.'

The Treasury seemed resigned to failure on this front. There was
only marginal scope for the more economical use of manpower, an
official minuted in June 1959. Only 'retrenchment of activities and
reconsideration of standards of service' would yield significant cuts,
but the problem was that such an exercise needed 'powerful backing
from the top – both Ministerial and official', and that ingredient was
lacking.

The figures speak for themselves. The 1960 total of non-industrial
civil servants was 380,000 (only 4,000 down on the 1956 figure) and the
trend was now upwards – there had been a 5,000 increase since 1959,

and the total had risen to 414,000 by 1964. It was the substantial cutback of the blue-collar industrial civil service workforce that accounted for the bulk of the total fall to 643,000 in 1960 – a 10 per cent overall cut since 1955, but a figure that was still almost twice the size of the civil service in 1939.

It was never going to be easy for the Conservatives to cut the size of the Whitehall bureaucracy when, rather than adopting an economic liberal platform, they were basically presenting themselves in the 1950s as better at running the Keynesian welfare state than the Labour Party. The pressures would inevitably be all the other way when, under Macmillan, a more interventionist stance was taken and public spending increased. The continuing expansion of the role of government and the size of the civil service also gave even more force to the criticisms of Whitehall's organizational and management shortcomings that were welling up at the end of the 1950s and in the early 1960s, as pressure mounted for a sweeping reform of the civil service from the outside.

Notes

1 Gavin Drewry, 'The Civil Service: from the 1940s to Next Steps and Beyond', *Parliamentary Affairs*, 47 (1994), p. 585.
2 Sir Edward Bridges, 'The Reforms of 1854 in Retrospect', *Political Quarterly*, 25 (1954), p. 316.
3 Richard Chapman and John Greenaway, *The Dynamics of Administrative Reform* (Croom Helm, London, 1980), p. 212.
4 Peter Hennessy, *Whitehall* (Secker and Warburg, London, 1989), pp. 88, 120, 125.
5 Rodney Lowe, 'The Second World War, Consensus and the Foundation of the Welfare State', *Twentieth Century British History*, 1 (1990), p. 172; D. N. Chester, 'The Central Machinery for Economic Policy', in D. N. Chester (ed.), *Lessons of the British War Economy* (Cambridge University Press, Cambridge, 1951), pp. 15, 33.
6 Alec Cairncross, *Years of Recovery: British economic policy 1945–51* (Methuen, London, 1985), p. 56; Alec Cairncross and Nita Watts, *The Economic Section 1939–1961* (Routledge, London, 1989); G. D. A. MacDougall, 'The Prime Minister's Statistical Section', in D. N. Chester (ed.), *Lessons of the British War Economy*.
7 Paul Addison, 'The Road from 1945', in Peter Hennessy and Anthony Seldon (eds), *Ruling Performance: British Governments from Attlee to*

Thatcher (Basil Blackwell, Oxford, 1987), p. 7; J. M. Lee, 'The British Civil Service and the War Economy. Bureaucratic Conceptions of the "Lessons of History" in 1918 and 1945', *Transactions of the Royal Historical Society*, 30 (1980); 'The Home Civil Service After the War', in PRO T162/931/E45491/06/2.

8 PRO T162/931/E45491/06/01.

9 J. M. Lee, *Reviewing the Machinery of Government 1942– 1952* (Birkbeck College, London, 1977), p. 22.

10 Lee, *Reviewing the Machinery of Government*, p. 142.

11 Lee, *Reviewing the Machinery of Government*, pp. 6, 75; Keith Middlemas, *Power, Competition and the State* vol. 1, *Britain in Search of Balance 1940–61* (Macmillan, London, 1986), pp. 32, 78–9.

12 Middlemas, *Power, Competition and the State*, p. 30; Lee, *Reviewing the Machinery of Governemnt*, p. 2.

13 PRO T162/931/E45491/06/1–2.

14 PRO T162/870/E45491/09/1.

15 Chapman and Greenaway, *The Dynamics of Administrative Reform*, pp. 162–4; Middlemas, *Power, Competition and the State*, p. 28.

16 Chapman and Greenaway, *The Dynamics of Administrative Reform*, p. 128; PRO CAB 87/75, MGO 74.

17 Peter Hennessy, *Cabinet* (Basil Blackwell, Oxford, 1986), p. 37; for a general discussion see: Kevin Theakston, *The Labour Party and Whitehall* (Routledge, London, 1992).

18 PRO T222/75, OM 383/1/03; PREM 8/17.

19 Hennessy, *Whitehall*, p. 138; Richard Chapman, *Ethics in the Civil Service* (Routledge, London, 1988); Lee, *Reviewing the Machinery of Government*, pp. 40, 144; Sir Douglas Wass, 'The Public Service in Modern Society', *Public Administration*, 61 (1983), p. 8.

20 PRO T162/969/E51965.

21 See: Hennessy, *Whitehall*, pp. 121–7; PRO T273/9.

22 PRO CAB 134/505.

23 Fifth Report from the Select Committee on Estimates, HC 143, 1946–7.

24 Chapman, *Ethics in the Civil Service*, pp. 210–12; PRO CAB 134/501, MG (48) 1.

25 D. N. Chester, 'The Efficiency of Central Government', *Public Administration*, 26 (1948), p. 12; Cairncross and Watts, *The Economic Section*; Alec Cairncross, *The British Economy Since 1945* (Basil Blackwell, Oxford, 1992), p. 289.

26 PRO T215/401; Dorothy Johnstone, 'Developments in the British Civil Service 1945–1951', *Public Administration*, 30 (1952), pp. 49–50.

27 PRO T216/488.

28 Bosworth Monck, *How The Civil Service Works* (Phoenix House, London, 1952), p. 68.

29 PRO CAB 129/14; CAB 129/18, CP (47) 121.

30 PRO CAB 129/40, CP (50) 124; T216/488.

31 Richard Chapman, *Leadership in the British Civil Service* (Croom Helm, London, 1984).

32 Hennessy, *Whitehall*, p. 159.

33 Eric Wigham, *From Humble Petition to Militant Action* (Civil and Public Services Association, London, 1980), pp. 100–1; Frank Dunnill, *The Civil Service: Some Human Aspects* (Allen & Unwin, London, 1956), p. 72; Hennessy, *Whitehall*, p. 157.

34 Kevin Theakston and Geoffrey Fry, 'The Party and the Civil Service', in Anthony Seldon and Stuart Ball (eds), *Conservative Century* (Oxford University Press, Oxford, 1994), p. 391; Anthony Seldon, *Churchill's Indian Summer: the Conservative Government 1951–55* (Hodder and Stoughton, London, 1981), p. 110; Sir Cuthbert Headlam et al., *Some Proposals for Constitutional Reform* (Eyre and Spottiswoode, London, 1946), p. 86.

35 R. A. Butler, 'Reform of the Civil Service', *Public Administration*, 26 (1948); Anthony Seldon, 'The Churchill Administration 1951–1955', in Peter Hennessy and Anthony Seldon (eds), *Ruling Performance: British Governments from Attlee to Thatcher* (Basil Blackwell, Oxford, 1987), p. 78.

36 Lee, *Reviewing the Machinery of Government*, pp. 113, 150.

37 PRO T215/297.

38 Royal Commission on the Civil Service 1953–5, Cmd 9613, 1955; W. J. M. Mackenzie, 'The Royal Commission on the Civil Service', *Political Quarterly*, 27 (1956); John Delafons, 'Working in Whitehall: Changes in Public Administration 1952–82', *Public Administration*, 60 (1982), p. 255.

39 Hennessy, *Whitehall*, p. 159; Geoffrey Fry, *Statesmen in Disguise* (Macmillan, London, 1969), pp. 32, 176.

40 Mackenzie, 'The Royal Commission on the Civil Service', pp. 135–8.

41 Wigham, *From Humble Petition to Militant Action*, ch. 14; Henry Parris, *Staff Relations in the Civil Service* (Allen & Unwin, London, 1973), ch. 7.

42 PRO T215/245; T273/227.

43 Parris, *Staff Relations in the Civil Service*, p. 187.

44 PRO T216/488.

45 *The Times*, 25 November 1953.

46 Seldon, *Churchill's Indian Summer*, p. 114.

47 PRO PREM 11/2244; T 216/488.

4 Reforming the Machine: Whitehall in the 1960s and 1970s

The bright and ambitious young graduates picked out by the Civil Service Commission as 'high-flyer' Assistant Principal recruits in the late 1950s were joining an institution that 'in its upper levels at least, considered itself an inviolable shrine of intellectual excellence, administrative competence and stability'. By the time they reached middle-age and more senior positions in the hierarchy – by the late 1970s – the civil service was an institution under siege.[1] It was being attacked by left and right as too powerful and unaccountable; at the top, it was alleged to be inbred, elitist and out-of-touch; accusations of amateurism, inefficiency and bad management had become routine. And the constant attempts at reform, rationalization and reorganization of the machinery and personnel of central government in this turbulent period led commentators to talk of an administrative 'revolution'.[2]

Government departments were created, merged, abolished and took on or lost functions at sometimes bewildering speed in the 1960s and 1970s. A wave of reform hit the civil service, affecting its organization, recruitment and training. New techniques of expenditure planning, policy analysis and management appeared on the scene. Governments of both parties tinkered with the Whitehall machine, under Prime Ministers – Harold Wilson and Edward Heath – who took an unusual interest in the reform of government. Whitehall's outside critics and would-be modernizers were vocal, but there was also an important reform impulse within the mandarinate itself. By the end of the 1970s, however, the results of all this upheaval were often written-off as unsuccessful, misguided, cosmetic or even counter-productive. The reformist optimism of the 1960s had turned sour. Whitehall had changed but in more evolutionary, piecemeal and modest ways than outside critics had wanted. The institutional self-confidence of the 1950s had been severely battered but, in many ways, behind the changes in organization, procedures and jargon in these two decades, the civil service's established order had survived and was still recognizable.

The Pressure for Reform

Britain's sluggish economic performance and 'stop-go' policies, together with the post-Suez problem of its changing place in the world, provided the context of national self-doubt and questioning for the 'what's wrong with Britain?' debate of the late 1950s and early 1960s. Disillusionment and decline prompted a search for scapegoats, and archaic institutions, attitudes and practices – including the public schools, Parliament, local government, and the civil service – were held to be obstacles to social and economic modernisation. Other countries seemed to do things better, and unfavourable comparisons were drawn with the dynamic and technocratic bureaucracy of French government in particular, with its confident economic planners and elite training schools like the *Ecole Nationale d'Administration* (ENA).

Established institutions were challenged by changing social attitudes and values. The social status and prestige of the civil service began to decline, and attitudes towards the values it embodied became more critical in the 1960s compared with the service's pre-war reputation and public standing. Hostility towards elitism and demands for greater equality in society (or at least 'equality of opportunity') grew. The growth of the social sciences fuelled an interest in 'rational' approaches to policy-making and new techniques of planning and decision-taking. Whitehall's neglect of the expert and its preference for pragmatic problem-solving strengthened the case for reform.

Another important factor was the shift to a managerial view of government in the 1960s. It was not that 'management' was a new conception for the civil service but hitherto, as we have seen, it had been regarded as a middle-grade executive-level activity. Private sector management methods and American innovations such as programme-budgeting now became fashionable and, with modifications, were copied in British government.[3]

Up until the mid-1970s these were years of growth for Whitehall. Civil Service numbers (excluding the Post Office) stood at 643,000 in 1961 and reached a post-war peak of 747,000 in 1975. Government spending accounted for 33 per cent of national income at the start of the 1960s and had reached over 45 per cent by 1975–6. This expansion made the need for reform all the more urgent, the critics argued. The mid-Victorian reformers had been spectacularly successful in fashioning an administrative system suitable for a 'nightwatchman' state. The charge in the 1960s was that the civil service had failed to adapt to the transformation in government's role from the passive and regulatory to the active and positive in the mixed economy welfare state.

Scathing evaluations of the administrative talent available to British governments were made in academic and media circles, but more importantly – and in contrast to the 1940s and 1950s – the leaderships of both main parties latched on to the issue of institutional modernisation in a new version of the pre-First World War campaign for 'national efficiency'. The running in the 1960s was made by Fabian critics of the civil service. Thomas Balogh's notorious and blistering (1959) attack on the civil service and the Treasury – this 'ignorantly dilettante bureaucracy' – was important because of his role in the Labour Opposition's network of policy advisers and his closeness to Harold Wilson. A 1964 Fabian group report, *The Administrators*, was particularly influential, its approach and proposals prefiguring Fulton's four years later.[4]

Inside Whitehall itself there was a growing sense of unease. There were reform-minded officials at Permanent Secretary level who felt that changes were needed in certain areas such as economic advice and the relationship between technical experts and administrators. Sir Lawrence Helsby, appointed Head of the Civil Service in 1963, felt it necessary to make cautious noises about the civil service not being able to or wanting to 'stand still'. Many younger civil servants had stronger views about what was wrong, as the First Division Association found when it organised an essay competition on the subject of civil service reform in 1964. Criticisms of the administrative class 'amateur attitude' (Fulton's use of this term later caused a storm), of the frequent job-switches 'on

Madhatter Tea Party lines', of the 'lack of managerial grasp', and of inadequate training abounded.[5]

In various ways, Whitehall *was* beginning to change under the Conservative government in the early 1960s. The 1961 Plowden Committee on the control of public expenditure was a watershed.[6] The Plowden report was very much an 'inside job', produced by a group of top civil servants and outsiders who had all been senior officials at one time, the driving force behind it being 'Otto' Clarke, a senior and controversial Treasury official. It was mainly concerned with the processes for planning and managing public spending, following parliamentary criticism of and growing internal Treasury concern about the short-term and disjointed approach of the existing system in the late 1950s. The public expenditure survey (PESC) system that was developed in the 1960s put the emphasis on medium-term (five-year) planning related to 'real resources'. In the mid-1970s, PESC was to be condemned for inflation-proofing public expenditure (via its constant prices or 'funny money') as the Treasury appeared to lose control of Whitehall spending, but in the 1960s the new system was hailed as a major step forward.

Accompanying this went an important reorganization of the Treasury (as from January 1963) into two 'sides', putting economic/financial and establishments/civil service management work under their own Joint Permanent Secretaries. This change made it easier for Fulton to later recommend the separation of the civil service from Treasury control.

The Plowden report was the starting point for the growing emphasis on the managerial role of senior civil servants over the following decades. It argued that Whitehall and the Treasury had not given the management function its proper priority. Administrators – up to and including Permanent Secretaries – needed to give more time and attention to management responsibilities, as opposed to policy-work. It called for the improvement of quantitative techniques in administration. And it recommended that the Treasury should take a more positive role in looking for managerial efficiency and developing management services and training. If the details were sparse and the immediate action limited, Plowden had at least set the ball rolling and marked the arrival of the management issue on to the official Whitehall agenda.

The early 1960s saw other significant administrative reforms and reorganizations. The Macmillan government's adoption of a policy of planning in 1961 led to the creation of the National Economic Development Council with a small supporting staff, a body which was however only a pale imitation of the French *Commissariat du Plan*. The start of more than a decade of major departmental reorganizations saw the creation of the Department of Education and Science (1963) and the arrival of the first 'giant' department in the shape of the merged Ministry of Defence (1964) with 111,000 staff. Macmillan instigated a review of overseas representation (carried out by a committee chaired by Lord Plowden again, 1962–3) which proposed the creation of a unified Diplomatic Service.

Post-Plowden, the outside critics of the higher civil service were, to some extent, shooting at a moving target. The setting up of the Treasury's Centre for Administrative Studies in 1963 represented a significant advance on the traditional approach to the training of administrators, for instance. The key factor seems to have been a change of opinion inside the Treasury in 1962, the idea of providing training in economics for administrators being urged by Sir Alec Cairncross, the government's Economic Adviser and head of the Economic Section, and by William Armstrong. Soon Assistant Principals were being put through a three–week course on the structure of government in their first year's service and, in their third year, a twenty–week course which included economics, statistics and management techniques. That this was possibly the first step towards the creation of the long called-for Civil Service Staff College was confirmed by the appointment in November 1965 of a Treasury working party to consider the next moves in management training.[7]

Plans were also being brought forward for expanded 'late-entry' recruitment to the administrative class, chiefly motivated by continuing shortfalls in Assistant Principal recruitment. By 1965–7, around thirty Principals a year were being recruited, mostly in their thirties, from industry, commerce and other walks of life. But this limited outside recruitment was hardly a major threat to what the Fabian group had called the 'closed monastic order' of the administrative class.

Outside critics wrote-off these innovations as minor and defensive modifications to the existing system which would leave its traditions and practices largely intact. That may have been their point, of course, as the Whitehall hierarchy felt it necessary and prudent to appear to

move with the times. However, for the politicians these were just
the first installments of change. Conservative Prime Minister Sir Alec
Douglas-Home was worried about the 'gross incompetence' revealed
in the 1964 Ferranti scandal (when an electronics firm made excessive
profits on a missile contract) and was privately considering further steps
to be taken, including appointing Enoch Powell to the Cabinet to push
through a shake up.[8] And Labour's new leader, Harold Wilson, had
made administrative modernization a key part of his political credo in
the run-up to the 1964 election.

The Appointment of the Fulton Committee

The Fulton report (1968) is undoubtedly a major landmark in the
historical development of the British civil service. For twenty years,
much of the debate about Whitehall and its reform was organised around
it. Developments in the civil service tended to be discussed in terms of
whether or how far they measured up to Fulton's proposals – as if the
report was something like the public administration equivalent of the
Bible instead of an input into a continuing process of administrative
adaptation and change.

As Norman Hunt (a leading member of the Fulton Committee – later
Lord Crowther-Hunt) saw it, civil service sabotage and obstruction
defeated 'the most determined effort this century to produce root and
branch change'. But others explained Fulton's apparently meagre legacy
in terms of shortcomings and weaknesses in the report's analysis and
prescriptions. The report was very much a product of the 1960s. It
took up long-standing Fabian ideas (going back to the 1930s) but added
a contemporary 'managerial' dimension. In many ways, argued Drewry
and Butcher, Fulton was opportunistic – 'in telling politicians what they
wanted to hear and in seizing upon existing trends and dressing them
up as something new'. Sir William Armstrong described the report as
an 'ice-breaker . . . a catalyst [that] enabled all kinds of ideas to come
through'. Behind its headline-catching criticisms, it is true, there were
far from radical proposals which actually assisted, encouraged and
accelerated developments already underway. The Treasury, in fact,
used the committee as an opportunity to advance proposals it had in
the pipeline or was already starting to implement.[9]

Fulton was a product of 'the brief period of Harold Wilson's techno-logical revolution, 1964–7'.[10] In many ways, Wilson was an admirer of the civil service, though it later turned out that as war-time 'temporaries' he (a statistician) and Lord Fulton had worked together and had discovered they had similar grudges against the traditional mandarin caste. Thomas Balogh had prepared a major document on Whitehall reform (including plans to split the Treasury) for him in 1963, and Labour planned several new ministries. But, though he agreed with many of the views expressed in the 1964 Fabian pamphlet, Wilson's pre-election public comments about civil service reform were fairly cautious and unspecific.

There was a flurry of machinery of government changes after Labour's narrow 1964 election victory, the new Prime Minister creating the Department of Economic Affairs, the Ministry of Overseas Development, the Ministry of Technology, the Welsh Office and a Ministry of Land and Natural Resources. Some of these were short-lived. Wilson seemed addicted to the manipulation of the Whitehall machine but his approach to rejigging departments gave priority to political factors and personalities and showed little in the way of strategic purpose or design.[11] The creation of the giant Department of Health and Social Security in 1968 owed much to the need to give a key minister (Richard Crossman) a big job.

There was no immediate shake-up in the civil service when Labour took office. In August 1965 the Commons Estimates Committee pro-duced a critical report on recruitment to the civil service, questioned the role of the administrative class, and called for a full-scale inquiry. The chiefs of the civil service, however, advised delay and a cau-tious approach, saying that Whitehall needed time to settle down after the rapid machinery of government changes of 1964. It is likely that the mandarins were waiting to see what would happen to the Labour government, which had a very small majority and would soon have to face the electorate again. With Labour seeking to create a reformist image by establishing commissions to review other national institutions, though, the civil service could not expect to wriggle off the hook and in February 1966 the prime minister announced the appointment of a committee of inquiry 'to examine the structure, recruitment and management, including training, of the Home Civil Service'.

Twenty years later Mrs Thatcher was to push through major civil service (and other) reforms without the cloak of an outside 'non-political' inquiry by the 'great and the good' or deference to established interests. By appointing two Permanent Secretaries to the Fulton Committee the Labour government aimed to make any changes it proposed more acceptable to and within Whitehall. But effectively, Fulton was a 'Labour' committee – key members were Labour supporters (and friends of the Prime Minister) and its reformist conclusions could be predicted in advance. Wilson wanted the committee to report quickly so that the government could be publicly seen to be doing something about reforming the bureaucracy.

Fulton's terms of reference excluded two crucial areas: relations between ministers and officials and the machinery of government. Norman Hunt thought that this was a civil service-imposed gag which the mandarins could use to undermine the committee's recommendations by arguing they neglected the wider picture. There is a suggestion, however, that William Armstrong had wanted a broader review of the organization and machinery of government first – a new Haldane – before looking at the people who would staff it.[12] Harold Wilson certainly wanted to keep outsiders off the machinery of government issue – decisions on this being a key prime ministerial power.

The Fulton Committee's strategy was described by its secretary as tossing a number of high explosive bombs at the civil service in order to justify a programme of supposedly radical change. The report's first chapter was deliberately provocative. The use of the loaded term 'amateur' to describe the top generalist administrators produced howls of outrage from Whitehall's defenders and alienated the very officials who would have to implement the report. But the rest of the report, 'though not without recommendations for change', Sir James Dunnett, one of the civil servants on the committee, said later, was 'broadly conservative'. Many of the report's 158 recommendations were in fact modest and uncontroversial. And, in a fundamental sense, Fulton was not hostile to the civil service *per se* (unlike Mrs Thatcher later). Labour MP John Garrett described Fulton as 'the last great Fabian public document', arguing that it was 'very sympathetic to the civil service . . . it believed in a big civil service'.[13] The report was based on collectivist assumptions about 'big government', emphasizing the need for management expertise in an era of rising public expenditure, the expansion of government activities and large departments.

Fulton's Analysis and Recommendations

Much of Fulton's attention was directed at the personnel of the civil service and particularly the mandarins of the administrative class.[14] One of the main weaknesses of the civil service, the committee declared, was that it was still essentially based on the 'obsolete' philosophy of the generalist. In the context of the great expansion of higher education underway in the 1960s and the growing emphasis on science, industry, technical training and business efficiency, the continued dominance of the 2,400–strong (1966 figure) administrative class inevitably attracted critical attention. The 'gifted layman' or 'all-rounder' – with his rapid job-changes, limited training and lack of in-depth knowledge – was condemned as ill-equipped for the managerial role required in the expanded state and as insufficiently innovative and dynamic.

Fulton believed that administrators had to become more specialized and it identified two broad areas – economic / financial and social policy – in which officials would receive training, build up expertise and pursue their careers. To break the hold of the arts-educated mandarins, a majority of the committee wanted, in recruitment, for preference to be given to graduates who had studied 'relevant' subjects.

But Fulton's failure to grasp that the generalist's role was – and would remain – essentially *political* was a damaging weakness. It did not properly acknowledge the way in which the characteristics and attitudes of the higher civil service were shaped by constitutional conventions (ministerial responsibility) and by the practices of Cabinet and parliamentary government. Ministers – amateurs themselves – needed the support of officials who were expert in working the government machine, had good political antennae, could synthesize different specialist contributions, and whose broad experience facilitated co-ordination within and across departments.[15] Significantly, the ministers and former ministers who gave evidence to Fulton - with the exception of Richard Crossman – did not seem fundamentally critical or hostile towards Whitehall.

The committee's second main criticism was that the horizontal and vertical divisions of its system of classes seriously impeded the civil service's work and limited individuals' career prospects. There were forty-seven general classes whose members worked in most government departments and over 1,400 departmental classes. The fact that in 1967,

39 per cent of the administrative class had been promoted or transferred from other civil service classes or grades suggested that, on the generalist side at any rate, the structure was not as rigid as Fulton supposed. The system did, however, generate vested interests, with staff associations and unions (there were 65 of these in the civil service) either trying to defend their territory or (like the IPCS representing specialists) arguing for reorganization to benefit their members' pay and prospects.

The Treasury was proposing to formally merge the administrative and executive classes into a general management group, and to introduce a form of open structure at the top of the service only, where the highest posts would be filled by the most suitable individuals from all groups. Fulton recommended the creation of a 'classless, uniformly graded structure covering all civil servants from top to bottom'.

The dominance of the generalist and the system of classes ensured the subordination of the specialists – who were 'on tap' but not 'on top'. The number of specialists in the civil service had increased dramatically since the war (the professional, scientific and technical classes totalling 80,000 staff in 1967) and they resented their status as second-class citizens. Robert Neild, a member of the committee, complained of economists and scientists being kept in back-rooms and treated like plumbers. Fulton wanted more training in management for specialists and opportunities for them to have greater responsibility and wider careers. The committee criticized the compartmentalization and cumbersome organizational forms which kept administrators in charge of the financial and policy aspects of the work of departments and sidelined specialists.

The 'cult of the generalist' was also a major factor in Whitehall's failure to recognize the need to build up new areas of specialist expertise. Fulton gave two examples of this. In 1963 there were only 19 economists in the whole civil service, and by 1967 only 106. There were only 309 accountants in the service in 1968, organized in a separate accountants' class which excluded them from financial control positions (a generalists' preserve).

As in the 'gentlemen' and 'players' conflicts in other institutions and settings, the attacks on the 'amateurism' of the administrative class also involved the enduring English preoccupation with class with a capital 'C'. Fulton went along with the standard 1960s' criticism that the mandarin class was too isolated and exclusive, and its social and educational base too narrow. It wanted Whitehall to pull in talent from a wider range of universities. Although the Labour Cabinet could be dominated by the Oxbridge-educated, it was undemocratic and unfair if the higher bureaucracy was too.

The two ancient universities had indeed a remarkable stranglehold over 'high-flyer' recruitment, despite their falling share of the total output of graduates. In the 1957–63 period Oxbridge accounted for 85 per cent of open competition direct entrants to the administrative class, though its share fell to 65 per cent in 1966 and 59 per cent in 1968. Fulton's social survey found that the intake had actually become more middle-class in the 1960s: 85 per cent being from social classes I and II in 1961–5. The proportion coming from state grammar schools (29 per cent 1961–5) was unchanged from the pre-war period, with the public school share increasing between the 1950s and 1960s.

In the Fulton report – as in much contemporary reformist thinking – there was in fact 'a fundamental ambiguity on the question of elitism'. The socially unrepresentative administrative class was criticized, but the stress on the need for greater professionalism and expertise 'implied elitism of a different sort'.[16] But Fulton never showed how the aim of making the civil service more efficient could be reconciled with making it more 'democratic', and nor did it address the question of whether a new-type, more expert bureaucracy could be in an even stronger power-position relative to the politicians.

Another area where Fulton did not move beyond the 1960s reformist conventional wisdom was the need for greater training. With the Centre for Administrative Studies already operating, and the (Osmond) Treasury working party on management training presenting its report as evidence to Fulton in 1967, it was no longer very radical for the committee to propose a Civil Service College. Even the civil service staff associations, which had opposed what they had felt would be an elitist Staff College in the 1940s, now strongly favoured the proposal.[17] The creation of a Whitehall version of the French ENA (providing two-and-a-half years' training) would have been a radical step, but Fulton's proposal was much less ambitious.

The recommendation that management of the civil service be taken away from the Treasury and located in a new Civil Service Department (CSD) was also hardly unexpected or particularly radical. The Treasury had indeed become 'a convenient symbol for all that was supposed to be stuffy or out-of-date in the civil service' in the 1960s, but criticisms of its control of the civil service and calls for a separate Ministry of Personnel could be traced back to Laski in the 1940s and the civil service unions' evidence to the Tomlin Commission (1929–31). The 1962 Treasury reorganization was not enough to satisfy outside critics, but inside Whitehall there was also some discontent at the Treasury's dominance and style. In his evidence to the committee, Sir William Armstrong gave powerful support to the proposal to carve out a separate department.[18] The relationship between Armstrong and Helsby as Joint Permanent Secretaries of the Treasury, heading its two 'sides', had not always worked smoothly. With Helsby – a grey figure – due to retire in 1968, it is likely that Armstrong was attracted by the idea of becoming a reforming Head of the Civil Service, with a separate department of his own to support him in that role.

Fulton was clear that a change was needed to signal a 'fresh start'. A new ministry was the fashionable option. The civil service unions wanted it. And Harold Wilson was always keenly aware of the presentational advantages of a Whitehall reshuffle. Fulton was pushing at an open door.

The Fulton Committee made some potentially far-reaching proposals about the organization of departments. What the committee said about departmental management was largely derived from the work of its management consultancy group. Too few civil servants were skilled managers, the committee maintained. 'Accountable management' should be introduced, it argued, making the heads of defined areas of executive work ('managerial commands') responsible for the performance of their units, measured in quantitative or financial terms, against budgets and other targets. For the policy and administrative work of departments, clear objectives and priorities should be set in a system of 'management by objectives'.

The possibility of 'hiving off' executive or managerial functions from the departmental machine to autonomous public boards or corporations was also considered by the committee, which had been impressed by the Swedish system of government agencies. It acknowledged that placing functions outside the day-to-day control of ministers and the scrutiny of Parliament raised machinery of government and constitutional issues beyond its terms of reference, and it recommended a further inquiry into these issues. This was the seed that later grew into the Next Steps initiative, but at this stage people seem to have been thinking of the limited application of the 'hiving-off' principle and not the massive reconstruction of the work of government that was started twenty years later.

Concerned that short-term administrative and parliamentary pressures crowded-out long-term planning and thinking ahead, Fulton recommended the creation of departmental planning units (including civil servants and outsiders), headed by a ministerial senior policy adviser. 'Planning' was of course a 1960s 'buzz word', its importance stressed by the Plowden committee and featuring prominently in the rhetoric of Wilson and the Labour Party. But Fulton's criticisms were not new: fifty years earlier the Haldane Committee (1918) had complained that 'adequate provision has not been made in the past for the organised acquisition of facts and information, and for the systematic application of thought, as preliminary to the settlement of policy and its subsequent administration'.

The Politics of Implementing the Fulton Report

On the day the Fulton report was published – 26 June 1968 – the Prime Minister announced that the government broadly accepted Fulton's analysis and that it had decided to accept its main recommendations: the creation of the CSD and of a Civil Service College, and the abolition of classes. This had not been a foregone conclusion. Members of the committee had carried out a great deal of high-level lobbying of ministers, senior officials and civil service unions, trying to sell their recommendations. Wilson wanted a quick response to the report and immediate acceptance of its key proposals. But Roy Jenkins, the Chancellor, who had received strong representations from officials, was furious at not having been consulted by Wilson over the removal of the management of the civil service from the Treasury. Pointedly excluded from the committee's pre-publication lobbying, Jenkins argued for delay and a cautious response. Other ministers cared little about the issues, only Tony Benn and Peter Shore initially supporting Wilson, and it took two meetings before Wilson could successfully manage the Cabinet to get the decision he wanted so that he could, in Crossman's words, 'improve his image as a great reformer'.[19]

After the Cabinet battle, there was little further top-level political attention given to Fulton, and the Whitehall machine was given the task of implementing the report, subject only to limited and episodic ministerial involvement. Civil service closing of ranks and opposition to new ideas hindered the Fulton reforms, according to John Garrett, but most importantly in his view 'they were thwarted by the lack of political interest in fundamental change. Ministers would not devote the time and attention to what most of them see as peripheral and boringly technical questions.'[20] Harold Wilson kept up a close interest for a year or so, but by 1969 his attention had been diverted elsewhere as other issues crowded in. Given Wilson's short-term horizons, and with *detailed* involvement in civil service reform (as opposed to the creation of a generalised modernizing image) offering only limited political returns, the eventual outcome was probably inevitable: a process of piecemeal adaptation and of reforms being implemented in a way entailing less fundamental change than outside critics had hoped.

Reviewing what he saw as the patchy and half-hearted implementation of the report's main proposals, Lord Crowther-Hunt argued that they had been ignored, distorted or watered down as the mandarins chose which recommendations to carry out and which to ditch or fudge in order to protect and even strengthen their power and position. 'How Armstrong Defeated Fulton', a chapter heading in the book he co-authored with Peter Kellner, graphically identified Sir William Armstrong, Head of the Civil Service from 1968, as the chief villain.

Certainly, no bureaucratic reform is possible without strong support from inside the machine. As suggested above, Armstrong had his own reasons for welcoming the establishment of a separate CSD. He described the Fulton report as 'a great opportunity' but, with mandarin circumspection, was careful not to publicly declare full support for its recommendations. He saw the need for change in a number of areas though he was also sceptical about some of Fulton's ideas, particularly unified grading. But to blame him for obstructing the Fulton reforms over-simplifies and over-personalizes the process. As Dillman put it:

> Armstrong was certainly not an obstacle to success. The reformers' disappointment can be explained in part by the interaction of union and official self-interest, lack of clear principles and goals in the report itself to guide the reforms, and lack of parliamentary-political interest at the implementation stage. Within an array of competing perspectives and interests, Armstrong worked to develop a consensus that could

be implemented. The truth is that while Armstrong looked to be a conservator of the status quo . . . he encountered opponents . . . who felt he was pushing for *too* much change . . . Armstrong was practising the art of the possible.[21]

It was the Prime Minister, Wilson, not 'obstructive' bureaucrats, who vetoed Fulton's proposal for 'preference for relevance' in recruitment. And the vested interests of the main civil service unions were also an important constraint and could be asserted in the National Whitley Council machinery (the civil service's system of joint consultation) that was used to discuss and oversee the implementation of changes, 1968–73. Unlike the Thatcher years, this was a period when the process of reform was handled in a consensual manner and union views and interests taken into account. This process gave an opportunity for the two largest unions, the Society of Civil Servants and the Civil and Public Servants' Association (representing rank-and-file executive and clerical staff), to work with the mandarins to keep out the specialists and maintain the 'vertical' barriers between classes protecting their members' jobs.[22]

Another factor affecting the implementation of the Fulton report was the change of government in 1970, only two years after the committee reported. In the 1980s and 1990s the Conservative government's long hold on office allowed their reforms to build up a powerful momentum. But 'the Fulton programme had hardly been started when the government changed and Civil Service reform took off in a new direction'.[23] Heath's planning was well-advanced when the Fulton report appeared, and the Conservative Opposition had developed their own ideas about reform of the machinery of government. Fulton's assumption that the state would continue to be 'the great provider' was not shared by the Conservatives, who were linking their plans for Whitehall with a reduction in the scale and scope of central government. Adding the upheaval of the 1970 departmental reorganizations to the work already underway on the Fulton changes threatened to overload the circuit. The result was William Armstrong's famous remark about the need to 'draw a line under Fulton'. Progress on the Fulton programme petered out or was halted on almost every front around 1972.

When Labour came back into office in 1974, attitudes at the top towards Whitehall reform were very different from the mood in the 1960s. Wilson in 1974 had none of the modernizing zeal of 1964.

Callaghan, Prime Minister after 1976, shared the caution and scepticism prevailing in the mid-1970s among senior politicians of both parties and among the top mandarins regarding the likely benefits of structural redesign in central government. Labour had lost all stomach for administrative reform and ministers appeared to be firm supporters of the Whitehall status quo, fending off calls for more 'open government' and for a renewed commitment to the Fulton reforms, and ditching radical recommendations from the Central Policy Review Staff for reform of the Foreign Office and the diplomatic service. The Expenditure Committee's 1976–7 investigation into the continuing defects of the civil service and the limited progress made on Fulton's agenda in terms of recruitment, training, grading, personnel management, the position of the generalist, planning units and the problems of the CSD, was 'a kind of inquest' or even a wake. By the late 1970s, it indeed seemed as if the post-Fulton reforming impulse was nearly spent.[24]

The Post-Fulton Reforms

(1) Unified grading

By the early 1970s, the labyrinthine complexities of the old civil service class structure had been replaced by new and simpler groupings, but the prime target of the 1960s critics and reformers – the administrative class – survived in all but name, and kept its hold on the key policy-making posts in Whitehall.

On 1 January 1972 the 'open structure' was created on the basis of a unified grading and pay structure for the 700 to 800 officials then in the top three grades of the administrative class and the equivalent specialist positions. Below that there were three major mergers abolishing a large number of the old classes and creating three new occupational groupings. The 200,000–strong administrative, executive and clerical classes were merged in January 1971 to form the 'administrative group' within the 'general category'. In September 1971 a 'science group' within the 'science category' was formed by merging the scientific officer class and its supporting classes. And in January 1972 the works group of professional classes and some of the supporting technical classes were brought together in the new 'professional and technical category'. By

1972, 50 per cent of the non-industrial civil service had been reorganised into these groups, and by 1976 a further 20 per cent of staff had been brought into the new structure.

These had been big changes but were a long way from a service-wide unified grading structure. Many restrictions on promotion within groups/categories had been removed. At the top of Whitehall the senior posts were open in principle to the best people from any group or category. But vertical barriers to staff movement of the kind criticized by Fulton still divided the service.

Although the open structure arrangements had been presented as a first step, William Armstrong persuaded Heath and his civil service minister Lord Jellicoe not to take unified grading any further. Robert Sheldon (who had strongly backed the idea as a member of the Fulton Committee) reportedly faced 'enormous resistance' when, in his brief stint as a CSD minister in 1974, he pushed for more progress.[25] The CSD line was that unified grading had come to a standstill because of the complexities of the restructuring task and because incomes policies after 1972 had restricted changes involving pay increases (which most did). The Expenditure Committee wanted the CSD to resume the process of unified grading, but the Labour government would only undertake to 'explore' the issue further, in consultation with the unions.

By the end of the 1970s it seemed as if the proposal to fully integrate the classes had been killed off. However, Mrs Thatcher's government unexpectedly pushed unified grading down two further levels of the hierarchy in 1984 and 1986 (to Principal or grade 7), but even then the 18,000 officials in the extended open structure represented less than 4 per cent of the non-industrial civil service. The government then took off in the opposite direction, and by the 1990s the civil service seemed to be moving away from, not towards, the sort of single unified structure that Fulton had wanted, as the creation of executive agencies threatened to break up the existing pay and grading structures.

(2) Generalists and specialists

The post-Fulton changes failed to dislodge the generalist. 'The top management of our large and technically complex departments of state is still dominated by generalist arts graduates from public schools and Oxbridge', John Garrett complained in 1980. That Treasury Under- and Assistant-Secretaries were averaging only 15–21 months in each post in the mid-1970s suggested 'musical chairs' carried to extremes.

Though multi-disciplinary project teams or corporate management teams were sometimes created, specialists remained essentially in advisory positions with administrators responsible for policy and financial aspects of the work. 'The pre-Fulton attitude on the role of the specialist remains firmly entrenched', the IPCS argued in 1976. Progress towards a new relationship between generalists and engineers, and a revision of their roles, was found to be limited and uneven across Whitehall in the ten years after Fulton.[26] Fulton had strongly backed 'integrated hierarchies', but a CSD report found that most departments were doubtful of their advantages and there were few major developments.

There was little movement of specialists into policy-making positions in the 1970s. The introduction of the open structure made little difference to the character of Whitehall's top ranks. In 1970, 62.5 per cent of the posts at Under Secretary and above were held by administrators, in 1976 the figure was 58.9 per cent; in 1970 scientists and technical staff held 17.1 per cent of posts at this rank, six years later 16.7 per cent. Virtually all those specialists were working in posts in their own discipline or professional field, not in mainstream policy jobs. Schemes designed to give management training and administrative experience to young specialists with the potential to reach senior positions and to designate 'opportunity posts' to encourage more flexible deployment of staff failed to have much impact.

Critics saw all this as evidence of the civil service's continuing 'discrimination against expertise'.[27] But private companies also apparently made little use of engineers, for instance, at senior management levels, suggesting that there were wider cultural factors at play. Most specialists recruited to the civil service looked primarily for careers in their own fields and the continuing difficulties Whitehall experienced in recruiting sufficient numbers of high-calibre specialists hardly suggested a service awash with talent. So long as senior civil servants' roles continued to be defined chiefly in terms of policy advice to ministers and dealing with the political environment in the widest sense, the generalists' predominance was unsurprising.

(3) High-flyer recruitment

Fulton's proposed recruitment reforms aimed at changing the social make-up and character of the higher civil service. The recommendation for an expanded 'late entry' came to little: the number of mature direct-entry Principals appointed averaged thirty-six a year between 1968 and 1976, and only seven were recruited in 1977. The rejection of 'preference for relevance' was an implicit endorsement of the traditional value system. In response to the recommendation for an inquiry into recruitment methods to consider 'possible ways of making the process of selection more objective in character', the Labour government set up the Davies committee which concluded in its 1969 report that there was no evidence of bias in the procedures or assessors and that the CSSB method was one 'to which the Public Service can point with pride', though Lord Crowther-Hunt subsequently denounced that 'white-washing conclusion' as running counter to the committee's own statistical evidence.[28]

New arrangements for an expanded graduate entry – the administration trainee (AT) scheme – were introduced in 1971. But the pre-Fulton elitism was largely perpetuated. Suspicions that the old-style 'officer class' would be retained were reinforced by evidence that, in many ways, the high-flyer 'fast-streamed' ATs were 'carbon copies of the former assistant principals'.[29] The figures were clear enough. In 1975 Oxbridge provided 60 per cent of external AT recruits (compared with 59 per cent in 1968); almost 50 per cent had been educated at private fee-paying schools (59 per cent in 1968); 78 per cent were from social classes I and II (82 per cent in 1968); and 50 per cent were arts graduates (54 per cent in 1968). In contrast, the graduate intake at executive officer was much more educationally and socially unrepresentative.

The left-wing minority of MPs on the Expenditure Committee scathingly criticized 'a bias of the civil service recruiting in its own image . . . and a bias of class, caste and cast of mind'. Whitehall sensitivity to allegations of bias in selection procedures was revealed by the commissioning of no less than three inquiries between 1978 and 1983 (and there was another review in 1994).

In 1982 the AT scheme was modified: a new grade of HEO (Development) was created, open to AT graduate recruits who passed their probation and to serving EOs and HEOs who went through an in-service selection procedure, and 'streaming' was ended. However, the number of AT vacancies had fallen dramatically, from 256 in 1974 and 160 in 1978 to only 44 in 1982 (about the level of Assistant Principal recruitment in the 1950s). And the Oxbridge dominance continued. A break-down of the 1986 figures showed that 15 per cent of initial applicants were Oxbridge, but 46 per cent of those appointed; one in ten of the original Oxbridge applicants became ATs or HEO(D)s, compared to one in fifty of the non-Oxbridge.

As Whitehall was seeking to recruit the most able people, it was to be expected that Oxford and Cambridge would supply a higher proportion of fast-stream recruits than other universities. If Oxbridge candidates still disproportionately came out on top of the competition in the 1980s and 1990s (59 per cent of the external entrants to the administrative fast-stream in 1993 were Oxbridge), much had changed since the late 1950s or early 1960s when they accounted for a staggering 85 per cent of the administrative recruits. But perceptions of bias continued to be a problem, and still worried Whitehall in the mid-1990s.

(4) The civil service college

The Civil Service College was opened in June 1970. In its early years it was widely seen as unsuccessful, particularly when measured against the ambitious aims of the Fultonite radicals. Resource constraints were one reason for this. Although civil service training provision was expanded in the early 1970s, departments remained responsible for most of the training effort, the College providing only 6 per cent in the mid-1970s (and only 3 per cent of the total in 1989–90, though it provided 30 per cent of the management training for grades 7 and above). Expenditure cuts in 1976 forced the closure of one of its three training centres (in Edinburgh) and the abandonment of plans to expand fast-stream training.

Another factor was a determination in Whitehall that the College would play only a modest role. It had not won the confidence of the civil service, according to the critical Heaton-Williams report (1974). Departments continued to believe that the best training for young administrators was to learn on the job – 'sitting next to Nellie', as it was called. Critics argued that the College was absorbed by the Whitehall machine as soon as it was set up, so that it became part of the civil service it was intended to reform. The College was further handicapped by a near-impossible brief. It was expected to provide a wide range of courses for staff at all levels of the service. The unions were opposed to an elitist staff college for the higher mandarins; Fultonites admired the French ENA; the College was caught in the middle. Many of its courses covered technical subjects (such as data processing and management services) and were taken mainly by fairly junior executive-level staff. Management training was laid on for specialists on the 'SPATS' course. Short seminars were arranged for senior officials in open structure grades. And the AT fast-stream programme absorbed about a quarter of the College's training effort in the mid-1970s (falling to about 5 per cent in the early 1980s).

The AT courses, first introduced in 1971, were heavily criticized and remodelled over the ears, eventually taking the shape of short modules totalling around twenty weeks spread over a number of years. Trainees and departments criticized the courses as over-academic and not relevant to their work; outside critics said they were too short and too superficial. Attendance was not mandatory and departments were often reluctant to release their high-flyers from key 'apprenticeship' posts (in private offices or busy policy divisions).

In the 1980s the College enjoyed a revival of sorts, with training boosted by the Financial Management Initiative and a new emphasis on personnel management and career development. The extension of unified grading to Principal level increased demand from specialists for management training. A new Top Management Programme, on which senior civil servants rubbed shoulders with managers from industry and commerce, was a success. The College became an executive agency and ran its courses on a repayment basis. However, Hennessy's judgement was that it was still 'more marginal to mainstream Whitehall life than it should have been', its peripheral place explicable in terms of the continuing influence of the generalist model and of the traditional mandarin view that practical experience counts for more than formal training.[30]

(5) The civil service department

The life-span of the Civil Service Department (CSD), established on 1 November 1968, turned out to be only thirteen years as Mrs Thatcher abolished the department in November 1981. With the powerful William Armstrong in charge, the early years of the CSD were an optimistic and dynamic period. The department was expected to work wonders and it was 'the temple of Fultonism, the repository of its ideals and ambitions'.[31] Implementing Fulton and working on Heath's major machinery of government changes in 1970 placed the CSD centre stage. It attracted able staff and boosted the importance and effectiveness of personnel management in the civil service.

By the mid-1970s, however, the atmosphere had changed and the CSD came under growing criticism. As civil service reform lost momentum and was downgraded on the political agenda after 1972, so the CSD seemed to run out of steam.

After 1972 William Armstrong was diverted into the economic and industrial policy field as Heath's right hand man and then retired under a cloud in 1974. His successors assumed a more modest role, concentrating on departmental CSD work and having much more limited access to and influence with the Prime Minister. Sir Ian Bancroft's relationship with Mrs Thatcher after 1979 was particularly uneasy and this further weakened the CSD.

The CSD enjoyed only limited political interest and support. Although the Prime Minister was formally designated minister for the civil service, successive premiers took little personal interest in the department's business. The ministers left in day-to-day charge tended to carry little political weight or to be preoccupied with other ministerial duties. It did not help that when the department did attract ministerial attention it was mostly because of problems generated by the growing industrial unrest in the civil service from the mid-1970s, when the tensions and contradictions between the CSD's two roles – promoting efficiency and reform in government and also representing and standing up for the interests of the civil service itself – were becoming more starkly exposed.

Lord Crowther-Hunt complained that CSD had 'an unduly limited concept of its role' and did not see itself as 'the spearhead of the drive for departmental efficiency'. The strength of departmentalism in Whitehall was critical here. The CSD went into departments by invitation only and the findings of its management reviews were purely advisory.

The relationship and the division of functions between the CSD and the Treasury soon came under the spotlight. CSD had been formed out of the pay and management side of the Treasury. There had been some

Treasury opposition to this split, but in the early years the fact that the CSD's staff were old Treasury hands helped the two departments work together. However, the separation of public expenditure responsibilities (Treasury) from control of establishments or manpower expenditure (CSD) was 'always a little illogical' or 'artificial' in Sir John Hunt's experience. 'Departments tend to regard their battle as with the Treasury and . . . having won that, they say, "We have agreed to do this. Now let us go and get the manpower from the CSD."' The CSD could not then 'start the policy argument all over again'.[32] As the economic climate worsened in the 1970s and cash limits were introduced in 1976, it became obvious that it was the Treasury which carried the biggest stick.

The various options for reorganizing the centre were aired during the hearings of the Expenditure Committee. MPs recommended transferring CSD's efficiency and manpower control responsibilities back to the Treasury, leaving CSD much more a personnel department. Prime Minister Callaghan was privately contemplating more extensive surgery but the Chancellor's opposition scotched his tentative plans.[33] The CSD had won only a temporary reprieve, however. Its future remained a live issue and a clear decision – whether to stick to the existing set-up but make it work better, or to go for more or less drastic reconstruction – could not be avoided for long.

(6) Departmental management and planning

Whitehall departments made only faltering steps towards introducing the new forms of organization Fulton recommended. Pilot schemes were started with units of accountable management. But the obstacles to significant progress soon became apparent and there was little political or bureaucratic will to tackle them.

William Armstrong told the Expenditure Committee that running a government department was not like running a bank (though on retirement he became chairman of the Midland Bank!). Public administration was different from business management because of its political dimension. Sir Derek Rayner described Whitehall as a mistake-avoiding culture: 'in business one is judged by overall success . . . the civil servant tends to be judged by failure', and that conditioned officials' approach to their work and the forms of organization adopted. The scope for delegation was limited by 'the conventions of public accountability, the highly centralized arrangements for the control of spending by the Treasury and of manpower and pay by the Civil Service Department, and the need for equity and consistency in the treatment of cases'.[34] Over large areas of government it was not possible for achievement or performance to be measured in quantitative or financial terms (though there was some progress in developing performance indicators). The information and budgeting systems needed to operate a proper accountable management regime did not exist.

Initially, rather more progress was made with management by objectives (MBO), a technique which had been very fashionable in the private sector in the 1960s. The CSD had launched 45 projects, covering 12,000 managers, by 1974 but the process then ground to a halt. Fulton had conceived of MBO as a tool for areas of administrative work, but CSD had tried it out in executive operations, quasi-commercial work and support services. Some of the schemes had apparently been over-elaborate and costly to install, but it is also clear that top administrators had not been enthusiastic and that the unions were concerned about the pressure put on low-ranking officials by target-setting and performance-monitoring arrangements.

A number of government functions were 'hived-off' to bodies or agencies outside departments in the early 1970s but, again, this was an approach applied in only a few parts of Whitehall.

The proposal for the appointment of senior policy advisers was stillborn. Planning units had actually started to appear around Whitehall in the mid-1960s and by 1972 ten departments had planning units of one sort or another, but none were outfits of the type envisaged by Fulton. The Whitehall view was that planning should largely be the responsibility of the mainstream policy divisions. Dismissive comments by the Permanent Secretary to the Department of Education in 1976 about 'the flabby type of futurological day-dreaming' showed that there were senior officials who did not take planning seriously.

Fulton: the Verdict

In the late 1970s the general verdict on Fulton was that the report had, on the whole, been a failure. Fultonites complained about 'the lost reforms'. John Garrett's view was that 'in general the Civil Service of 1980 is not much different from the Civil Service of 1968 . . . The top management of our large and technically complex departments of state is still dominated by generalist arts graduates from public schools and Oxbridge.' Whitehall had not been static, of course, but 'there has not been any sense of pushing through the great strategy for development which Fulton envisaged. After 1969 no politician with sufficient weight cared sufficiently to understand the strategy or to see the importance of reform.' 'Fulton was a joke', a civil servant told Peter Hennessy in 1975. ' . . . They accepted everything he said and then did what they wanted to.' Less flippantly, academic observers talked of the administrative system's 'remarkable capacity to absorb and transform reform proposals, adapting them subtly to its perception of what is tolerable'.[35]

If the Fulton programme seemed stalled by the late-1970s, a decade later a more favourable audit of the effects of the report could be framed. After 1979 Mrs Thatcher abolished the CSD but provided the political clout necessary to make progress with Fulton-style management reforms (her Financial Management Initiative extending the principle of accountable management, and hiving-off executive functions to agencies in the Next Steps initiative) as well as extending unified grading. However, the Thatcher government had most unFabian views about the merits of a big civil service – an important contrast to Fulton's assumptions.

The official Whitehall view in the 1980 and 1990s was that Fulton had been a 'milestone' on the way to the 'lasting reforms' of the Thatcher years, that it had 'laid a trail for many of the key changes in the civil service over the next two decades'. Looking back on their work after twenty years, some members of the Fulton Committee inclined to that view also. Fulton's influence on this view had been indirect. Its proposals were coming to fruition with the sort of twenty-year time-lag seen after Northcote–Trevelyan.[36]

'Lots of foundations were laid by the Fulton Committee', judged its secretary, Richard Wilding, with an eye on the Thatcher government's creation of agencies. 'Without accountable management, it would not be possible to contemplate the Ibbs changes.' But it may be more accurate to say that while these changes may have been foreshadowed by Fulton (the 'planting the seeds' argument), they were not generated by that report. Thatcher had her own agenda, as did her successor. Nor was

Fulton the only source of ideas about the reform of the civil service even before the Thatcher/Major era, let alone during it.[37]

Heath's 'New Style of Government'

Edward Heath, Conservative Prime Minister 1970–4, appeared fascinated by the machinery of government. Like Wilson, he had actually been a civil servant and, in many ways, would have made an outstanding top Permanent Secretary. His approach to government was managerial, rational, and problem-solving. Critics attacked him as 'a civil servants' Prime Minister' (his key advisers were top civil servants rather than politicians, party advisers or political cronies), and it is true that he had a high regard for the civil service as an institution, though he was also convinced of the need for reform to make government more efficient and improve the quality of decision-making.[38]

Probably no political party has entered office with such extensive and detailed plans for overhauling the structures and processes of the administrative machine as the Conservatives in 1970. Heath had strong and well-thought-out views on the issues; he 'hankered after a French-style Civil Service with highly-trained officials not afraid to take a strong line'. The party's preparations in Opposition had been extensive and had involved the party's policy group (which formulated proposals for a new pattern of departments), the Public Sector Research Unit (which worked on new analytical, budgeting and managerial techniques pioneered in US government and in the private sector), and a team of businessmen. Former senior civil servants also advised Heath on the organization of a possible Prime Minister's Department and a new central planning staff.[39] The Conservatives' aim was for 'less government, but better government', with a more 'rational' departmental structure, executive functions 'hived-off', and clear objectives and systematic control supported by new decision-taking methods and by a stronger and more strategic central direction.

Whitehall was receptive to these ideas and senior civil servants had been thinking in broadly similar terms themselves. The idea of large, 'functional' departments had wide support in political and bureaucratic circles (with the outgoing Labour government's plans for new departments well-advanced). Treasury officials were coming to the view that more effort had to be put into evaluating individual spending programmes and their results in the annual PESC round. William Armstrong and Burke Trend had been discussing the need for a 'central capability' unit which could look to the long-term and take a strategic view. As Hennessy says, 'Heath's reformers were preaching to the converted'.

The government's ambitious plans were set out in a White Paper, *The Reorganization of Central Government*, in October 1970.[40] In many ways, this was a very Fabian blueprint and its explicit theorizing about the machinery of government and its reform called to mind the Haldane report of 1918. The main reforms included two new 'giant departments' (Trade and Industry [DTI], and Environment [DOE]), the introduction of Programme Analysis and Review, a commitment to 'hive-off' and relinquish some departmental functions, and the establishment of the Central Policy Review Staff (CPRS).

Heath had long wanted a smaller Cabinet committed to a clear set of priorities and a system of larger, 'federal' departments. His departmental amalgamations – making nine departments into four – resulted in a Cabinet of eighteen compared to Wilson's twenty-one. The advantages claimed were the elimination of duplication and overlap, a capacity to develop a clear strategy for related functions, and the resolution of policy conflicts within a unified line of management rather than by inter-departmental compromise or fudging.

In practice, the DTI proved unwieldy from the start, not because of its size (only 18,000 officials) but because of the range and heterogeneity of its functions and the wide spread of its policy responsibilities. It soon had a top-heavy team of nine ministers and four Second Permanent Secretaries. The 'super-departments' really needed a new breed of executive minister to run them, but only Peter Walker proved effective, at DOE (1970–2) and then DTI (1972–4). The different 'wings' of the DOE began to drift apart after 1972.[41]

The departmental pattern of 1970 had started to unravel even before Heath had left office. A second Cabinet minister was appointed to DTI in 1972 and, to deal with the energy crisis, a separate Department of Energy was carved out in January 1974. Wilson and Callaghan completed the demolition: DTI was dismembered in 1974 and Transport removed from DOE in 1976. By the mid-1970s, ministerial and Whitehall opinion had swung against the idea of 'giant' departments.

Programme Analysis and Review (PAR), introduced from 1971, was supposed to involve the systematic and critical analysis of objectives, costs, outputs and new options. The aim was to help ministers to examine what was going on in a department, so that they could decide whether it was still necessary and receiving the right priority.[42]

As a tool of more 'rational' government, PAR was a failure. It fell victim to Whitehall's bureaucratic politics and power-play. The original plan to base PAR in the CSD floundered on Treasury opposition, but while the Treasury took it over it was not enthusiastic about PAR. Treasury caution and the compromises brokered on the inter-departmental steering committee (PARC) meant that only a dozen or so programme were reviewed each year. The Treasury inevitably saw the point as expenditure-reduction and did not take kindly to CPRS involvement sometimes complicating the picture with arguments that more resources would boost the effectiveness of a programme. Spending departments reacted defensively and tried to protect their programmes from cuts. PAR did not produce savings on the scale anticipated.

Another problem was that there was little heavy-weight political support behind PAR; most ministers did not find PAR studies useful or relevant in making their political judgements.

The Heath government's 'U-turn' and its rapid expansion of public spending from 1972 completely undermined the PAR system, which had even less 'bite' when its political clients were no longer interested in 'rolling back the state'. It lingered on under the Labour government after 1974, but was formally abolished by Mrs Thatcher in November 1979. The best that can be said for PAR is that the seeds were planted and lessons learnt for Rayner's more effective 'efficiency strategy' after 1979.

Only limited progress was made with 'hiving-off', with the Civil Aviation Authority being established in 1971. The civil service unions were strongly opposed to this policy and the government decided that few activities were suitable (i.e. were largely self-financing, were not politically-sensitive, etc). The Ministry of Defence's Royal Ordnance Factories were instead put on a 'trading fund' basis (with profit and loss accounts). No major public sector functions were privatized in the Heath years. And for all the talk about cutting the number of civil servants, Heath's government brought about an overall reduction of only about 5,000 (with the number of non-industrial civil servants actually increasing).

More success was had with the establishment of 'departmental agencies' – separate units of accountable management operating within a departmental framework. The Defence Procurement Executive was established in the MoD in 1971 (with Derek Rayner as Chief Executive); the Property Services Agency was set up in the DOE in 1972; and the Employment Services Agency and the Training Services Agency were created in the Department of Employment, with the Manpower Services Agency (initially opposed by officials) appearing in January 1974 – the creation of the latter appeared to cut the size of the civil service by 18,000 but, following protests, the staff regained their civil service status in 1975.

The Central Policy Review Staff (CPRS) – the think-tank – was the most imaginative and successful of Heath's reforms. Starting work in early 1971, it generated a certain amount of media hype because of the independent style and singular personality of its first head, Lord Rothschild (a scientist and ex-head of research at Shell), and because of its apparently glamorous role as a group of young and brilliant licensed free-thinkers at the heart of the government machine. The think-tank was a small but high-powered outfit, its staff of 15–20 a mix of outsiders and civil servants. Its official brief covered the clarification and monitoring of the government's overall strategy, the establishment of priorities, and the analysis of alternatives and long-term problems. Its staff defined its role in more subversive terms as thinking the unthinkable and the grit in the machine, sabotaging the over-smooth working of Whitehall.[43]

Some Conservatives had wanted the new 'central capability' to be primarily a resource for the Prime Minister, but senior officials had been clear that it had formally to serve the Cabinet as a whole. In practice, the Prime Minister was the CPRS's most important 'client' and the think-tank was very dependent on prime ministerial support to survive and function effectively in Whitehall. Rothschild established a close relationship with Heath and became one of his most influential advisers. The head of the CPRS and his deputy were given the right – unique for civil servants – to attend and speak at Cabinet committee meetings.

The CPRS operated in a number of ways. Heath was concerned that ministers were well-briefed on departmental business but, as members of the Cabinet, had no independent advice about the proposals of other ministers or about the wider problems of the government. Accordingly, the CPRS fed-in around fifty 'collective briefs' a year to the whole Cabinet – short notes analysing urgent issues or reviewing departments' papers (pointing out drawbacks, weak spots and special pleading). These interventions often irritated departments, who resented what they saw as meddling by dilettante outsiders, and ministers mostly remained departmentally-oriented, but this was an innovative attempt to address a genuine problem about collective ministerial decision-taking.

The CPRS was also deployed on more detailed and longer-term projects, including problems that cut across departmental boundaries. It produced reports on energy policy, Concorde, the role of the City of London in the economy, population, roads and transport, nuclear power, and many other problems, having an indirect and long-term influence on Whitehall thinking on some key issues.

The Treasury saw off CPRS attempts to get involved in fiscal policy and open up budget policy-making (the think-tank once calculated that 50 per cent of the previous year's budget could have been leaked without any economic damage), but it was centrally involved in the annual public expenditure round and was a key 'player' on general economic policy issues (particularly prices and incomes policy in the 1970s).

Heath also gave the CPRS the role of guardian of the government's overall strategy. It organized six-monthly presentations to the Cabinet at Chequers, using slides and charts, mapping out how the government had performed in relation to its declared aims and where it had fallen short of its objectives, and also looking at big problems looming over the horizon. 'Rubbing ministers' noses in the future' was how some insiders saw these exercises. CPRS warnings on inflation at the May 1972 Chequers seminar have been credited as having a major influence on the Heath government's development of a statutory incomes policy.

One of the reasons why Labour was so suspicious of the think-tank as a 'Tory Trojan Horse' was because it could seem to be playing a party-political role as guardian of the government's strategy. After 1974 the newly-created Prime Minister's Policy Unit took over that role. Right-wing critics of Heath questioned the constitutional propriety and political wisdom of permitting a civil service unit to apparently take over what should be the Cabinet's central responsibility. It was ironic that a government so committed to a resolute and 'strategic' approach should, in the event, launch such a spectacular policy 'U-turn' in 1972.

After 1974 the CPRS and its subsequent heads (Sir Kenneth Berrill

1974–80, Sir Robin Ibbs 1980–2, John Sparrow 1982–3) did not enjoy the same wide-ranging role and influence as had been the case in the think-tank's early years. The Chequers strategy sessions were ended. The Downing Street Policy Unit gave Wilson, Callaghan and Thatcher more personally- and party-oriented advice, as did the special advisers to Cabinet ministers, now appointed in greater numbers than before. The CPRS was absorbed into the Whitehall machine and pushed more into producing one-off reports (particularly on industrial issues under Ibbs).

It became clear that a unit like the think-tank could achieve little without the full backing of the Prime Minister. None of Heath's successors gave it such strong support: Wilson and Callaghan were agnostic, Thatcher had little use for it. The CPRS reflected a view of policy-making as a rational, analytical and data-driven process which was perhaps always flawed and over-optimistic. In the 1970s, politicians lost interest in the long-term and in overall strategy, and were forced into crisis-management. Mrs Thatcher came close to abolishing the CPRS in 1979 and her style of 'conviction' politics further reduced its influence and the scope of its work. Already badly damaged by the political furore over its controversial 1977 report on the diplomatic service, the think-tank was further undermined by a spate of leaks in the early 1980s. One of Mrs Thatcher's first acts after the 1983 election was to abolish the CPRS.

Overall, the results of Heath's reforms of the machinery of government turned out in practice to be something much less than the 'new style of government' so optimistically talked about in 1970. The new giant departments were broken up or lost major functions within a few years. PAR was a damp squib. Little was hived-off. Only the CPRS stands out as a really successful innovation and even its lustre had faded some time before it was axed in 1983.

Douglas Hurd, Heath's Number 10 political secretary, believed that 'Because of his justified respect for his senior advisers Mr Heath tended to exaggerate what could be achieved by new official machinery . . . a little more scepticism about machinery would have been wise'. John Campbell detected 'an element of wishful thinking' in Heath's belief that 'institutional tinkering was a solution to deep-seated economic problems'. Heath's approach and thinking, and Wilson's, were similar in this sense at least, whatever the differences in terms of character and personal style.[44]

And like Wilson, Heath seems to have lost interest in his reforms soon after their initiation as his attention was diverted away from reshaping Whitehall.

In some ways, Heath's attempted reforms were ahead of their time and laid the groundwork for the changes of the Thatcher period. This was the case with the use of businessmen in government, the interest in accountable management and the idea of separating policy and management functions and setting up agencies. These came onto the agenda again after 1979, and Mrs Thatcher's interest in and commitment to overhauling the machine did not slacken. She took a much more robust and confrontational attitude than did Heath to the civil service as an institutional interest and, crucially, maintained tight control over budgets to keep up the pressure to find more efficient, streamlined and economical methods.

Malaise and Crisis

The mid and late 1970s were a crisis period for the civil service. Its size, its power, its (in)efficiency, and its perceived 'privileges' (particularly inflation-proofed pensions) all came in for critical scrutiny from politicians of left and right and the press. The wider economic crisis – 'stagflation', the 1973–4 oil shock, the recourse to the IMF in 1976 – meant that for the civil service, like other parts of the public sector, 'the party was over'. The emphasis was now put on economy, cost-control, cutbacks and the search for greater efficiency. The Treasury's cash limits system made short-term control of spending rather than medium-term planning the priority. The CSD mounted a 'cost of central government review' and the long-term growth of the civil service was checked with 15,000 jobs cut between 1976 and 1979.

At the same time, civil servants were starting to feel as if they were on a political and organizational roller-coaster. 'There had been the disheartening spectacle for civil servants of the habitual volte-face by mnisters, as much within the life-span of a single administration as the product of two-party adversary politics. The trauma of frequent policy changes had ben exacerbated by continuous administrative upheaval.' Wilson's break-up of the DTI in 1974 provoked unprecedented public complaints from civil servants that they were 'tired of being pushed around from pillar to post'. The notion of 'overloaded government' gained ground – a feeling (shared by some senior officials) that the government machine had sucked in too many functions and responsibilities and was being clogged up with detailed administrative and managerial issues.[45]

Concerned about growing staff discontent in the lower and middle grades, the CSD set up the Wider Issues Review Team in July 1973 which produced a report on *Civil Servants and Change* in 1975. Aiming to challenge the stereotype of the middle-aged, male, bowler-hatted, umbrella-carrying Whitehall mandarin, the report pointed out that a third of all staff were under 30, two-thirds of clerical staff were women, and less than a fifth worked in inner London. (The success of the *Yes, Minister* television series in the 1980s suggested that the popular image remained strongly entrenched however!)

The character and tone of the civil service had changed, and wider social and economic forces were affecting Whitehall. The civil service had become increasingly a regional and local service, and many lower-ranking staff never moved away from their local area and did not naturally associate themselves with the business of government in London. Before the war recruitment had been highly competitive, but now there were plenty of other career opportunities. Many civil servants did not regard themselves or the service as very special; the civil service was just a job like many other jobs and not necessarily an attractive one as the social standing and the earnings of civil servants had fallen behind relative to other jobs and sectors. Wider changes in social values and attitudes towards authority were reflected in the outlook and behaviour of the younger generation of officials. The staff associations had become more militant and had started to act like other trade unions.

The report put forward a programme for improving staff relations and conditions. The Wider Issues exercise signalled an important shift of emphasis away from the traditional civil service establishments approach (concerned with costs and negative controls) towards a more modern 'human resources' approach to personnel management.[46] Unfortunately, the report could not have appeared at a more inauspicious time. A more positive and innovative managerial regime was not easy to promote in a context of public expenditure crisis, cash limits, staff cuts, poor (and deteriorating) labour relations, and growing public hostility.

The old model of government as a 'good employer' was one of the casualties of the worsening economic environment. The Priestley pay system, embodying that idea and designed to take civil service pay out of politics with its 'fair comparisons' principle, came under increasing strain. Conservative and Labour governments' incomes policies in the 1970s limited, deferred or 'staged' civil service pay increases. Governments were determined to set an example in the public sector, even if they could not hold down the pay of other workers. In 1976 the Labour government suspended pay research (it was restored two years later, but abolished by the Thatcher government in 1980). The Treasury's cash limits now set the parameters for pay bargaining and settlements.

The pay squeeze and the attitudinal changes charted by the Wider Issues Review transformed industrial relations in the civil service in the 1970s. Up to the late 1960s civil service industrial relations had seemed relatively calm; as fifty years of Whitleyism were celebrated in 1969, Whitehall's system of joint consultative councils (at national, departmental and local levels) appeared to make for consensus and stability in 'staff relations'. But by the end of the 1970s Whitleyism was on its knees and civil service industrial relations had become among the worst in the country.[47]

The civil service is highly unionised. In the 1970s the previously relatively unassertive staff associations began to behave more like mainstream trade unions, pressing their interests with greater militancy and willing to use the strike weapon – something seen right across the public sector in that period. Symbolically, the civil service 'staff side' Whitley label was replaced by the 'trade union side' and the umbrella organization was called the Council of Civil Service Unions from 1980. Even the First Division Association (FDA) representing the senior grades decided to affiliate to the TUC in 1977 and took a higher profile.

The first civil service strike occurred in 1973 as a protest against the Heath government's incomes policy. In 1979 a series of selective strikes and disruption defeated the Labour government's civil service pay policy. The new confrontational attitude meant that 'Whitleyism [was] dead, in spirit if not in body.'[48]

It is worth emphasizing that 'this harsher climate had taken its toll in the civil service before the Conservative Party returned to office' in 1979. John Garrett wrote in 1980 that 'the innovative and optimistic atmosphere of the late 1960s has given way to a sour hostility between the Civil Service unions and the government and between politicians and the Service'.[49] While the problems of low morale, discontent over pay, and poor industrial relations may have been intensified under Mrs Thatcher, they had not been created by her.

Notes

1 John Garrett, *Managing the Civil Service* (Heinemann, London, 1980), p. 1; Peter Kellner and Lord Crowther-Hunt, *The Civil Servants* (Macdonald, London, 1980), p. 16.

2 Geoffrey Fry, *The Administrative 'Revolution' in Whitehall* (Croom Helm, London, 1981).

3 Nevil Johnson, 'Change in the Civil Service: Retrospect and Prospect', *Public Administration*, 63 (1985), pp. 418–19.

4 Kevin Theakston, *The Labour Party and Whitehall* (Routledge, London, 1992), ch. 4.

5 Anthony Sampson, *Anatomy of Britain Today* (Hodder and Stoughton, London, 1965), pp. 264, 282–3.

6 *Control of Public Expenditure*, Cmnd 1432, 1961; D. N. Chester, 'The Plowden Report: Nature and Significance', *Public Administration*, 41 (1963).

7 Richard Chapman and John Greenaway, *The Dynamics of Administrative Reform* (Croom Helm, London, 1980), pp. 151–3.

8 *Independent on Sunday*, 1 January 1995; Peter Hennessy, *Whitehall* (Secker and Warburg, London, 1989), p. 174.

9 Kellner and Crowther-Hunt, *The Civil Servants*, p. 23–4; Gavin Drewry and Tony Butcher, *The Civil Service Today* 2nd edn (Basil Blackwell, Oxford, 1991), p. 54; Expenditure Committee, *The Civil Service*, HC 535, 1976–7, q. 1499. For a general discussion see: Geoffrey Fry, *Reforming the Civil Service* (Edinburgh University Press, Edinburgh, 1993).

10 Garrett, *Managing the Civil Service*, p. 11. See also: Theakston, *The Labour Party and Whitehall*.

11 Christopher Pollitt, *Manipulating the Machine* (Allen and Unwin, London, 1984), p. 49.

12 Expenditure Committee, *The Civil Service*, q. 1501.

13 Sir James Dunnett, 'The Civil Service: Seven Years After Fulton', *Public Administration*, 54 (1976), p. 372; *Contemporary Record*, Summer 1988, p. 51.

14 *The Civil Service*, Cmnd 3638, 1968.

15 David Judge, 'Specialists and Generalists in British Central Government: A Political Debate', *Public Administration*, 59 (1981).

16 Barry Jones and Michael Keating, *Labour and the British State* (Clarendon Press, Oxford, 1985), p. 147.

17 Chapman and Greenaway, *The Dynamics of Administrative Reform*, pp. 154–8.

18 R. G. S. Brown and D. R. Steel, *The Administrative Process in Britain* 2nd edn (Methuen, London, 1979), p. 50; Fry, *Reforming the Civil Service*, pp. 87–8, 94.

19 Hennessy, *Whitehall*, pp. 199–202; Fry, *Reforming the Civil Service*, pp. 241–4; Kellner and Crowther-Hunt, *The Civil Servants*, pp. 55–8.

20 Garrett, *Managing the Civil Service*, p. 191.

21 Expenditure Committee, *The Civil Service*, q. 1497; David Dillman, 'The Paradox of Administrative Power: John Macy and William Armstrong', *Public Policy and Administration*, 5 (1990), p. 14.

22 Kellner and Crowther-Hunt, *The Civil Servants*, pp. 66, 68, 73.

23 Garrett, *Managing the Civil Service*, p. 23.

24 W. H. Greenleaf, *The British Political Tradition, vol. 3 A Much Governed Nation part I* (Methuen, London, 1987), p. 237; Nevil Johnson, 'Editorial: The Expenditure Committee on the Civil Service', *Public Administration*, 56 (1978).

25 Fry, *Reforming the Civil Service*, pp. 272–3; *Contemporary Record*, Summer 1988, p. 48.

26 Expenditure Committee, *The Civil Service*, p. 532; K. Gillender and R. Mair, 'Generalist Administrators and Professional Engineers: Some Developments Since the Fulton Report', *Public Administration*, 58 (1980).

27 Garrett, *Managing the Civil Service*, p. 47.

28 Expenditure Committee, *The Civil Service*, p. 1091.

29 Chris Painter, 'The Civil Service: Post-Fulton Malaise', *Public Administration*, 53 (1975), p. 431.

30 Hennessy, *Whitehall*, p. 529.

31 Anthony Sampson, *The New Anatomy of Britain* (Hodder and Stoughton, London, 1971), p. 239. For a general discussion, see: Richard Chapman, 'The Rise and Fall of the CSD', *Policy and Politics*, 11 (1983); John Greenaway et al., *Deciding Factors in British Politics* (Routledge, London, 1992), ch. 7.

32 Expenditure Committee, *The Civil Service*, qs. 1823–4.

33 Hennessy, *Whitehall*, pp. 265–6.

34 Expenditure Committee, *The Civil Service*, q. 1510; Garrett, *Managing the Civil Service*, p. 132.

35 Kellner and Crowther-Hunt, *The Civil Servants*, ch. 5; Garrett, *Managing the Civil Service*, p. 3; Hennessy, *Whitehall*, p. 205; Nevil Johnson, 'Recent Administrative reform in Britain', in A. F. Leemans (ed.), *The Management of Change in Government* (Martinus Nijhoff, The Hague, 1976), p. 294.

36 Sir Robert Armstrong, 'Taking Stock of our Achievements', in *Future Shape of Reform in Whitehall* (Royal Institute of Public Administration, London, 1988), p. 13; [Sir] Robin Butler, 'The Evolution of the Civil Service', *Public Administration*, 71 (1993), p. 396; *Contemporary Record*, Summer 1988, pp. 50–1.

37 Fry, *Reforming the Civil Service*, pp. 257, 259.

38 For a general discussion see: Kevin Theakston, 'The Heath Government, Whitehall and the Civil Service', in Stuart Ball and Anthony Seldon (eds), *The Heath Government 1970–74: A Reappraisal* (Longman, Harlow, 1996) and the authoritative study by John Campbell, *Edward Heath: A Biography* (Cape, London, 1993).

39 Hennessy, *Whitehall*, p. 238; Pollitt, *Manipulating the Machine*, pp. 83–8; Edward Heath and Anthony Barker, 'Heath on Whitehall Reform', *Parliamentary Affairs*, 31 (1978).

40 *The Reorganisation of Central Government*, Cmnd 4506, 1970.

41 James Radcliffe, *The Reorganisation of Central Government* (Dartmouth, Aldershott, 1991).

42 Andrew Gray and Bill Jenkins, 'Policy Analysis in British Central Government: the Experience of PAR', *Public Administration*, 60 (1982).

43 See: Tessa Blackstone and William Plowden, *Inside the Think Tank* (Heinemann, London, 1988); Peter Hennessy, Susan Morrison and Richard Townsend, *Routine Punctuated by Orgies: the Central Policy Review Staff 1970–83*, Strathclyde Papers on Government and Politics, no. 31 (Glasgow, 1985); Simon James, 'The Central Policy Review Staff 1970–1983', *Political Studies*, 34 (1986).

44 Douglas Hurd, *An End To Promises* (Collins, London, 1979), pp. 92–3; Campbell, *Heath*, p. 222.

45 Painter, 'The Civil Service: Post-Fulton Malaise', p. 434.

46 Painter, 'The Civil Service: Post-Fulton Malaise', pp. 436–40; Garrett, *Managing the Civil Service*, pp. 152–60.

47 Henry Parris, *Staff Relations in the Civil Service* (Allen and Unwin, London, 1973); Geoffrey Fry, *The Changing Civil Service* (Allen and Unwin, London, 1985), p. 122.

48 Drewry and Butcher, *The Civil Service Today*, p. 124.

49 Chris Painter, 'Civil Service Staff Militancy: Joining the Mainstream of Trade Unionism', *Public Administration Bulletin*, 40 (1982), p. 25; Garrett, *Managing the Civil Service*, p. 191.

5 The Civil Service at the Crossroads: Thatcher, Major and Whitehall since 1979

Like the guns at Singapore, the Whitehall mandarins were caught facing the wrong way in 1979. They had long feared that the major assault on them would come from the political left, not the right. But for all that Fabians and left-wing socialists have over the years talked about civil service reform, it is actually the Thatcher and Major Conservative governments – rather than any of their Labour predecessors – that set about making some of the most far-reaching changes this century in the way in which the civil service operates and is organized.

As in many other areas of public policy, the practices of the Conservative government in relation to the civil service in the 1980s and 1990s embraced both radical as well as conservative behaviour, with the coherence of its policies towards Whitehall often being exaggerated by supporters and opponents alike. On one view, the changes in the civil service after 1979 added up to the equivalent of an administrative revolution – in fact, the most profound upheaval since Northcote–Trevelyan and the most ambitious attempt at civil service reform this century. A more sceptical view is that what we saw was rather a continuation of reforms grounded in the 1960s managerial thinking that had so influenced Fulton and Heath, with Mrs Thatcher simply giving a new impetus to the pace of change. However, the scale and pace of change in Whitehall disappointed the radical right economic liberals, whose criticism was that the government was not going far enough in tackling the inefficiencies and political pretensions of the civil service, or in remodelling government along private business lines and introducing the disciplines of the market.

'Handbagging' the Civil Service

Mrs Thatcher's 'anti-civil service bias' was central to her political identity. In many ways, she was an 'outsider' and an anti-Establishment figure, loathing those institutions that she felt had 'failed' Britain – the City, the unions, the BBC, the Church of England, as well as the civil service. 'Detest[ing] senior civil servants as a breed', she believed that clever and energetic people should be making profits not working in the public sector. Rejecting the 'centralizing, managerial, bureaucratic, interventionist' style of other post-war governments, she had no truck with the 'gentleman in Whitehall knows best' approach and abhorred the mentality exemplified in the remark that the task of the British civil service was the 'orderly management of decline'. Her policies of curbing public spending, cutting the size of the public sector and unleashing market forces inevitably challenged the Whitehall status quo and gave a sharper edge to the push for civil service reform. Mrs Thatcher delighted in 'handbagging' traditional institutions, and the civil service proved to be no exception. Harold Wilson and Ted Heath had seemed to lose their interest in and appetite for Whitehall reform soon after work had started on Fulton and on the 1970 initiatives respectively. Mrs Thatcher was different. She did not let go of this issue and, in fact, she became more, not less, radical in office, providing sustained political 'clout' to help realize the reforms of the 1980s. It is not an exaggeration to say that 'but for her the changes would probably not have occurred'.[1]

Mrs Thatcher's impact on the civil service was, in the event, greater than that of any peacetime premier since Gladstone. But there was no blueprint or coherent strategy regarding its reshaping evident in 1979. There were Mrs Thatcher's gut-instincts or prejudices, and a general Conservative faith in the superiority of business methods ('public sector bad: private sector good'). The process of change then developed piecemeal, in an incremental and even haphazard fashion. Although civil service unions complained about ministers' 'ideological hatred of the public sector', the influence of 'New Right' thinking should not be exaggerated, certainly in the early 1980s when the government's motives were more practical and political. Later in the decade the government's actions were often presented as an ideologically coherent programme, often with reference to American 'public choice' theories, but even then ideology was just one factor and probably not the most important. The fact that the key 1980s management reforms won all-party backing, and were to some extent based on ideas espoused by the Fulton Report which had been endorsed by Labour governments, also suggests that they should not be seen as a simple 'right-wing' phenomenon. Nor was Britain's experience in the 1980s unique for other countries (Australia, New Zealand, Canada, the USA and many European states), under governments of left and right, embarked upon broadly similar public service reforms (an international trend labelled the rise of 'new public management'). A common factor here was the experience of economic 'hard times' and financial crisis in prompting efficiency drives, as indeed had been the case (albeit reluctantly) with the Labour government in the 1970s.[2]

The 1979 Conservative manifesto promised a reduction of 'waste, bureaucracy and over-government'. 'Rolling back the frontiers of the state' meant that cutting the number of civil servants had to be one of Mrs Thatcher's top priorities. When she came to power, the civil service numbered 732,000. The white-collar non-industrial civil service had increased in size by 14.8 per cent since 1970 (from 493,000 to 566,000). An immediate recruitment freeze was ordered and in 1980 a target was set to cut the civil service to 630,000 by April 1984 – the reductions achieved actually exceeded plans – and further across-the-board cuts were then specified. As a result, the civil service was one-fifth smaller in 1988 (579,000) than it had been in 1979. Although there was an 12,000 *increase* in numbers between 1991 and 1992 (to 565,000), the downward direction was resumed again in 1993, with the Major government in 1994 (when the total stood at 533,000) anticipating staffing levels being 'significantly' below half-a-million by 1998.

The staff cuts fell disproportionately on the blue-collar industrial civil service with over 100,000 posts shed in the first three Conservative terms (from 166,000 in 1979 to 61,000 in 1992), while the number of non-industrial civil servants fell by only 60,000 in that period (from

566,000 to 504,000), remaining at about the level it had been in 1945 and significantly above its size in the mid-1950s. Civil service white-collar staff had actually been cut-back more severely in the 1920s (the Geddes Axe) and in the decade after the end of the second world war than under Mrs Thatcher.

The 1980s cuts were achieved in a number of ways, some of them fairly arbitrary and crude. Some government functions were discontinued, others cut-back or hived-off, or eliminated by efficiency reviews. Naval dockyards were closed, the Royal Ordnance Factories privatized, the Property Service Agency's staff slashed. Computerization of PAYE saved 4,600 Inland Revenue posts. Some of the reductions were cosmetic – for instance, the staff at Kew Gardens were no longer classified as civil servants but continued to do the same jobs as before.

The Treasury claimed that, where comparisons could be made, productivity improvements in Whitehall in the 1980s were at least as great as in the private sector. But in some cases the pressure on staff numbers did seem to affect the quality of public services: the social security system was reported as facing breakdown in 1986 with a 10,000 increase in staff needed to clear a massive backlog of claims. And the cut-back fetish could seem managerially irrational in cases such as the Revenue departments, where employing more staff would produce increases in tax-revenue well above their employment costs. Ministers spoke of 'cutting out the fat' and, by forcing departments to consider how to 'do more with less', manpower cuts were a spur to greater efficiency. But a more critical view was that the civil service had emerged 'leaner but not necessarily fitter . . . not so much slimmed down as hacked at around the edges'.[3]

The Thatcherites' denigration of public servants and the government's intention to 'deprivilege' the civil service placed it outside the conventional Fabian/'liberal' reforming tradition. Mrs Thatcher was, by post-war standards, radical in her refusal to recognize the career civil service as an interest in its own right. Top civil servants' public anguish over charges of parasitism, the damaging stereotyping and plummeting morale cut no ice with her. On the one hand, the government was riding the wave of growing press and public hostility that had built up through the 1970s about the size and perceived 'privileges' (pay, pensions, job security) of officialdom in a context of economic retrenchment and cut-back. And on the other hand, aggressive public sector unionism was an integral part of the wider 'union problem' the government was determined to tackle.[4]

The government had hoped to abolish the Heath-bestowed index-linking of civil service pensions but was thwarted by the report (in 1981) of an inquiry it had commissioned. On civil service pay, it acted unilaterally in 1980 to abolish the Priestley pay arrangements, tearing up the existing agreements and repudiating the 'fair comparison' principle. In response, industrial action by the civil service unions dragged on for 21 weeks in 1981 (then the longest strike since 1926), costing the government over £350 million in interest charges to cover delayed and uncollected taxes. Mrs Thatcher took the lead in facing down the strike to demonstrate the government's tough stance, threatening resignation rather than accepting (as some ministers wanted to) a compromise formula. After this defeat, the civil service unions were very much on the defensive in the 1980s, powerless to prevent wages falling behind relative to the private sector (by the late 1980s there were claims that civil service pay had slipped 30 per cent behind the position in 1979). Senior mandarins, however, received large increases (with a controversial big hike in 1985), and between 1979 and 1987 top civil servants' salaries increased from six times the basic civil service minimum to 15.5 times. Although progress in moving towards a new pay system was slow, the government's aim of breaking-up the national pay bargaining system and its preference for market forces, performance-related pay, productivity incentives and regional variations was clear.[5] As every £1 billion extra on the civil service pay bill was the equivalent of another penny on income tax, its interest in limiting increases was understandable. On top of pay grievances, industrial relations in the civil service were further soured in 1984 when the government banned union membership at the Government Communications Headquarters (GCHQ) eavesdropping intelligence station, spurning the unions' offer of a 'no-strike' deal.

The Civil Service Department (CSD) was a casualty of the Thatcher government's determination to impose a tougher managerial regime on Whitehall. Unlike Heath, Mrs Thatcher was sceptical about the value of recasting the departmental geography of Whitehall, preferring to concentrate on getting the right policies and the right people in place. It was not that her years in Downing Street saw no change to the structure of departments – CSD was abolished in 1981, the Departments of Trade and Industry were amalgamated in 1983, Health and Social Security was split into two ministries in 1988 – but the main motive behind the changes that occurred was political rather than a self-conscious 'style of government' or explicit theory of organisation.

The CSD had looked increasingly vulnerable in the 1970s. Mrs Thatcher's appointment of Sir Derek Rayner as her personal adviser on efficiency (see below) was a personal vote of no confidence in CSD. The prime minister and her supporters did not want a central department that saw its role as, in some sense, 'looking after' the interests of the civil service. The CSD's perceived weakness in the face of the civil service unions' strike action in 1981 sealed its fate. The Treasury took over responsibility for civil service numbers and pay, while CSD's responsibilities for management, efficiency and personnel policy went to a new Management and Personnel Office (MPO), grouped with the Cabinet Office. The 1983 Cassels report emphasized departmental responsibility for personnel management and reduced the centre's role. And the MPO itself lasted only until the autumn of 1987 when the Treasury absorbed most of the its functions and staff, with the rump going to the Office of the Minister for the Civil Service (OMCS) in the Cabinet Office. (In 1992, OMCS itself disappeared as John Major created the Office of Public Service and Science.) Something like the traditional Treasury control of the civil service had been restored, but the Cabinet Office and Downing Street had muscled in to this territory in a way not seen before and took some of the key initiatives in civil service management reform in the 1980s and 1990s.

Information Technology

Alongside Mrs Thatcher's impact, the microchip's effect on the civil service in the 1980s should not be underestimated. In the 1950s and 1960s government departments had developed computer systems to handle large-scale number-crunching tasks in the social security and tax fields. The introduction of desk-top computers, new computerized networks and databases, and fax machines transformed the way in which administrative work was done. Central government became the country's leading user of information technology (IT) systems, with major computerization projects (the Social Security Department's 'Operational Strategy' and the Inland Revenue's computerization of

PAYE) ranking among the biggest in Europe. The computer system at the DSS's Newcastle Central Office is one of the world's largest: there are 35,000 terminals installed in all its local benefits offices, and 18 million benefit inquiries a year are handled; the PAYE system involves 18,000 terminals linking 600 offices and processing 27 million taxpayer records.

Information technology (IT) brought advantages and problems. The management reforms of MINIS and the FMI (see below) were facilitated by IT as was the relocation of civil service jobs, with computer networks permitting the removal of 'back office'/claims assessment functions from some local benefits offices for instance. The automation of repetitive and routine clerical tasks would increase job satisfaction, it was claimed, but low-level DSS staff frequently complained that they had become mere 'text inputters' instead. At more senior levels the 'increased pace of transmission of information left less and less time to think through and respond to questions and demands', said former-Permanent Secretary, Sir Terence Heiser. But the 'two-cultures' divide remained: IT issues tended to be handled by departments' 'operational management' and not the most senior mandarins or ministers (Sir Robin Butler was reported to dislike computers!).[6] From the citizen's point of view, concerns about civil liberties and personal privacy were only partially met by the 1984 Data Protection Act.

Whitehall's experience with IT projects in the 1980s was not a good advertisement for its supposedly greater management efficiency. The National Audit Office produced several critical reports pointing to delays, cost escalation, mismanagement and waste. DSS's 'Operational Strategy' eventually cost around £2.6 billion rather than the original estimate of £570 million; the Inland Revenue abandoned a major IT project in 1985, incurring losses of £16.5 million; £48 million was lost when a planned computer system for the Training and Enterprise Councils was abandoned. Because of a shortage of civil service staff with IT skills, outside consultants were used in large numbers, but these cost four or five times more than 'in-house' staff (in 1987–8 a third of government's IT staff costs went on buying-in outsiders). Industrial action by civil service IT staff prompted ministers to contract out to private sector firms the running of some computer installations, using the justification of trying to minimize the risk of strikes and disruption. And at the end of the day, IT's record in terms of improvements in efficiency and quality of service was decidedly mixed (e.g. speedier processing of benefits claims but no improvements in error-rates).[7]

The 'Efficiency Strategy' and the FMI

The government had declared that it was committed to 'better management' in government, though it had not entered office with any detailed plans about what this meant or how it could be achieved and its 'efficiency strategy' was developed by stages and in a fairly pragmatic fashion. In the first instance, Mrs Thatcher took with her into Downing Street Sir Derek (later Lord) Rayner, from her favourite department store Marks and Spencer, to head a small Efficiency Unit reporting direct to her. As well as bringing private sector business expertise Rayner knew his way around Whitehall, having run the MoD's defence procurement organization in the early 1970s. A programme of narrowly-focused 'efficiency scrutinies' was started, using departmental officials to put selected blocks of work under the spotlight, looking to reduce costs and streamline procedures. The scrutiny programme undoubtedly uncovered areas of inefficiency and mismanagement. One of the best-known examples concerned the Ministry of Agriculture laboratory breeding its own rats for research purposes at a cost which worked out at £30 per rat – private sector rodents cost £2 each! And until Rayner's team came up with the figure no one knew how much it cost to run government – in 1981 civil service 'gross running costs' were calculated to be £3 per week for each man, woman and child in the country.[8]

Administrative inertia or resistance and external political constraints (the sub-postmasters' lobby frustrated plans to make large savings in the way social security benefits were paid, for instance) blunted some of the impact of 'Raynerism'. An Efficiency Unit report in 1985 found that only half the planned savings from scrutinies ever materialized, with their implementation taking twice as long as expected. But between 1979 and 1983 (when Rayner was succeeded by Sir Robin Ibbs as the PM's efficiency adviser), 155 scrutinies had led to savings of £300 million a year. By the end of Mrs Thatcher's second term of office, the cumulative savings of the continuing scrutiny programme were reported as around £1 billion, and by 1993 the Efficiency Unit was claiming that total savings since 1979 were more than £1.5 billion. Another of Rayner's achievements was the review that led to the abolition of 27,000 Whitehall forms and the redesign or simplification of another 41,000.

Critics of Raynerism (including the civil service unions) portrayed it as a narrow cost-cutting exercise, looking for short-term financial savings and staff cuts and ignoring the impact on service-quality or effectiveness. That running a government was not like running Marks and Spencer was an obvious argument against Rayner, though it was one he acknowledged: 'government has to provide services which no sane business would undertake' he conceded. Rayner was also far from being a crude Thatcherite 'bureaucrat-basher': he was generous in his praise of the range of talent available in Whitehall (though he felt that it was not properly used) and he wanted more investment to improve officials' working conditions.

Rayner's longer-term, strategic goal was to achieve fundamental change in the culture of Whitehall. 'Good management of the state' would become a policy in itself; the mandarin's job would be transformed from a policy-making into a managerial one. Institutional changes were necessary too, he argued, to provide the information and budgeting systems to permit greater delegation of management responsibilities 'down the line' to individual civil servants actually running government programmes. To some extent, Rayner was pushing at an open door because within the civil service itself there were signs of a shift in attitudes since the 1960s and a growing feeling that 'the time had come for these ideas'.[9]

Michael Heseltine, appointed Environment Minister in 1979, proclaimed the role of the minister-as-manager. He was dismayed to find that he did not really know what was going on in the DOE – who was responsible for doing what, why, at what cost and with what results? – and he set up in 1980 the MINIS management information system, designed to provide ministers with the information they needed to establish political control over the bureaucracy.[10] MINIS was not a bloodless management tool: it worked to serve up a menu of alternatives for politicians looking where to cut staff numbers (DOE had shed 15,000 jobs by 1983). In 1983 DOE's management structures were further overhauled with the introduction of 120 'cost-centres' and a computerized budgeting system. (When Heseltine became Secretary of State for Defence in 1983 he quickly introduced a MINIS system to that department too and went on to push through a major management reorganization of the MoD.)

Heseltine's innovations had few supporters elsewhere in Whitehall or the Cabinet, however. Most ministers were not interested in civil service management issues and had not gone into politics to be managers. But MPs on the Commons Treasury and Civil Service Committee were impressed and in their (1982) report on *Efficiency and Effectiveness in the Civil Service* they recommended the adoption of MINIS across the board in Whitehall. Inside government, Mrs Thatcher's backing made the vital difference. She wanted to press on with the Rayner/Heseltine agenda and the Conservative's management shake-up gathered momentum with the launching of the Financial Management Initiative (FMI) in 1982.[11]

The FMI, in effect, aimed to institutionalize the 'business methods' approach: FMI documents used the language of departments' 'businesses' and 'customers'. However, the thinking behind this new push towards a system of accountable management was not all that new: Fulton had prescribed something similar for Whitehall in the 1960s and giant US corporations had taken this path several decades earlier. MINIS-style 'top management systems' now sprang up around Whitehall to provide an information base for ministers' and top officials' decisions about priorities and resources (the acronyms proliferated: the Ministry of Agriculture set up MINIM, the Home Office APR, the Department of Health DMA, the Lord Chancellor's Department LOCIS, and so on). And a move towards 'decentralized budgetary control' saw middle- and lower-level managers running blocks of departmental work being made accountable for their budgets and performance (the DHSS, for instance, set up over 800 cost centres, many of them local social security offices).

The traditional civil service approach, as represented by the DHSS's Newcastle Central Office 'paper-factory' for instance, was one in which 'control mechanisms . . . were highly centralized and remote from operational management', there was 'little incentive for savings and efficiency at local unit level', 'operational managers had no idea what resources their commands were consuming', and 'there was no formal system of setting objectives, allocating resources to achieve those objectives and monitoring the outcome'.[12] The government was right to want to improve departmental management in this sense.

More emphasis was put on financial and management training at all levels in the service. A new six-week course for senior officials promoted to under secretary, the Top Management Programme, was launched in

1985 which brought civil servants together with high-flyers from other public services and the private sector to brainstorm about the challenges of management and radical change, though there were criticisms that this was 'too little, too late' for officials who had been immersed in the traditional Whitehall culture for perhaps twenty years. After a study revealed that staff at principal level and above received on average only one day's training a year, a management development programme was introduced, aiming for an increase to five days' training.[13]

From the start, the FMI was intended to be a flexible programme that departments would tailor to their own circumstances and needs, but this carried the drawback that its implementation was, inevitably, rather patchy and slow. The commitment to delegated budgeting ran up against the reluctance of departmental finance and establishments divisions, not to speak of the Treasury's expenditure controllers at the centre, to let go of their power. The Treasury was anxious to encourage greater cost-awareness in government but was concerned that decentralizing budgetary powers carried the danger of loosening the purse-strings. Continued central controls over staff costs (pay and grading) and accommodation costs, and manpower ceilings (though these were formally dropped in 1988 and the emphasis switched to 'running costs controls', giving greater flexibility) meant in practice limited 'freedom to manage'. 'The amount of delegation of eventual control was at most five per cent' complained one official.[14]

The administrative costs of central government itself (running costs) were the main focus of the FMI, rather than total spending on programmes (i.e. £13 billion out of a total of £100 billion in 1986/87). The FMI's focus was narrow in another sense in that it was, in Gray and Jenkins's words, 'obsessed with costs at the expense of performance.' As with Rayner's efficiency scrutinies, 'value for money', reduced inputs and financial restraint all had a higher priority in practice than policy outputs or programme-effectiveness, as the FMI dealt with what was more easily measurable and controllable. The civil service manager, FMI-style, would know the cost of everything but the value of nothing quipped one critic, while others talked of 'an impoverished concept of management'.[15]

That the FMI did not add up to anything like a fundamental change in the civil service, its methods and its culture, was apparent to insiders and outsiders alike by 1986–7. In many ways it had only scratched the surface. Continued central controls were limiting managerial delegation, producing delays and frustration. Form was triumphing over substance and the FMI was not delivering many of the promised benefits. If it was not to become little more than a paper exercise then the fuller realization of its principles would mean calling into question the continuation of a centralized career civil service with standardized terms and conditions of service. The extension of Fulton-style unified grading down to the senior principal grade from 1984 and the principal grade from 1986 (see below) conflicted with the thrust of the FMI reforms, for instance.[16]

The 'Open Structure' (numbered grades first introduced in 1984)

Grade 1	Permanent Secretary
Grade 1A	Second Permanent Secretary
Grade 2	Deputy Secretary
Grade 3	Under Secretary
Grade 4	Executive Directing Bands (and corresponding Professional and Scientific grades)
Grade 5	Assistant Secretary (and corresponding grades)
Grade 6	Senior Principal (and corresponding grades)
Grade 7	Principal (and corresponding grades)

The FMI was supposed to be about flexibility, not uniformity. There was a feeling that the Rayner-inspired efficiency strategy had more-or-less reached its limits. If the Conservatives had lost office in 1987, the FMI could well have ended up on the scrap-heap. In fact, the managerial reformers were preparing to push on with a bolder initiative, building on the foundations laid by the FMI and confronting some of the issues and obstacles it had shirked.

The Next Steps Initiative

By the autumn of 1986 the Prime Minister and her Efficiency Adviser, Sir Robin Ibbs, had become concerned that the government's management reforms had run out of steam. A small Efficiency Unit team was given the task of assessing the progress achieved since 1979, identifying the obstacles to more efficient management, and coming up with new ideas. Its report, delivered to Mrs Thatcher in the spring of 1987, was dynamite:

Despite the real achievements of the Rayner years, it showed how little in the way of *real* financial and management responsibility had been devolved down the line; how meddlesome the Treasury and Cabinet Office remained; how dominant was the Whitehall culture of caution; how great was the premium placed on a safe pair of hands; and how rarely were proven managerial skills perceived as the way to reach the top of the bureaucratic tree.[17]

With an election imminent, it was not surprising that the Prime Minister ordered that a study which undermined the government's boasts about improvements since 1979 and which proposed fundamental managerial and constitutional changes should be kept secret.

It was not until February 1988 that the Efficiency Unit report *Improving Management in Government: the Next Steps* was published, with the Prime Minister announcing that the government had accepted its main recommendations (though sometimes referred to as the Ibbs report, its authors were identified as Kate Jenkins, Karen Caines and Andrew Jackson). The government's decision had come after months of tremendous behind-the-scenes arguments between Whitehall's Young Turk 'managerial radicals' and the so-called 'Treasury consolidators'. Some of the Efficiency Unit's original ideas were watered-down (initially, it put the emphasis more on massively cutting the size of the civil service than on management improvement) and the published version of its report fudged some key issues (see below). Though Sir Robert Armstrong and Sir Robin Butler lent crucial support, bureaucratic infighting dictated the limited scope and the cautious step-by-step approach of the early stages of the initiative.[18]

The functions of government were too disparate and the civil service too big and too diverse to manage as a single entity, the Ibbs report argued. Whitehall should, in fact, be treated as a collection of separate businesses. Five years after the launch of the FMI, the pressures on departments were still mainly directed at keeping within budgets, the report stated, with too little attention paid to the results achieved with resources. Centralized and detailed rules and regulations still imposed a straightjacket on individual civil service managers' ability to manage. The advantages of a unified civil service were increasingly seen as outweighed by the practical disadvantages, the report claimed. The Efficiency Unit team recommended that the way forward was to move towards a thorough-going separation between a core civil service of ministerial policy advisers and a range of executive agencies employing the bulk of officials (who totalled 95 per cent of the civil service) engaged in service-delivery and operational tasks. The advantages claimed for this scheme were the reduction of overload at ministerial level and greater freedom for the heads of the new agencies to manage within clear departmentally-determined policy frameworks. Managerial autonomy would allow agency chiefs more control over the recruitment, grading, organization and pay of their staff in order to meet their particular targets.

The parallels with the Swedish model of government were not lost on commentators, nor that twenty years previously the Fulton Committee had made similar proposals (accountable management and 'hiving off'), which had been shelved. What was different this time around? Next Steps was revolutionary *and* evolutionary. It built on and extended the principles and the mechanisms developed in the 1980s; in the late 1960s the financial management infrastructure (information, budgeting, accounting and computer systems) necessary to make the agency idea workable just did not exist. Another important factor was the emergence of a new breed of managerially-minded senior officials. The top mandarins at the time of Fulton had entered Whitehall in the 1930s and 1940s and made their careers during the halcyon post-war period when resource-constraints were loose. The new breed joined in the 1960s, took Fulton seriously, were more cost-conscious and more open to change than their predecessors. The civil service unions were weaker in the late 1980s than in the 1960s/70s and less able to resist proposals threatening their interests. There was also, of course, the very strong political push from Mrs Thatcher behind Next Steps. Back in the early 1970s, one of her political soul-mates, Nicholas Ridley, had given a 'new-right' ideological gloss to ideas very like those later to surface in the Ibbs report. And the Next Steps changes also made sense in terms of the government's determination to maintain political control over policy-making, while fitting in with its aims of cutting the size of the civil service, moving away from nationally-determined pay rates, and breaking-up the public sector.[19]

The Next Steps report did not provide a detailed blueprint for reform (nor had it presented detailed evidence supporting its diagnosis): according to one insider, 'it had described an idea, and sketched out – but no more – how it might be put into effect'. It was the bold and evangelical manifesto of a new breed of civil service reformers, just as the Northcote–Trevelyan Report of 1854 had been. The policy had to be worked out as it was being implemented, but this was something which had its advantages in terms of the successful management of change inside government.[20]

The first changes were small-scale, but they were intended to be the thin end of a very big wedge. Initially twelve blocks of work, accounting for 70,000 civil service jobs, were identified as candidates for agency status but a confidential Cabinet Office report was said to have set a target of 100 agencies. By the end of 1988, however, only three Next Steps agencies had been set up – the Vehicle Inspectorate, Companies House and HMSO, which employed barely 6,000 staff between them – and by the end of 1989 there were only ten, employing 7,700 officials. Most of these early agencies were small and already distinct, technical or self-contained operations; applying the Next Steps principles to larger organizations running politically-sensitive programmes proved more tricky – the 35,000-strong Employment Service Agency was launched a year behind schedule in April 1990. But the momentum behind the drive to introduce executive agencies rapidly built up: by October 1990 there was a total of 34 agencies, employing 80,000 staff, and by June 1991 there were 50 agencies in existence, employing 183,000 civil servants. By May 1992, the number of agencies had grown to 72, and 290,000 civil servants (half the total) worked in agencies and other organizations operating on Next Steps lines. Following fierce arguments, the big battalions of the revenue departments had been reorganized on a Next Steps-like basis in 1991 and 1992, with Customs and Excise establishing 30 'executive units' and Inland Revenue 34 'executive offices'. By the end of 1993 the agency count had reached 92 and as of May 1994, 96 agencies employed 280,000 staff; adding in the tax-gatherers, 348,000 staff were covered by the Next Steps, 60 per cent of the total civil service. The agency programme was expected to be virtually complete by 1995–6, when it would cover 78 per cent of the total civil service. The remaining 'core' civil service left in departments would then number around 50,000 – roughly the size of the Whitehall bureaucracy in 1900.

The remarkable pace of change following the Ibbs report – with most civil servants working in agencies within five years of the launch of the Next Steps programme – stands in contrast to allegations that earlier attempts to reform Whitehall (particularly Fulton) were smothered by

Table 5.1 The changing structure of the Civil Service

	1980		1994	
	No.	% of staff	No.	% of staff
Main departments	23	90%	23	25%
Small departments	31	10%	27	10%
Executive agencies	–	–	96	65%

Note:
There were organizational changes between 1980 and 1994; it is a statistical coincidence that the number of main departments is the same.

Source:
Michael Geddes, 'Recruitment and Assessment Services, the Commission and the market', paper to 1994 PAC conference, University of York.

civil service obstruction. There had been quick and decisive action rather than extended 'navel-gazing' or pilot schemes followed by thorough evaluation of results, though this 'bull-headed' approach was risky.[21] The result was that the structure of the civil service was fundamentally altered (see table 5.1)

Supported by a small unit located in the OMCS which chivvied departments to identify possible agencies and put in the detailed work needed to set them up, Sir Peter Kemp was the key Whitehall figure behind the Next Steps shake-up. He was far from being a stereotypical fast-track civil service mandarin, which is probably why Mrs Thatcher picked him out to become Next Steps 'project manager' (and the Permanent Secretary head of the OMCS). Kemp had left school at age 16 and had not gone to university. A qualified accountant, he was a late entrant to the civil service, joining the Department of Transport as a direct entry Principal in 1967 and switching to the Treasury in 1972, working as the Deputy Secretary in charge of civil service pay 1983–8. An enthusiastic and impatient mould-breaker, he established a high-profile, delighting in one MP's description of him as the 'SAS of Whitehall'. Kemp was a forceful champion of the Next Steps inside the government machine, keeping up the pressure for change and wearing down departmental resistance. (In contrast, responsibility for the FMI had been left with an inter-departmental unit of middle-grade officials.) This role put him in an exposed position and won him enemies, however. When William Waldegrave decided to dismiss Kemp as head of the restyled Office of Public Service and Science in 1992, Whitehall's elite did not close ranks to protect him and he was forced into premature retirement (Kemp himself suggested that a factor in his demise may have been the threat he posed to the Whitehall 'empire'). The official version of the Kemp sacking was that Waldegrave felt he had the right qualities to launch Next Steps, but a different sort of person was needed to consolidate the initiative and run the new OPSS department. Stories of a personality clash and policy differences soon circulated, though. And there are suggestions that following Kemp's removal the drive to give agencies more operational freedoms and to change the engrained cultures lost some of its impetus, with the Major government putting the emphasis on its *Citizen's Charter* and market-testing policies instead.[22]

The development of the Next Steps programme was, from the start, publicly and closely monitored by Parliament's Treasury and Civil Service Select Committee (TCSC). Perhaps the implementation of the Fulton Report would not have run into the sands in the way that it did if there had been similar sustained parliamentary interest and support twenty years previously. The TCSC, operating through a sub-committee chaired by Labour MP Giles Radice, produced a series of reports on Next Steps, and its regular inquiries undoubtedly helped to shape the form of the initiative and brought some of the principles underlying the Ibbs report into clearer focus. Whitehall was anxious to bring along the TCSC behind the Next Steps, recognizing that its backing was important in forging all-party support for the reform as a piece of 'transferable technology'. Senior officials spoke of 'building for the state', not just for one particular government, and their reward came in May 1991 when the then-shadow chancellor John Smith confirmed that Labour would not simply kill off the Next Steps agencies – the changes to the Whitehall landscape were to be permanent.[23]

Executive Agencies: Problems and Implications

The introduction of Next Steps agencies, though often presented as offering a model of government for the twenty-first century, in fact raised some familiar administrative dilemmas and problems: the absence of a clear black-and-white distinction between 'policy' and 'operational' (or managerial) questions, and the play-offs and tensions between account-ability and autonomy. The practical experience of the Morrisonian public corporation model was hardly such as to create confidence in the workability of the arm's-length principle, but here it was being tried again (ditching in the process the early 1980s notion of the 'minister as manager').

The 'hands-off' rule could only work if ministers were able and willing to make it work. But would political pressures drive them to intervene in day-to-day management decisions, perhaps covertly and free from effective scrutiny (as they had done with the nationalised industries)? With 69,000 staff and a budget of £75 billion (1992–3 figures), together with its huge clientele, the Benefits Agency is a crucial test of the Next Steps model. Tony Newton, Social Security Secretary 1989–92, told Patricia Greer that Next Steps had not reduced the number of politically-loaded managerial issues that crossed his desk, though his successor Peter Lilley apparently tried to stand back more from day-to-day operations. But the difficulties here were seen with the political flak directed at the Child Support Agency in 1993–4 (culminating in the resignation of its chief executive), which inevitably pulled Social Security ministers into detailed involvement with its business. Further controversy surrounding the Prison Service agency – beset by riots, break-outs and criticism of the decision to transfer a number of IRA prisoners to jails in Northern Ireland in 1994, days after the IRA cease-fire announcement (producing a Downing Street inquiry into why ministers had not been told) – also provoked accusations of blurred accountability and buck-passing. When 'operational' decisions generate political storms or ministerial embarrassment, the Next Steps arrangements will come under immense strain.[24]

The policy/management line is blurred in those cases where an agency chief executive's role is defined as including a policy-advice input (e.g. the Employment Service) and where departments are reluctant to let go and define policy 'downwards' into the managerial sphere. The Fraser Report, produced by the Efficiency Unit in 1991, argued that 'sponsoring' departments had to reappraise their size, structures and methods of working, and adopt a more disengaged and strategic role, urging that Whitehall should move towards the private sector 'holding company' model. Two changes would underpin this shift. First, operating constraints should be specified and justified by departments wishing to retain them rather than agencies always having to fight for managerial discretion. Second, over-detailed monitoring and intervention would be prevented, and greater delegation to agencies encouraged, by reducing headquarters staff numbers (particularly in the personnel and finance divisions) by 25 per cent.[25]

Not surprisingly, departments showed little enthusiasm for these ideas. In the Social Security Department (98 per cent of whose total staff now worked in agencies), central staff apparently fell from 4,000 to 1,200 but it turned out that the other 2,800 had simply been transferred onto an agency's books and were doing the same jobs as before. Three years after the Fraser Report there had been few significant reductions in headquarters staffs around Whitehall and a Treasury/OPSS-commissioned investigation (the Trosa Report, March 1994) found that there had been little progress in terms of reshaping department/agency relationships along the lines recommended by the Efficiency Unit. Overlaps, confusion and tensions remained. Departments were still trying to 'second-guess' agencies, did not want to 'let go', were still intervening in management decisions and had not adopted a 'strategic' role; at the centre, the Treasury and the Cabinet Office/OPSS also needed to delegate more and adopt a new role.[26]

However, plans for substantial staff cuts being prepared in different parts of Whitehall could provide the lever needed to redefine the functions and roles of headquarters departments. The July 1994 White Paper (see below) set out the government's aim to remove 'unnecessary layers of management' and further reduce the size of the civil service. On one estimate, departmental reviews could result in the elimination of one-third of the 3,000 mandarins at grade 5 and above. The Departments of Transport, Health and Trade and Industry, and the Home Office, were preparing to shed large numbers of staff. And a report published in October 1994 gave details of a major restructuring of the Treasury and a reduction of 25–30 per cent in its senior staff. There would be more delegation to departments and the Treasury, it was planned, would play a more strategic role, setting the framework and the objectives, rather than getting involved in the nitty-gritty of departmental and agency business. The Treasury's own cuts and restructuring were widely seen as an example to other departments and may well mark the start of the process whereby the Next Steps revolution transforms the Whitehall 'core'.[27]

The Treasury had initially been sceptical, even hostile, towards the Next Steps, fearing a loss of control over public spending and a diminution of its power. It appeared 'unwilling to trust in the capacity of . . . agencies to manage properly', and feared that they would inevitably press for additional resources to fund better quality services. But there was a shift towards cautious support of the initiative when the Treasury realized that Next Steps could help it establish better control arrangements.[28] In some ways the Treasury's power was reinforced: it took on a central role in the planning and launching of individual agencies, sets their financial targets, monitors their performance and interferes with them directly, as well as dealing with their parent departments. At the same time, and egged on by OPSS, it began to gradually loosen the apron strings and allow some agencies greater financial and personnel flexibilities when it was confident that rigorous monitoring and reporting systems were in place. The Civil Service Management Functions Act was passed in 1992 to facilitate the greater delegation of personnel management functions to departments and agencies, opening the way for a redefiniton of the managerial role of the centre of Whitehall and suggesting that the Treasury had finally accepted the logic of the Next Steps project.

The Next Steps brought the notion of government by contract and a more performance-oriented approach into Whitehall, with 'framework documents' and 'business plans' specifying what agencies were expected to achieve within given levels of resources. The government claimed that marked improvements in performance were being delivered. The Passport Agency, for instance, cut the average time taken to process an application from three-and-a-half weeks to one. The Benefits Agency bettered tough targets set for it on clearance-times and accuracy rates for paying income support. At the centre, OPSS monitored performance and published an annual review, showing that agencies met around three-quarters of their targets in 1991–2 and 1992–3 for instance. There were some criticisms of the targets themselves, however. The TCSC was concerned that too much stress had been given to financial performance as opposed to wider notions of efficiency or – crucially – quality of service. The Public Accounts Committee pointed to weaknesses in the Vehicle Inspectorate's efficiency index and suggested that there was no clear proof that the agency's performance had actually improved. Agencies started talking about their 'customers' and carrying out customer satisfaction surveys and market research, though the head of the Benefits Agency had to admit that social security claimants were the 'customers' of a monopoly supplier and had no consumer choice over which local office to go to. Some London Business School research suggested that, in any case, the shift to agency status did not by itself bring about significant changes in performance – what was important were other managerial and organizational improvements which could, in principle, be gained without Next Steps.[29]

The spectre of privatization loomed over the initiative from the start. The Ibbs report had raised the possibility of some agencies being outside government and the civil service. Mrs Thatcher was not willing to rule out the possibility of privatization in the longer-term but took the line in public that Next Steps was primarily about those activities which were to remain within government. A series of 'prior options' tests were applied, with privatization or contracting-out considered as options before the decision could be taken to create an agency. Nevertheless, civil service unions and the Labour Opposition were suspicious that the move to agencies was a preparatory stage in the creeping privatization of White-hall functions. Behind-the-scenes, that was exactly why Nigel Lawson, Mrs Thatcher's then-Chancellor of the Exchequer, and an enthusiastic privatizer, had in the end reluctantly backed the Next Steps change. As the official history of the Next Steps commented, 'introducing more business-like arrangements' (such as commercial-style accounts and tighter financial systems) could increase the marketability of civil service activities.[30] There were press leaks in 1991 that John Major's Policy Unit was working on plans for the sale of some agencies and after 1992, with the Conservative's fourth successive election victory, the ousting of Kemp and the market-testing programme gathering pace (see below), the privatization option loomed ever larger. Initially, transfer to the private sector was announced or planned for a handful of fairly small and specialized units such as DVOIT in the information technology field, a number of the DTI's research laboratories, and the Transport Research Laboratory. But in 1993 the government invited outside organizations to take part in the regular agency review exercises which reconsider the 'prior options' and rewrite framework documents, a move which suggested to critics that it hoped that the private sector would step in and take over more agencies or parts of their operations.

Back in the 1960s, the Fulton Committee had recognized that devolving management responsibility to agencies would raise parliamentary and constitutional issues. There were frequent complaints that the government was too blasé or even disingenuous about the implications of the Next Steps changes for parliamentary and public accountability, issues which the Ibbs report had dealt with only perfunctorily. Ministers remained responsible for policy, but if they were to be no longer responsible for 'operational' questions then ways had to be found to allow MPs to monitor the detailed working of agencies. Not surprisingly, the TCSC repeatedly focused on this problem in its regular inquiries into the progress of the initiative, forcing ministers to concede that chief executives should be regarded as the accounting officers answerable to the Commons Public Accounts Committee and pressing for select committees to have the right to summon agency heads to give evidence. Critics got particularly steamed up about the handling of MPs' queries about agencies. Ministers would reply to parliamentary questions (PQs) on policy matters, the theory went, but chief executives would reply to PQs on operational matters. Chief executives' replies were originally placed in the Commons Library and the Public Information Office which meant, it was argued, that a significant amount of important information previously easily accessible through Hansard was no longer in the public domain in any meaningful sense – the government eventually having to agree to print chief executives' answers to PQs in Hansard. (This storm in a teacup has to be kept in perspective: chief executives actually answer only about 2 per cent of PQs overall – though the figure is more like 60 per cent in the case of the Benefits Agency.[31])

The Next Steps changes were, for the most part, pushed through by executive action rather than by statute (something that would surprise constitutional lawyers in other countries) and with little in the way of parliamentary debate. Legislation to permit the creation of new Trading Funds was an exception in this respect – twelve agencies were operating on this commercial basis by 1994, which meant that they could be run with greater financial freedoms and with profit and loss accounts. But this also meant that parliament's budgetary oversight and control powers were reduced for those agencies.

The official line was that Next Steps preserved, even strengthened, the chain of accountability to parliament and brought greater transparency. Breaking with the past practice of the civil service, identifiable officials were now directly answerable for their administrative actions. It was claimed that Next Steps ended 'the myth of the old system' that ministers were 'omnicompetent beings who knew everything about [departmental] operations'.[32] The government also pointed to a significant increase in the volume of information available to MPs and the public through the publication of agency framework documents, annual reports and business plans.

For the government's critics, though, the established principles and mechanisms of parliamentary accountability were being diminished or destroyed: 'the system is closing its doors' said Labour MP Gerald Kaufman. There was a danger of buck-passing by ministers and chief executives to avoid criticism, and a reduction in MPs' power to scrutinize government and obtain redress for constituents. But the real problem, perhaps, and one that posed uncomfortable questions for ministers and MPs alike, was the need to reappraise what the Labour think-tank the Institute of Public Policy Research (IPPR) called 'the faded convention' of ministerial responsibility, recognize its limitations and put in place a new framework of accountability. The managerialist philosophy of Next Steps and the traditional doctrine of ministerial responsibility were incompatible, the IPPR argued, and accountability through parliament needed to be augmented by a strengthening of administrative law, FoI legislation, the development of complaints procedures, ombudsmen arrangements, user councils and public compensation schemes (i.e. accountability to the public as 'customers' and as citizens). The underlying problem was that the Next Steps project was launched by a government that 'was mistaken in believing that the administration of government could be restructured without tackling its theoretical basis'.[33]

As with the problem of accountability, the Ibbs report had brushed aside the issues involved in the shape of the post-Next Steps civil service. It was soon obvious that the logic of its changes spelt the end for a national career bureaucracy of the type built up earlier in the century. 'A "unified civil service" really is not compatible with the way we are going', the PM's Efficiency Adviser, Sir Angus Fraser, candidly explained to the TCSC in 1991. The Ibbs report had said it was important that there should not develop two classes of civil servants but the introduction of agencies promised just that and 'reinstigates the policy versus administration cultural and skill divide which Fulton tried so hard to remove'.[34]

Next Steps had the advantage for the government of encouraging movement away from national pay agreements negotiated with the civil service unions. It also reinforced the Treasury's drive to vary pay according to location, skills and individual performance. Chief executives' salaries were linked to meeting agency targets. HMSO led the way in breaking loose from the established civil service pay and grading system in 1990, but progress in extending to other agencies significant pay and grading 'flexibilities' (e.g. introducing staff bonus schemes) was initially slow because of Treasury caution. However, from April 1994 twenty-one of the biggest agencies (with 2,000 or more staff) and the two Revenue departments, accounting for over half the staff in the civil service altogether, were given responsibility for their own pay and grading structures (the Employment Service abolished the old EO–SEO executive-level grades and replaced them with new pay bands, for instance) and the Treasury authorized other agencies employing more than 500 staff to propose their own schemes too. The government's 1994 civil service white paper (see below) announced that from 1996 all pay and grading responsibilities would be left to agencies and departments.

Changes in the responsibilities and operation of the Civil Service Commission meant that from April 1991 agencies and departments could fill all their own posts except for those at grade 7 and above and fast-stream entrants (95 per cent of posts). As with the movement away from uniform civil service terms and conditions, devolved recruitment arrangements may well make sense for agencies looking for people with particular skills or operating in particular labour market conditions but could, over time, further fragment the civil service. The civil service unions were concerned that the Next Steps would create barriers to the movement of officials between different parts of the civil service. Of course, most officials have always spent their whole working lives in just one department, but for the top-most ranks and the 'high-flyers' the concept of a 'unified' service has had more meaning and the creation of additional obstacles to the acquisition of 'managerial' as well as 'policy' experience by future top mandarins conflicted with the stated aims of the Next Steps project. Traditional ideas about civil service career patterns were also challenged by the way in which chief executives were appointed. Not only were they on short-term contracts, but of the 98 appointments of this type made by the end of 1993, 65 involved public advertisement and open competition and 35 of those posts were filled by outsiders (from the private sector, local government, the NHS, etc).

A number of other developments buttressed these Next Steps changes.

The *Working Patterns* report prepared by Dame Anne Mueller (Second Permanent Secretary at the Treasury responsible for civil service pay and conditions), and leaked at the end of 1987, challenged the whole basis of the career civil service by proposing a large increase in part-time and temporary staff contracts and in flexible working hours.[35] Applying these measures to executive and routine clerical operations could offer, it was suggested, big savings in pay, national insurance and pension costs (though perhaps finally killing-off the notion of government as a 'good' employer). The number of part-timers in the civil service did increase from 16,000 in 1984 to 43,000 in 1992. Plans also circulated in Whitehall for a major new programme of job dispersal from London, leaving a drastically slimmed-down core of senior mandarins (and their support staff) in the capital, with executive and clerical work relocated in the regions. This shift would generate cost-savings and ease middle- and lower-grade recruitment difficulties experienced in the south-east. The Department of Health's NHS Management Executive and the Benefits Agency headquarters were moved to Leeds. Taken together, the Next Steps, the Mueller plan and the dispersal of jobs would open-up a divide (or perhaps widen an already existing divide) in the civil service between an elite policy 'core' of largely London-based career mandarins and a provincially-based operational/managerial 'periphery' with different (for the most part, worse?) terms and conditions of employment.

Peter Kemp was openly prepared to envisage that the result of these changes would effectively create 'a very large number of civil services'. The Head of the Civil Service, Sir Robin Butler, maintained that the civil service of the future would be 'unified but not uniform'. But what would hold it together? Butler said in 1988 that it was vital that the 'traditional strengths' of the civil service were maintained: 'equity, accountability, impartiality and a wide view of the public interest'. The worry was obviously that the managerial upheavals would undermine the public service ethos. It was also essential, Sir Robin Butler insisted, to maintain 'a degree of cohesion across the [civil] service as a whole'. Departments and agencies must not 'become simply different unconnected elements in the overall public sector, with little in the way of staff transferability, and no real working mechanisms for policy co-ordination'.[36] The Fraser report had similarly pointed to the civil service's 'unity of purpose in serving collective Cabinet government'. The criticism that the government was reluctant to publicly address problems of this nature in the early years of the Next Steps initiative was justified. Fundamental changes in the structure and workings of government, and the character of the civil service, were being introduced piecemeal and without full public discussion of all the implications. This problem was compounded when another wave of reforms hit Whitehall as the Major government pressed on with the Next Steps agenda and at the same time introduced changes that cut right across it.

The Citizen's Charter

Civil service reform did not slip off the government's agenda following Mrs Thatcher's replacement by John Major in November 1990. There was no let-up in the implementation of the Next Steps initiative, as we have seen. And Major had his own ideas about the reshaping of public services – his government's reforms actually became increasingly radical and the pace of change increased in momentum. There were soon three teams of officials working away in the Cabinet Office on particular policy initiatives – the Next Steps Team, the Citizen's Charter Unit, and the Efficiency Unit working on 'market testing' – with Major and William Waldegrave (civil service minister 1992–4) visibly committed to reform and anxious for quick results. Ministers presented their schemes as a comprehensive and coherent package which involved nothing less than a fundamental reappraisal of the role of government. However, there was concern at the top of Whitehall about possible 'initiative fatigue' as well as wariness about the extent of Conservative privatization ambitions. The government's critics talked of the dismemberment of the civil service and of the substitution of ideology for strategic thinking. Ministers had 'embarked on the fragmentation of government without knowing what they're doing' complained one insider. Plowden's explanation for what was happening in terms of 'the frustration of a government at its failure to solve the substantive problems of the day . . . turning to questions of administrative reorganization as a surrogate' called to mind parallels over a thirty-year period.[37]

The Citizen's Charter, published in July 1991, was Major's 'Big Idea' for the 1990s. It marked something of a change of direction and an attempt to make Conservative policies towards public services more positive and appealing. The new emphasis was on raising the quality of public services and making them more consumer-sensitive: the focus would be on the outputs and the users of public services rather than on inputs and service-producers. These concepts echoed developments in private sector management thinking in the 1980s, with management gurus like Peters and Waterman stressing the themes of excellence and quality, and they had been aired in a little-noticed Cabinet Office publication called *Service to the Public* in 1988. But the politics of *The Citizen's Charter* were paramount. The Charter was, in part, a vehicle for Major to establish his own political identity and 'show both continuity with, and a departure from, Thatcherism' before the next election, argued Bruce Doern. (Mrs Thatcher was reported to be scathing about the Charter.) It was also the Conservatives' answer to their Labour and Liberal Democrat opponents policies of increased public spending and wider political and constitutional reform. It prompted a fair amount of 'me-tooism', with Labour proclaiming that it too was committed to improving the quality of public services and even insisting it had invented the term 'citizen's charter' (first used by Labour-controlled York City Council in 1988). Labour claimed that £10 million of taxpayers' money was being used to launch glossy Tory election propaganda and there were reports of doubts in Whitehall about the party-political aspects of the Charter exercise. There had apparently been protracted arguments between the political zealots of the Number 10 Policy Unit and unenthusiastic officials in departments who had raised practical objections and pointed out drawbacks.[38]

The Charter programme was, to some extent, just a repackaging of a number of existing but separate initiatives, but there were some new ideas too. It was aimed at public services generally – the health service, local government, the police, railways, education, public utilities – as well as services delivered by the civil service; by 1993 over thirty charters had appeared for different parts of the public sector. The basic idea was to provide consumers of public services with more information about service-standards they could expect and about performance against those targets; to strengthen complaints procedures and provide redress when things went wrong; and to use the mechanisms of privatization, contracting-out and competition to provide more consumer choice. Symbolizing the new approach, and jettisoning the 'faceless bureaucrat' image, civil servants dealing with the public would henceforth wear name badges (though some officials protested about personal safety implications). A 'Taxpayer's Charter' set out what people could expect of the 'services' provided by the Inland Revenue and by Customs and Excise (they would be impartial, fair, collect only what was due under the law, etc.) and targets were set for the time taken to reply to customers' letters. The Benefits Agency and the Employment Service also produced charters.

The civil service *did* need to become more responsive to the public-as-consumer. 'Civil servants were dedicated to the public service in the abstract. That somehow failed to translate into service to the individual citizen', as *The Economist* put it. 'The "public" service was notoriously ponderous and customer-unfriendly.' But the Charter project was attacked on a number of grounds. The government's concept of 'citizenship' appeared very narrow and limited – it had confused consumerism with citizenship argued its critics. The Charter(s) had not, for the most part, given citizens any more legal rights than they had already and nor were they enforceable in the courts. Also, it seemed pitched at the individual citizen but the 'customers' for some key government activities (e.g. regulatory functions) are the wider community. Furthermore, ministers and the Treasury were adamant that there was no extra money available to fund the Charter and that it was, in the jargon, 'resource neutral'. Services had to be (and could be) improved within existing resources. For those who did not accept this argument, the Charter was about 'dressing up the front-line official, a "have a nice day McPublic Servant"' as a sop and to deflect criticism away from underfunding and the failures of government. The Charter's claim to be about extending accountability led to criticisms of the absence of any commitment in it to freedom of information legislation.[39]

The Charter's not-so-hidden agenda concerned the furthering of market values in the public services. The government stated its determination to 'drive reforms further into the core of the public services' and signalled its intention to extend 'contracting-out' and 'market-testing' in central government. This was a green light for the radical right. Madsen Pirie, a leading champion of privatization, joined the prime minister's *Citizen's Charter* advisory panel and Graham Mather, of the right-wing think-tank the Institute of Economic Affairs, saw the opportunity to move towards a new model of 'government by contract'.[40]

Market Testing

Central government had failed to practise what it had preached to others in the 1980s. Privatization had meant dismantling the nationalised industries, and local councils had been compelled to put services out to tender. But Whitehall had remained 'in the competitive tendering stone age', argued William Waldegrave. Departments had privatized or contracted-out support services such as cleaning, catering and security. A Treasury report, *Using Private Enterprise in Government* (1986), had recommended the extension of competitive tendering in central government but by the early 1990s only about £25 million of work was being tested against the market each year. In the *Competing for Quality* White Paper published by the Treasury in November 1991, the government's plans for expanding competition in the public sector were set out. 'Public services will increasingly move to a culture where relationships are contractual rather than bureaucratic', it predicted. Contracting-out in Whitehall would be taken beyond the traditional support functions to areas 'closer to the heart of government', involving clerical and executive operations and many professional and specialist services, with departments and agencies set targets for market testing and contracting-out (the former involving the comparison of bids from in-house providers and outside would-be contractors, the latter referring to cases where a department/agency decides not to continue as the provider itself and chooses between competing private sector bids). In addition, the government wanted Whitehall to develop its own 'internal market', with a charging regime developing for services provided by one department or agency to another (e.g. services provided by HMSO, the Central Office of Information, the PSA) and encouraging charging for 'common services' inside departments (DTI put its central support services on a market basis, giving its managers budgets they could spend on internal or outside suppliers).[41]

The 'prior options' exercises at the start of the Next Steps initiative had included consideration of contracting-out but in the late 1980s the presumption seems to have been that activities would remain within the public sector; after 1991 the emphasis changed. In the autumn of 1992 Treasury minister Stephen Dorrell ordered departments to come up with candidates for privatization: they had to list their 'core' and 'non-core' functions and privatization was not ruled out even for the 'core'. In a speech to the right-wing Centre for Policy Studies he talked of a 'long march through Whitehall' involving the transfer to the private sector of activities which were not part of 'the inescapable core of government'. In *Competing for Quality* the government had claimed it had 'no dogmatic preference' for either public or private sector provision (though the presumption was that entirely new services would normally be contracted-out). But this was followed up with an internal paper ('Selling government services into wider markets') circulated around Whitehall which openly declared a prejudice in favour of the private sector.[42]

With the Next Steps programme the government had seemed to concede that civil servants could manage efficiently, given the right structures. Now – in the middle of the drive to create agencies – it was declaring that exposure to market forces, competition and, ultimately, privatization was the only way to make public services more efficient. The Fraser report had promised chief executives more managerial freedom but they were now being ordered to market test/contract-out agency functions. Agency heads were reported to be resentful and disillusioned by this destabilizing political interference. But the sacking of Sir Peter Kemp in 1992 (see above) had marked a victory for John Major's new efficiency adviser, Sir Peter Levene, in a behind-the-scenes tussle over the priority to be given to the policy of competitive tendering in central government. With a new civil service minister, William Waldegrave, needing to make a big splash to rescue his Cabinet career and a new Conservative back-bench intake dominated by 'Thatcher's children', the climate of political opinion in 1992 favoured a new privatization drive, this time directed at Whitehall itself.[43]

The government's reforms would certainly lead to a smaller public service, William Waldegrave admitted, and he anticipated financial savings averaging around 25 per cent from market testing/contracting-out. He talked of a new role for government: concentrating on what it really needed to do and no more, separating the purchaser and provider roles and introducing competition and management by contract into the provision of services. Ministers and top officials took to citing the latest American best-seller, *Reinventing Government* by Osborne and Gaebler (1992), with its notion of government 'steering' rather than 'rowing'. The purchaser/provider split had figured in Lord Rothschild's report on government departments' use of Research and Development in 1971 but in other respects the administrative conventional wisdom of the early 1970s had been abandoned: the fashion in the 1990s was for 'small rather than large-scale organization, for diversity rather than uniformity, and for uncoupling previously unified institutional responsibilities'.[44]

Initial reports were that every department and agency had been ordered to draw up plans for up to 25 per cent of their activities and staff (130,000 posts across the civil service as a whole) to be put out to competitive tender before the next election, but a target of 15 per cent was nearer the mark. The scale of the exercise convinced critics (in and outside Whitehall) that the real aim was not so much better management as 'a cost-saving jobs purge' or to 'dismantle the civil service altogether'. In the event, departmental foot-dragging meant that the government did not meet the ambitious targets for its market testing programme. The target had been a fifty-fold increase in the the amount of work market-tested – £1.5 billion by September 1993. In fact, 389 individual market tests with a total value of £1.1 billion had been completed by the end of 1993, mostly covering support services (typing, payroll, libraries, printing, and particularly IT and computing) but also including the MoD's atomic weapons establishment, the Police National Computer and the National Lottery. In-house civil service teams won 68 per cent of the work they were permitted to bid for. But in 113 test exercises in-house bids had not been allowed and the work had been contracted-out to a private firm; these cases accounted for £768 million of work. Savings of £135 million were claimed (ministers had forecast savings of £375 million), with over 14,000 civil service jobs going (successful in-house bids leading to a 24 per cent reduction in posts in the operations concerned). In November 1993 a new target to market test £800 million of work (covering 35,000 civil service jobs) over the next twelve months was announced.[45]

By January 1995, ministers were claiming savings of £400 million a year over the past two years from the market testing programme, representing average cost savings of 20 per cent. More than £2 billion of government work had been reviewed since April 1992, with more than £1 billion of it transferred to the private sector. A total of 54,000 civil service jobs had been reviewed and 26,000 posts lost – including 10,600 transferred to the private sector, 6,500 redeployed in the civil service, 2,100 gone by natural wastage, and 3,300 made voluntarily or compulsorily redundant. Half the work had been put out to the private sector without any competing in-house civil service bid; in-house teams had, however, won 73 per cent of the contracts they had been allowed to tender for. Another £1.1 billion worth of work was to be reviewed and subjected to tendering and competition over the next twelve months.[46]

'The opportunities for the private sector can be enormous' Waldegrave had predicted in 1992, and the figures just quoted bear out that claim. Ministers had given the contract for selling personalized car number plates to a private company despite the in-house DVLA bid being £2 million cheaper. However, controversy surrounded the extent to which European law, in the shape of the so-called TUPE (transfer of undertakings/protection of employment) regulations, would undermine private firms' ability to undercut publicly-run services by cutting wages and eroding conditions of service. The private sector also benefited from the sharp increase in government spending on external consultants which rose four-fold between 1985 and 1990 to run at about £500 million a year. An Efficiency Unit report in 1994 pointed out duplication of work done for different departments (the FDA said that one management consultancy was being consulted simultaneously by eight different departments on performance-related-pay), argued that expensive consultants were used to do jobs civil servants could do just as well, and recommended savings of £130 million on this spending over a three-year period.[47]

The government clearly intended to press on with the contracting process, the crucial questions being how far it could be taken beyond the obvious support services, whether it would extend to contracting-out policy work, and the size and scope of the Whitehall 'core' that would remain (perceptions of what this is or should be likely to change over time and to be the subject of ideological disagreement). Contracting-out would, for all practical purposes, be likely to be a one-way-street, to be an 'irreversible' move. 'If the public service ceases to carry out a function, the staff and the facilities to do it disappear. Even if a contract were only fixed term, it would be very difficult for any in-house tender to be put together', the FDA argued. And ministers were clear that testing the comparative efficiency of public and private sector operators would not involve allowing successful Next Steps agencies to expand their businesses and take on new functions. If chief executives felt they could out-perform the private sector and wanted their organizations to grow, the proper course was to privatize agencies.[48]

The problems and dangers of the move to government by contract and competitive tender tended to be brushed aside by the government. Osborne and Gaebler themselves noted that the contract tool is one of the most difficult for governments to use because writing and monitoring contracts requires so much skill; Whitehall's mandarin cadre has little experience of those skills. Waldegrave argued that the government's reforms would strengthen accountability, but critics maintained they would impair it. Clients (departments) and contractors might blame each other for what went wrong; vital information might be stamped 'commercial in confidence' and withheld from the public. Outside employers could not be required to follow civil service best practice in the field of equal opportunities (though they would have to meet normal legal obligations), and so the progress made by Whitehall since the late 1980s in this area could be undermined by large-scale contracting-out, the civil service unions feared.

If market testing was to be a 'shopping around' process, was there sufficient competition and choice of potential service-providers for the market's invisible hand to deliver improved services? In the IT field, choice seemed limited and, more generally, doubts were raised about the dangers of government being at the mercy of a private sector monopoly or cartel. There was concern, too, at what the FDA called the 'general erosion of what used to be thought of as a politically-neutral non-commercialised public service'. Among the dangers here were safeguards for confidentiality (e.g. private contractors having access to information about individuals' and companies' tax affairs). The potential for corruption was increased. Would companies that made political donations be allowed to bid for civil service work? There was the problem of conflicts of interest: private sector consultants inevitably have other clients who might be interested in securing contracts for government work; politicians might sit on the boards of companies tendering for contracts. Would commercialization weaken the traditional public service ethos as private contractors brought a different culture and a different style of behaviour into government? That these were not abstract considerations was shown by an unprecedented Public Accounts Committee report in early 1994 which talked of a departure from time-honoured standards of public conduct. Instancing cases of irregularities and improper spending, the PAC said that outsiders coming into Whitehall had to understand that 'public money is different from private money' and criticized the government for not doing enough to prevent corruption in the civil service. The Comptroller and Auditor General, Sir John Bourn, complained that market testing made the job of telling whether public money was being spent properly or efficiently more difficult because the National Audit Office had no right to examine the books of private companies that had won contracts to deliver public services. The underlying question was: were private sector business practices really better?[49]

The End of the Civil Service?

It was not just the threats to its integrity which alarmed observers of the Whitehall machine: the continued existence of the civil service itself seemed to be at stake by the mid-1990s. Market testing and contracting-out added to the destructive impact of Next Steps upon the traditional unified and centralized career civil service. In the name of managerial flexibility, for instance, the common system of recruitment was ended. Lower-grade recruitment had been progressively delegated to departments from the 1960s and by 1982 85 per cent of civil service recruitment (broadly to posts below Executive Officer level) was a departmental responsibility. In 1991 centralized EO recruitment was abandoned, meaning that departments and agencies would be responsible for 95 per cent of all recruitment; the Civil Service Commission was replaced by a Recruitment and Assessment Services agency which could contract to recruit for departments and executive agencies; and the Civil Service Commissioners kept responsibility for recruitment at grade 7 and above and the 'fast stream' entry, otherwise monitoring the work of over 3,000 'recruitment units' to ensure compliance with rules laid down by the Minister for the Civil Service to provide for fair and open competition. A Cabinet Office review in 1994 recommended even more delegation, proposing that the Commissioners should only be directly involved in appointments to agency chief executive posts and senior Whitehall grades, with departments/agencies recruiting at grade 7 and above, ending the Commissioners role in 'fast stream' recruitment, but clarifying their role as custodians and monitors of the principles of openness, fairness and merit for all recruitment.[50]

In the 1960s, said the report, the assumption had been that 'the service needed to recruit people with broadly common qualities, grade for grade' and that 'there was a common, if not uniform, structure into which they would be recruited'. Now there was a different approach, particularly in agencies, and a belief that 'each "business" should recruit the kinds of people *it* needs', that 'for many jobs, business or functional expertise is more important than traditional, generalist skill', and that senior managers should be directly involved in getting the right people into the right posts. The danger, as the review team recognized, was that the extensive delegation of recruitment responsibilities to small, local units, together with the greater use of private sector suppliers of recruitment services, made it more difficult to 'embed openness, fairness and merit as constant principles in a changing Civil Service culture'. It was an open question whether the high standards previously expected and achieved by the Civil Service Commissioners could be maintained in the new set-up.[51]

Whether the higher civil service, the elite corps of senior officials, could survive in its traditional form also became a subject of debate. It was probably only to be expected that, having introduced competition and contracting-out to civil service executive operations, the government would face pressure to apply these methods to the central policy-making core of Whitehall. Ten years earlier, the mandarins had 'seen off' the attacks of John Hoskyns; this time it was not so clear that 'a protective exclusion zone' could be drawn around the highest reaches of the civil service.[52]

In July 1992 Sir Robin Butler and Sir Peter Levene commissioned a study by the Efficiency Unit of recruitment to the senior open structure (the top three grades, covering the 600 most powerful officials). The *Career Management and Succession Study* report (or the Oughton report, after the head of the Efficiency Unit), published in November 1993, was a classic civil service holding-operation: critical of some of the existing practices, promising important changes, but defending traditional principles (e.g. impartiality, non-politicization), and disappointing the really radical outside critics.[53] Recommendations that high-flyers should gain more experience of management and of the operational end of the work of government to better prepare them for top-level jobs were hardly novel.

That the higher civil service had 'sometimes confused job rotation with career development' was also a long-standing criticism, with the Oughton report calling for more depth, rather than breadth, of experience, linked to a couple of 'career anchors' or areas of special expertise. However, it was clear that ministers and permanent secretaries continued to value the traditional Whitehall skills of the versatile policy-adviser adept at 'political management' and experienced in working the government and parliamentary process.

Using private sector practice as justification, the report said that there should be a clear statement that the expectation was to appoint from within for the top jobs – the civil service should 'grow its own timber'. Advertisement and open competition should be considered as an option for every appointment to the highest grades, to 'ventilate' the top structure, but not every post would be filled in this way (the Cabinet Office should publish an annual results tally). The report did not specify a target, but noted that over the previous three years 14 per cent of senior open structure vacancies had been advertised and 10 per cent of the posts had been filled by people who were not career civil servants. The Senior Appointments Selection Committee (SASC) should include at least one woman and one outsider in future, the report recommended, but this was unlikely to weaken the power of the most senior permanent secretaries and the Head of the Civil Service over top appointments or open-up the mysterious and hidden process through which they were made. And the report recommended that senior open structure officials be placed on contracts but ruled out fixed-term contracts.

In the months after the Oughton report appeared there were fierce arguments inside Whitehall and among ministers about the next moves. Sir Peter Kemp talked of 'wayward barons' at the top of the civil service pulling in different directions. A ministerial committee on civil service reform was deeply divided. Foreign Secretary Douglas Hurd (a former diplomat) tried to exercise a restraining influence; he had pointedly warned the Tory Party conference against an overly-dogmatic or ideological approach to the role of the state and public servants (the dangers of a Mao-style 'permanent cultural revolution'). Kenneth Clarke, the Chancellor, and Michael Heseltine, President of the Board of Trade, pressed for a more radical approach: big cuts in the number of senior officials, universal fixed-term contracts, automatic open advertising of all top jobs. The need for a single civil service at all was even questioned:

each minister/department could recruit their own staff. But Sir Robin Butler was reported to have 'dug his heels in' and John Major to have eventually opted for the 'more emollient approach'.[54]

The general media reaction was that the top mandarins had beaten-off the most radical reform ideas. 'The consolidators have won' was the verdict of Giles Radice, the chairman of the TCSC's inquiries into Whitehall, when the government's White Paper, *The Civil Service: Continuity and Change*, was issued in July 1994. 'The evolutionaries have routed the revolutionaries' was how *The Economist* put it, arguing that the White Paper contained 'lots of reassuring continuity and fewer-than-expected proposals for change.' But, in many ways, the White Paper was a 'clear compromise between the hardline reformers and the consolidators'.[55]

It seemed as if the top mandarins had defended their own territory and fought-off the threat to do to them what they had done to hundreds of thousands of other public servants: open-up their jobs to contracting-out and external competition. The government's response to Oughton was (from 1996) – the creation of a new Senior Civil Service, comprising the 3,500 officials at grade 5 and above and all agency chief executives. The government envisaged that most of these top posts would continue to be filled by insiders, and the White Paper appeared to rule out a dramatic increase in the recruitment of outsiders – it would allow only that 'departments and agencies will always *consider* advertising openly posts at these levels when a vacancy occurs, and then will use open competition whenever it is necessary and *justifiable* . . . ' (emphasis added). Behind the blandness, however, an important principle had been conceded and future ministers could set targets to increase outside recruitment (a Conservative government might want more businessmen, but Labour could use this provision to set quotas for women, trade unionists or ethnic minorities).[56]

The 'fast-stream' would remain as an inside track to posts in the elite corps, as a separate Cabinet Office study argued that the civil service could not withdraw from 'the top end of the graduate market', though it recommended regular external audit of the selection process because of continued perceptions of Oxbridge bias.[57] Officials in the Senior Civil Service would have individual (but not fixed-term) contracts. There would probably be fewer top civil servants (because of management reviews eliminating posts), with less job security, but with higher pay:

permanent secretaries in different departments may be paid at different rates, maximum salaries for grades 2 and 3 were increased, and pay would reflect individuals' responsibilities and performance.

In some ways, *The Economist* observed, 'the White Paper represents a retreat from the civil service revolution of the past few years'. In what was interpreted as a retreat from the commitment to the centrally-imposed market testing programme, departments and agencies were to draw up annual 'efficiency plans' (scrutinized by the Efficiency Unit and the Treasury) and decide themselves on the best mix of measures – including privatization, contracting-out and putting work out to tender – that would most effectively meet their own needs and deliver efficiency gains within the government's three-year freeze on running costs. Central targets for market-testing would no longer be set, but it is not being abandoned as a management tool. Agencies and departments could be expected to press on with it and, in some cases, even expand its use. As a result, the division between the top cadre and the rest of the civil service will be further entrenched. As Andrew Marr put it:

> from now on, the protected elite of the Senior Civil Service . . . will get promotion and pay awards based partly on their success in squeezing the rest of the system. Market testing will represent golden opportunities for the SCS: the interests of the mandarins and of tax-cutting politicians will be identical and will fall heavily on the incomes and security of the lower ranks.[58]

To allow them greater stability, Next Steps agencies would henceforth be reviewed every five years, instead of every three, to see if they could be privatized. At the same time, the delegation of greater management flexibility from the centre of Whitehall (Treasury and Cabinet Office/OPSS) to departments and agencies would continue. Already 60 per cent of officials were covered by delegated pay bargaining arrangements at departmental/agency level. From 1996 responsibility for pay and grading of all staff below the senior corps would be delegated to departments and agencies, marking the end of the existing national pay agreements. And although no specific manpower targets were set, the government anticipated that its policies would lead to a reduction in the civil service jobs total from 530,000 to under 500,000 over a four-year period.

The first two terms of office of the Conservative government (1979–87) were described as a 'traumatic' period for the civil service and the blows continued to rain down on it after 1988. If the 'old civil service' still recognizably survived in 1987, the talk in the mid-1990s was of the 'end of the civil service'. Sir Robin Butler spoke of the 'glue which holds the civil service together. The political context, the public accountability and consequent requirements of integrity and impartiality, the expectation that we will set an example and the public expenditure controls are all unique.' But the common system of recruitment organized by the Civil Service Commission had gone; agencies and contracting-out had introduced massive organizational fragmentation; managerial delegation was spawning different pay and grading arrangements in different parts of the service. It would be difficult to disagree with Andrew Marr's comment that 'that giant community, linked by grades and public codes, that national system which was the post-war Civil Service is dead'.[59]

Sir Robin Butler himself admitted that he did not know what the final shape of the civil service would be as a result of the changes that were taking place. Jones and Burnham argued that the clock was being put back: 'the fragmentation of the British civil service into separately-managed units has taken it back beyond the incomplete Fulton reforms of the 1960s and 1970s unifying "specialists" and "generalists", beyond the unitary, centrally-managed civil service created in 1920, to before the Northcote–Trevelyan reform of 1870 introducing central, uniform, non-partisan recruitment through open competition.' It had taken more than fifty years, starting in the 1870s, to create a unified career civil service; it had been dismantled in about fifteen years in the 1980s and 1990s.[60]

The civil service in the mid-1990s was certainly in a state of profound crisis. That the government's changes were felt to be raising constitutional as well as managerial issues was reflected in the wide-ranging Treasury and Civil Service Committee report published in November 1994 and in calls from many observers for an independent Royal Commission on the Civil Service. Administrative fashions could change in the years ahead and a new government might bring its own ideas about public-service reform. But there could be no doubt that the Conservative's Whitehall revolution of the 1980s and 1990s had produced massive, and in some areas probably irreversible, changes and that the process of reshaping the civil service and central government machine had by no means come to a halt.

Notes

1 Peter Hennessy, *Whitehall* (Secker and Warburg, London, 1989), pp. 591–2; Margaret Thatcher, *The Downing Street Years* (HarperCollins, London, 1993), pp. 6, 46; G. W. Jones, 'A Revolution in Whitehall? Changes in British Central Government since 1979', *West European Politics*, 12 (1989), p. 244.

2 Peter Hennessy, 'The Civil Service', in Dennis Kavanagh and Anthony Seldon (eds), *The Thatcher Effect* (Clarendon Press, Oxford, 1989), p. 114; Geoffrey Fry, 'The Thatcher Government, the Financial Management Initiative and the "New Civil Service"', *Public Administration*, 66 (1988), p. 2; G. W. Jones and June Burnham, 'Modernising the British Civil Service', Discussion paper no. 19, Centre for European Studies, Nuffield College, Oxford, 1992, pp. 8–9.

3 Spencer Zifcak, *New Managerialism: Administrative Reform in Whitehall and Canberra* (Open University Press, Buckingham, 1994), p. 15; Clive Ponting, *Whitehall: Changing the Old Guard* (Unwin Hyman, London, 1989), p. 68.

4 Fry, 'The Thatcher Government, the Financial Management Initiative and the "New Civil Service"', p. 1; Chris Painter, 'The Thatcher Government and the Civil Service: Economy, Reform and Conflict', *Political Quarterly*, 54 (1983), p. 296.

5 Ian Kessler, 'Pay Determination in the British Civil Service Since 1979', *Public Administration*, 71 (1993).

6 Sir Terry Heiser, 'The Civil Service at a Crossroads?', *Public Policy and Administration*, 9 (1994), p. 16; Christine Bellamy and John Taylor, 'Introduction: Exploiting IT in Public Administration – Towards the Information Polity', *Public Administration*, 72 (1994), p. 7; Stephen Dorril, *The Silent Conspiracy: Inside the Intelligence Services in the 1990s*, paperback edn (Mandarin, London, 1994), p. 379.

7 Helen Margetts, 'The Computerisation of Social Security: the way forwards or a step backwards', *Public Administration*, 69 (1991); Leslie Willcocks, 'Managing Information Systems in UK Public Administration: Issues and Prospects', *Public Administration*, 72 (1994); David Collingridge and Helen Margetts, 'Can government information systems be inflexible technology? The operational strategy revisited', *Public Administration*, 72 (1994).

8 Les Metcalfe and Sue Richards, *Improving Public Management*, 2nd edn

(Sage, London, 1990); Alan Bray, *The Clandestine Reformer: A Study of the Rayner Scrutinies* (Strathclyde Papers on Government and Politics, no. 55, 1988).

9   Zifcak, *New Managerialism*, p. 14.

10   Andrew Likierman, 'Management Information for Ministers: the MINIS system in the Department of the Environment', *Public Administration*, 60 (1982).

11   Andrew Gray and Bill Jenkins, 'The Management of Change in Whitehall: the Experience of the FMI', *Public Administration*, 69 (1991); Andrew Gray and Bill Jenkins, 'The Civil Service and the Financial Management Initiative', in Christopher Pollitt and Stephen Harrison (eds), *Handbook of Public Services Management* (Basil Blackwell, Oxford, 1992), pp. 168–78.

12   S. F. Thorpe-Tracey, 'FMI in practice: Newcastle Central Office', *Public Administration*, 65 (1987).

13   Geoffrey Gammon. 'The British Higher Civil Service: Recruitment and Training', *Public Policy and Administration*, 4 (1989).

14   Colin Campbell, 'Public Service and Democratic Accountability', in Richard Chapman (ed.), *Ethics in Public Service* (Edinburgh University Press, Edinburgh, 1993), p. 124.

15   Andrew Gray and William Jenkins, *Administrative Politics in British Government* (Wheatsheaf, Brighton, 1985), p. 125; Metcalfe and Richards, *Improving Public Management*.

16   Fry, 'The Thatcher Government, the FMI and the "New Civil Service"'; Geoffrey Fry, 'Outlining the Next Steps', *Public Administration*, 66 (1988).

17   Hennessy, *Whitehall*, p. 620.

18   Efficiency Unit, *Improving Management in Government: The Next Steps* (HMSO, London, 1988); Sue Richards, 'Management in Central Government: the Next Steps', *Public Money and Management*, 8 (1988); Zifcak, *New Managerialism*, p. 71.

19   Patricia Greer, *Transforming Central Government: the Next Steps Initiative* (Open University Press, Buckingham, 1994); *FDA News*, October 1991; Nicholas Ridley, 'Efficiency Begins at Home', in William Niskanen, *Bureaucracy: Servant or Master?* (Institute of Economic Affairs, London, 1973), pp. 87–93; C. Sladen, 'The Agency Game and the Civil Service: an inside view', *Teaching Public Administration*, 12 (1992).

20   Diana Goldsworthy, *Setting Up Next Steps* (HMSO, London, 1991), pp. 8, 34; Greer, *Transforming Central Government*, p. 6.

21   Barry O'Toole, 'Editorial: Permanent Secretaries, Open Competition and the Future of the Civil Service', *Public Policy and Administration*, 8 (1993), p. 3; Zifcak, *New Managerialism*, pp. 89–90.

22 Greer, *Transforming Central Government*, pp. 47–8; *Guardian*, 30 January 1991, 22 July 1992; *Independent*, 5 May 1993, 27 May 1993.

23 Treasury and Civil Service Committee: *Civil Service Management Reform: the Next Steps*, HC 494, 1987–8; *Developments in the Next Steps Programme*, HC 348, 1988–9; *Progress in the Next Steps Initiative*, HC 481, 1989–90; *The Next Steps Initiative*, HC 496, 1990–1; *Guardian*, 9 May 1991.

24 Geoffrey Dudley, 'The Next Steps Agencies, Political Salience and the Arms-Length Principle: Barbara Castle at the Ministry of Transport 1965–8', *Public Administration*, 72 (1994); Greer, *Transforming Central Government*, p. 55; *Independent*, 24 September 1994, 6 January 1995.

25 Efficiency Unit, *Making the Most of Next Steps: The Management of Ministers' Departments and their Executive Agencies* [Fraser Report] (HMSO, London, 1991).

26 *Next Steps: Moving On* (Cabinet Office/OPSS, 1994); see also: Elizabeth Mellon, 'Executive Agencies: Leading Change from the Outside-in', *Public Money and Management*, 13 (1993).

27 *Guardian*, 18 October 1994; *Independent*, 20 October 1994; *Financial Times*, 20 October 1994; Treasury and Civil Service Committee, *The Role of the Civil Service*, HC 27, 1993–4, paras 236–40.

28 Zifcak, *New Managerialism*, p. 84; Greer, *Transforming Central Government*, pp. 48–51.

29 Treasury and Civil Service Committee, *The Next Steps Initiative*, HC 496, 1990–1, pp. 108–11.

30 Nigel Lawson, *The View From Number 11* (Bantam Press, London, 1992), pp. 390–3; Goldsworthy, *Setting Up Next Steps*, p. 18.

31 *Next Steps Review 1993*, Cm 2430, 1993, p. 7; Treasury and Civil Service Committee, *The Role of the Civil Service*, p. 231.

32 Greer, *Transforming Central Government*, p. 82.

33 *Independent*, 31 March 1993; *Guardian*, 7 December 1992, 14 June 1993; Anne Davies and John Willman, *What Next? Agencies, Departments and the Civil Service* (Institute for Public Policy Research, London, 1991), pp. 24, 26–7, 35, 72–5.

34 Greer, *Transforming Central Government*, p. 96.

35 Fry, 'Outlining the Next Steps', pp. 435–6.

36 *FDA News*, October 1991; Sir Robin Butler, 'The evolution of the civil service', *Public Administration*, 71 (1993), p. 404.

37 William Waldegrave, *Public Service and the Future: Reforming Britain's Bureaucracies* (Conservative Political Centre, London, 1993); Richard Mottram, 'Developments in the Public Sector', paper to the PAC conference, University of York, 1993; William Plowden, *Ministers and Mandarins* (Institute of Public Policy Research, London, 1994), p. 15.

38 *The Citizen's Charter*, Cm 1599, July 1991; Michael Connolly et al, 'Making the Public Sector More User Friendly? A Critical Examination of the Citizen's Charter', *Parliamentary Affairs*, 47 (1994); G. Bruce Doern, 'The UK Citizen's Charter: Origins and Implementation in Three Agencies', *Policy and Politics*, 21 (1993); *Guardian*, 1 July 1991, 24 July 1991.

39 *The Economist*, 19 March 1994; David Farnham, 'The Citizen's Charter: improving the quality of the public services or furthering market values?', *Talking Politics*, 4 (1992); Doern, 'The UK Citizen's Charter', p. 27; Norman Lewis, 'The Citizen's Charter and Next Steps: A New Way of Governing?', *Political Quarterly*, 64 (1993), p. 316.

40 Graham Mather, *Government by Contract*, IEA Inquiry no. 25 (Institute of Economic Afairs, London, 1991).

41 Waldegrave, *Public Services and the Future*, p. 15; HM Treasury, *Competing for Quality: Buying Better Public Services*, Cm 1730, November 1991.

42 Tony Stott, 'Market Testing and Beyond: Privatisation and Contracting Out in British Central Government', *Teaching Public Administration*, 14 (1994), p. 38; *FDA News*, July 1992, January 1993.

43 Jones and Burnham, 'Modernising the British Civil Service', pp. 18–19; Sue Richards and Jeff Rodrigues, 'Strategies for Management in the Civil Service: Change of Direction', *Public Money and Management*, 13 (1993), p. 36.

44 Chris Painter, 'Public Service Reform: Reinventing or Abandoning Government?', *Political Quarterly*, 65 (1994), p. 260.

45 *FDA News*, July 1992; *Independent*, 15 November 1993; Plowden, *Ministers and Mandarins*, p. 14; *The Citizen's Charter: Second Report 1994*, Cm 2540, 1994.

46 *The Times*, 10 January 1995; *Independent*, 10 January 1995.

47 *Guardian*, 15 July 1992; *Observer*, 15 August 1993; *FDA News*, February 1993; *Independent*, 20 May 1994; *Financial Times*, 6 April 1994, 5 August 1994.

48 *FDA News*, November 1992; *Independent*, 23 March 1994.

49 Stott, 'Market Testing and Beyond', p. 47; *FDA News*, July 1992, November 1992; *Guardian*, 15 July 1992; Public Accounts Committee, *The Proper Conduct of Public Business*, HC 154, 1993–4; Barry O'Toole, 'The British Civil Service in the 1990s: Are Business Practices Really Best?', *Teaching Public Administration*, 14 (1994).

50 *Responsibilities for Recruitment to the Civil Service*, Cabinet Office/OPSS, July 1994.

51 Richard Chapman, 'The End of the Civil Service?', *Teaching Public Administration*, 12 (1992), p. 3.

52 *Observer*, 15 August 1993.

53 Efficiency Unit: *Career Management and Succession Planning Study* (HMSO, London, 1993).

54 *Independent*, 8 October 1993, 15 November 1993, 19 May 1994; *The Economist*, 28 May 1994, 16 July 1994; *The Times*, 14 July 1994; *Daily Telegraph*, 14 July 1994.

55 *The Civil Service: Continuity and Change*, Cm 2627, 1994; *Financial Times*, 14 July 1994; *The Economist*, 16 July 1994; Andrew Massey, 'Old Wine in New Bottles', *Parliamentary Brief* vol. 2, no. 10, 1994.

56 Massey, 'Old Wine in New Bottles'.

57 *Review of Fast Stream recruitment*, Cabinet Office/OPSS (HMSO, London, 1994).

58 *Independent*, 14 July 1994.

59 Fry, 'The Thatcher Government, the FMI and the "New Civil Service"', pp. 15, 18; Chapman, 'The End of the Civil Service?'; *FDA News* November 1991; *Independent*, 14 July 1994.

60 Butler, 'The Evolution of the Civil Service', p. 395; Jones and Burnham, 'Modernising the British Civil Service', p. 7.

6 Whitehall Accountability and Control

The extension of state activities after 1945 and the growth of far-reaching government controls (imposed during war-time and its aftermath) called into question the adequacy and effectiveness of the democratic checks on the government machine. The Attlee government did nothing to strengthen the existing channels of accountability or to create new ones, and some socialists as well as that government's Conservative opponents were concerned about the problem of 'bureaucracy' in the late 1940s. After 1951 Conservative ministers did not, it must be said, set about creating rods for their own backs, or helping their competitors in the struggle for power, by releasing more information or by greatly improving Parliament's capacity for scrutiny and control. Only in the 1960s, with the appearance of the parliamentary ombudsman and the introduction of specialized Commons select committees (and the development of a proper system of these had to wait until 1979), were steps taken to reinforce the traditional methods of holding the executive to account. In the 1970s and 1980s, attention focused on the open government/freedom of information issue as the key reform needed to secure more effective control over the state apparatus, but the struggle to reduce Whitehall secrecy was still far from over in the early 1990s.

The tradition of strong government, dominating Parliament and pushing through the party's electorally legitimated programme, appealed to both Labour and Conservative parties in the post-war period, though both parties contained those suspicious of the power and prerogatives of the executive. In this sense, the Attlee government and the Thatcher government had a common approach and philosophy – moreover, one that was shared by the higher mandarinate. In a classic essay published in 1964, *Representative and Responsible Government*, A. H. Birch contrasted to the Liberal view of the constitution (a model giving primacy to Parliament and to democratic accountability), a top-down, government-centred perspective which he labelled the Whitehall view – 'the view of the constitution held by those in power', the language or governing code used by ministers and senior civil servants. This was an apt distinction, still valid nearly fifty years after the Second World War. In 1918 the Haldane Committee had argued that increases in government efficiency must be matched by increases in the power of Parliament, but the emphasis in recent decades has always been more on the first than the second of these elements – even civil service reformers and outside critics (for instance at the time of Fulton) have often in effect accepted the 'Whitehall view'.

Ministerial Responsibility

Over the post-1945 period there has been a move away from talking about the doctrine of individual ministerial responsibility in, so to speak, hushed and reverential tones, and a growing recognition that this piece of constitutional furniture is threadbare and in urgent need of renewal and modernization, a task, however, for which no government has had the stomach. Successive governments have in fact used the doctrine as a talisman to ward off a range of democratic improvements, from the ombudsman, to select committees and open government reform.[1]

The theory of ministerial responsibility was devised in the nineteenth century and the textbooks tell us that it relates to ministers' responsibility for their personal behaviour (a relatively unproblematic aspect of the convention – ministers quitting because of personal errors or scandals) and for the work of their departments (a matter of dispute and controversy). In principle, ministers carry responsibility for all the actions of their departments; civil servants are simply ministers' anonymous agents. The two main aspects of the doctrine are, first, that the responsible minister is expected to answer in Parliament for the work of his or her department, and, second, that the minister must 'carry the can' for decisions or policies which are criticized, if necessary by resigning after serious failures of departmental policy or administration. On both counts, the doctrine has come under pressure since 1945.

Ministers remain the most authoritative exponents and defenders of their policies, and so responsible or answerable in the first sense. But the development since the 1960s of investigative select committees of MPs, to whose inquiries civil servants frequently give evidence, and of the Parliamentary Commissioner for Administration (or ombudsman), raised the question of the extent to which officials could be regarded as having, *de facto* if not *de jure*, a direct answerability of their own to Parliament and public. Whitehall guidelines drawn up in the 1970s – the so-called 'Osmotherly Rules' – showed, though, that the authorities were determined to stick to a traditional and minimalist interpretation of civil service accountability (see below).

Ministerial responsibility for the actions of departmental officials and the resignation sanction of the second element of the doctrine has been an additional area of uncertainty and difficulty. Ministerial resignations for the mistakes or failures of their departments are few in number, which is why the doctrine is sometimes labelled a constitutional myth. However, it would be wrong to imagine that there is a lost 'golden age' when ministers did shoulder responsibility and honourably resign after departmental mistakes.[2] For political reasons the Prime Minister and Cabinet may rally round a departmental minister under fire, in effect extending the cover of the government's collective responsibility. Alternatively, some instances where ministers have resigned in apparent vindication of the doctrine may in reality be exercises in limiting the political damage of a crisis to the Prime Minister and the government as a whole (the 1982 Falklands Foreign Office resignations and Leon Brittan's 1986 Westland resignation are cases in point).

The famous Crichel Down case, involving the resignation of the Minister of Agriculture in 1954, was for a long time widely interpreted as a classic case of a minister taking on himself responsibility for his civil servants' mistakes as a sacrificial victim, the whole episode usually being presented as a story of bureaucratic arrogance and abuse of power. Recent research has, however, put the civil servants involved in a better light and has suggested that Sir Thomas Dugdale was forced out of office primarily because his decision on the Crichel Down issue provoked angry Tory back-benchers into demanding his head and the party chiefs decided to let them have it. As Norman Chester argued at the time, Crichel Down was essentially a failure of political sensitivity on the part of the Conservative government.[3]

Absolute claims, such as Herbert Morrison's in 1954 that 'the Minister is responsible for every stamp stuck on an envelope', have given way in the post-war period to a recognition that 'ministerial responsibility is, at best, a matter of line-drawing, and the precise location of the line at any time owes much more to political pragmatism than to constitutional dogma'.[4] The massive scale and complexity of government business means that it is now widely acknowledged that ministers may be answerable to Parliament but that they cannot be held responsible for actions taken in their name which they would not have approved of if they had been personally consulted by their officials. As Sir John Hunt, then Secretary to the Cabinet, put it in 1977: 'The concept that because somebody whom the Minister has never heard of has made a mistake means that the Minister should resign is out of date and rightly so.' But this development can leave civil servants in an exposed position: named and blamed or scapegoated in official inquiries, their careers perhaps damaged, but denied the opportunity to respond to criticism (as over Crichel Down, in the Vehicle and General case in the 1970s, and in the Maze and Brixton prison break-outs in 1983 and 1991).[5]

The Westland case (1985–6) made this a live political issue and strained the traditional doctrine almost to breaking point. The government blocked the officials at the centre of the affair from giving evidence to the Defence Select Committee. MPs on the Treasury and Civil Service Select Committee (1986) were not satisfied: 'who ought to resign or to be penalised if mistakes are made?' they asked. 'If it is not to be Ministers, it can only be officials.' And the committee suggested that 'a mechanism must be provided to make officials, in cases in which Ministers deny responsibility for their actions, answerable to Parliament.' Like its predecessors, however, the Thatcher government preferred to repeat orthodox constitutional formulae rather than face up to the difficult task of modernizing constitutional thinking and practice in this area, something made all the more necessary after the launch of that government's Next Steps initiative (as we saw in chapter 5).

Recently, the government, and Sir Robin Butler in particular, have made much of the distinction between 'accountability' and 'responsibility'. Ministerial accountability involves a minister's duty to account to Parliament for the work of his department: 'in the last resort . . . Ministers can be challenged about any action of the Civil Service'. But that does not mean that ministers must take the blame for every wrong decision of their subordinates. 'They cannot and should not take the blame for decisions of which they know nothing or could be expected to know nothing', insists Sir Robin. Responsibility, according to the government, 'implies direct personal involvement in an action or decision, in a sense which implies personal credit or blame for that action or decision'. Officials, on this view, can be held responsible for certain actions and can be delegated clearly-defined responsibilities, but are not directly accountable to Parliament for their actions.

The Treasury and Civil Service Committee, in its 1994 report, believed that this distinction was unconvincing. It was argued that the distinction was untenable in practice because of the way ministers responded to events and external pressures, and because the government's restatement still did not acknowledge a shared responsibility (between politicians and officials) for decisions. 'Ministerial preparedness to resign when Ministerial responsibility for failure has been established lies at the very heart of an effective system of Parliamentary accountability', insisted the MPs.[6]

All the same, by introducing the accountability/responsibility distinction, the first steps may have been taken towards defining a more satisfactory constitutional framework for reconciling parliamentary accountability with (civil service) freedom from ministerial control. Reluctance to admit the direct accountability of civil servants has always been the major stumbling-block, but if that can be achieved (perhaps through agency chief executives being regarded as directly and personally accountable to select committees), then responsibility (including blame and sanctions) and accountability can be more closely aligned in clearly-defined spheres. But this is likely to remain an unsettled and controversial frontier of constitutional development in the 1990s.

Parliament and the Civil Service

'Silly bladders! Self advertising, irresponsible nincompoops. How I *hate* Members of Parliament. They embody everything that my training has taught me to eschew – ambition, prejudice, dishonesty, self-seeking, light-hearted irresponsibility, black-hearted mendacity.' So wrote the Permanent Secretary to the Foreign Office in a revealing diary entry in the 1940s. Similarly dismissive – if less violently-expressed – comments about MPs could be heard from other Permanent Secretaries forty years later.[7]

'The MP is often seen [by civil servants] as an actual or potential adversary, to be helped as little as possible', according to Kellner and Crowther-Hunt. 'There seems to be considerable merit in keeping as quiet as possible about this politically sensitive issue', a DTI official minuted in 1988 as civil servants advised ministers on how to get round the guidelines on arms sales to Iraq and how best to present policy so as to keep MPs, journalists and the public in the dark. The documents released to the Scott inquiry into the arms to Iraq scandal showed, as Lawrence Freedman, put it, 'the government machine working normally. This includes telling Parliament as little as possible in order to preserve freedom of manoeuvre.' The Scott inquiry revealed a thinly-veiled contempt for Parliament, and exposed Whitehall cynicism, dissembling and dishonesty (on the part of ministers and officials).[8]

Although the *Questions of Procedure* rule-book for ministers makes it clear that they should not deceive or mislead Parliament and that they should give 'as full information as possible', Sir Robin Butler told the Scott inquiry that 'half an answer' could be accurate when replying to parliamentary questions and that it was sometimes necessary to give an 'incomplete' answer that fell short of the whole truth. 'Government activity is much more like playing poker than it is like playing chess. You do not put all the cards up all the time', William Waldegrave candidly explained in March 1994, provoking controversy over his claim that it was acceptable 'in exceptional cases' for ministers to lie to Parliament.[9]

The higher civil service has an executive mentality and believes strongly in the right of government to govern, often regarding Parliament as a nuisance. In December 1971 it was revealed that officials in the Department of the Environment had, at the request of ministers, prepared a 'bank' of parliamentary questions to be distributed among Conservative backbenchers to 'crowd out' Labour MPs' questions. After an outcry, instructions were issued to ensure that this did not happen again but not before the Head of the Civil Service, Sir William Armstrong, had cheerfully admitted that, under all parties, civil servants had been involved in various 'strategems', worked out with ministers, to manage the parliamentary process in ways that would favour the interests of the government and handicap the Opposition.[10]

The parliamentary system moulds Whitehall's mistake-avoiding culture and accounts for the paramount bureaucratic aim of avoiding embarrassment to ministers. This is seen in the way the civil service handles the flood of parliamentary questions (PQs) which pours into departments – great care is taken when drafting the answers, with the aim of giving away as little information as possible. H. E. Dale, a senior civil servant between the wars, gave the classic definition of the perfect answer to a PQ as 'one that is brief, appears to answer the question completely, if challenged can be proved to be accurate in every word, gives no opening for awkward "supplementaries", and discloses really nothing'.[11] Sir Robert Armstrong's notorious remark during the *Spycatcher* affair about being 'economical with the truth' shows the durability of this mindset. These mandarin arts have had to cope with a massively increased number of PQs (particularly ones for written answer) in the post-1945 period: 21,000 PQs were on the Order Paper in 1945–6, 72,000 by 1987–8, with a major escalation occurring in the 1980s. MPs' letters to ministers, mostly on constituents' problems, and usually requiring attention at Assistant Secretary level, have also increased in number. A Cabinet Office note of 1949 complained of the greater volume of correspondence compared to the inter-war years, and the load continued to grow: in the early 1960s 50,000 letters a year passed between MPs and ministers, the figure in the late-1970s was around 100,000; in 1970 the Department of Health and Social Security dealt with 15,000 letters a year from MPs, by 1975 the figure was 25,000 a year.[12] The introduction of Next Steps agencies was intended to free Whitehall policy-advisers and ministers from the burden of this executive case-work.

Select committee scrutiny of departmental policies and administration was rather patchy and uneven before the creation in 1979 of a new Commons select committee system. Parliamentary reformers had long championed the creation of all-party investigative committees and the Crossman reforms in the 1960s saw experiments with a number of specialized committees. Norman St John Stevas, then Leader of the House of Commons, managed to persuade a sceptical Conservative Cabinet in 1979 to create fourteen departmental select committees.

There was much early euphoric talk about redressing the balance of power between Parliament and the executive: 'the pips are beginning to squeak in the Treasury', said one retired Permanent Secretary. The new committees undoubtedly improved Parliament's capacity to scrutinise Whitehall, but their effectiveness should not be exaggerated. They have generated large amounts of information about the work of government, with civil servants regularly being quizzed in public as witnesses. But the 'Osmotherly Rules' (drawn up in the 1970s) effectively conceal from scrutiny the whole policy-making process of government: MPs are not to be told about the advice given to ministers, inter-departmental exchanges, or the work of Cabinet committees, for instance. Some committees have had a hard time trying to squeeze information out of departments: the Ministry of Defence hoped 'to get away with (what) nobody would notice', complained the chairman of the Defence Committee. 'We can never disclose the advice to ministers . . . whether we gave advice or not is itself advice', said one Permanent Secretary refusing to answer a committee's questions. Lack of adequate research back-up is a further limitation. The committees can sometimes embarrass government but they cannot realistically expect to deflect it from the course it has chosen.[13]

In addition to the appearance of the new departmental select committees, the 1980s also saw important developments in state audit in Britain. The Public Accounts Committee (PAC), backed-up by the Comptroller and Auditor-General (CAG) and the staff of the Exchequer and Audit Office, go back to the 1860s and were traditionally concerned to oversee the stewardship of public funds and to check for waste and extravagance (looking to the regularity and propriety of departmental spending). Permanent Secretaries would appear before the PAC in their capacity as departmental Accounting Officers (with the right to ask for written ministerial directions if they think that a particular item of expenditure could not be justified in front of the PAC – disputes between Tony Benn and his Industry Department officials over financial support for a workers' co-op resulted in the leaking of an Accounting Officer's Minute in 1975, and in 1994 it was disclosed that ministers overruled the Permanent Secretary at the Overseas Development Administration to pump British aid into the Pergau dam project, linked to arms sales to Malaysia).

There was criticism from the 1960s of the scope, aims and lack of independence of the audit arrangements (the Treasury overseeing the CAG and his staff), but successive governments showed no interest in an overhaul of the system. A private member's bill in 1983 finally brought change: making the CAG an officer of the Commons, and establishing a National Audit Office (NAO) with a broader remit to investigate the efficiency and effectiveness of public spending programmes. With a staff of 850 (over half of whom are accountants), the NAO has put increasing emphasis on its 'value for money' probes, which yielded savings and economies totalling £397 millions over 1989–92, for instance. The work of the PAC could be dismissed in the 1970s and earlier as like archaeology – uncovering the past – but the NAO has added a sharper edge to its investigations, probably increasing its deterrent effect on departments and providing a stimulus to better management of spending programmes.

Redress of Grievances

The Crichel Down affair hit the headlines in 1954 just in time to spoil the centenary celebrations of the Northcote–Trevelyan Report. The case had an important effect on the outlook and methods of working of the civil service in its dealings with members of the public. It 'influenced the collective consciousness of the civil service . . . [illustrating] how not to treat the public and what can happen if you do'. The then Head of the Civil Service, Sir Edward Bridges, sent a letter to all civil servants pointing out the need for respect for the individual citizen's rights and feelings.[14] And the concern over administrative behaviour and for the way in which decisions were carried out led the Franks Committee on Administrative Tribunals and Enquiries (1957) to emphasise the importance of the three key principles of openness, fairness and impartiality in the conduct of administration.

What the row over Crichel Down showed, Whitehall's critics contended, was the failure of the traditional machinery for the redress of grievances in the British system of government. Disquiet about the growth of administrative power and about the limitations of established methods of control fuelled an interest in the Scandinavian ombudsmen in academic and legal circles from the late 1950s, culminating in the *Justice* organization's recommendation of the creation of a Parliamentary

Commissioner in an influential report in 1961, a proposal which the Macmillan Cabinet turned down, despite Conservative diatribes against 'bureaucracy'. The Labour Party took up the idea, however, and the Wilson government established the Parliamentary Commissioner for Administration (PCA), supported by a Commons select committee, in 1967.

The PCA's role was to investigate 'maladministration' (defects in administrative procedures: arbitrariness, bias, delay, incompetence, and so on). Although successive PCA's have broadened the focus of their inquiries, questions of policy or the merits of decisions have remained outside their jurisdiction. The PCA was given no powers to issue orders to the bureaucracy or to compel departments to provide remedies for aggrieved citizens, but his recommendations are usually accepted by the government. Citizens cannot approach the PCA direct, but must route their complaints through an MP. The office is, thus, hedged about with restrictions. But early critics who wrote it off as an 'ombudsmouse' or a gimmick were wrong. To be sure, the PCA has investigated fewer than 200 cases a year in recent years (usually rejecting three-quarters of the complaints referred to him as outside his jurisdiction), but in 40 per cent or more of these cases over the last decade, the complaints have been upheld (this figure being only 10 per cent in the early years of the PCA). Inevitably, ministries with extensive dealings directly with the public – Social Security and the Inland Revenue – appear at the top of the PCA's league table of errant departments. As important, the PCA has a preventative or deterrent influence on administrative procedures and attitudes which cannot be measured simply by examining the size of his case-load.[15]

There are other channels open to citizens who want to challenge official decisions and actions or seek redress. Administrative tribunals have proliferated over the course of the century, adjudicating for instance in conflicts between departments and citizens over social security claims or tax assessments. The Pliatzky Report in 1980 identified sixty-seven different 'tribunal systems'. Following the 1957 Franks Report, improvements were made to the operation of tribunals, but there are still grounds for criticism of their procedures and doubts expressed about the standards of justice they dispense and their independence from departmental influence.

The courts, since the mid-1960s, have been increasingly willing to review and challenge administrative actions. Applications for judicial review of administrative and ministerial decisions rose from 160 in 1974, to 491 in 1980 and 2,439 in 1992, with about fifty per cent being granted. 'For Thatcherite Whitehall, the judges were a curse', argued Hugo Young. Official concern about this trend led to the production of a booklet by the Treasury Solicitor in 1987 entitled *The Judge Over Your Shoulder*, advising civil servants on how to avoid what it suggested was the nuisance of judicial review. The scale and impact of this development must be kept in proportion, however. Judicial review has in fact remained marginal to the administrative process. Rawlings has likened the situation to 'a state of guerrilla warfare between judiciary and administration':

> For much of the time, given the intermittent emergence of case-law, all is quiet, but, of a sudden, wholly unpredictable raids are made by the judiciary, and administrative decisions, if not to the terror then surely to the annoyance of the administrator, come under severe attack, such that public servants may be told that they have acted "unlawfully, irrationally and procedurally improperly" in the conduct of their duties . . . It must seriously be doubted whether this constitutes "control of government" in any meaningful sense.[16]

The machinery for the redress of grievances in Britain has developed in a characteristically piecemeal and haphazard fashion and lacks coherence. The existence of many different channels for pursuing complaints may well make 'the system' appear even more complex and confusing to citizens who want their problems dealt with. The additional mechanisms and methods for handling complaints and grievances provided in the move to agencies and by the *Citizen's Charter* (see chapter 5) are surely welcome but will further complicate the picture.

Secrecy and Open Government

Britain's tradition of government secrecy has proved to be remarkably durable. In the 1980s Whitehall's defences against what policy-makers clearly regard as the deadly virus of freedom of information were, if anything, strengthened, while in many other countries open government laws were being introduced. Britain, argued James Michael 'is about as secretive as a state can be and still qualify as a democracy'. Section 2 of the Official Secrets Act of 1911 – which made the unauthorized release (and receipt) of *any* official information a criminal offence (including, in theory, the amount of tea consumed in Whitehall offices) – was a major target of open government campaigners from the 1960s onwards. But even after it was scrapped and replaced with the 1989 Official Secrets Act, a Whitehall trawl revealed that there were over 200 other statutes with secrecy provisions.[17]

The presumption in favour of 'closed' rather than 'open' government has had other supports. Since the 1880s the civil service's internal discipline rules have set out an absolute ban on the unauthorised communication of *any* official information. A statutory right of access to information has been rejected as a constitutional novelty incompatible with the accountability of ministers to Parliament. However, the experience of other 'Westminster'-style systems (Australia, Canada and New Zealand) which have introduced freedom of information (FoI) measures suggests that this is a spurious argument. A deferential civic culture may have continued to sustain a closed policy-making elite for some time after 1945, but the decline of mass deference from the late 1960s and a growing distrust of policy-makers and institutions lay behind the open government movement.[18]

The culture of the Whitehall insiders (ministers and officials) has, however, remained saturated with the values of secrecy. Secrecy is regarded not as a problem but as an essential feature of 'good government'. There is, of course, no such thing as 'open government' even inside Whitehall: information is rationed on a 'need to know' basis. Government 'in a goldfish bowl', the insiders have argued, is impossible and undesirable. Critics have countered that preventing political embarrassment, rather then protecting national security, is often the real aim. As James Callaghan candidly told the Franks Committee in the 1970s, the attitude of ministers in an adversarial parliamentary system is: 'We are not going to tell you anything more than we can about what is going to discredit us.'[19] And instead of secrecy underpinning effective government (by permitting free and frank discussion between policy-makers), open government campaigners have insisted that it is actually an obstacle to good policy-making: as a Fabian group put it in 1964, 'it prevents the tapping of a sufficiently wide range of expert advice and . . . it narrows public discussion of policy issues'.

Secrecy was put on to the reform agenda in the 1960s, and as the pressure for a more open style of government developed there turned out to be some pretty strange bed-fellows on the different sides of the argument. Retired Permanent Secretaries could be found calling in suitably discreet and guarded tones for some relaxation of the level of secrecy. Impatient radicals of the left, such as Tony Benn, and of the right, such as Sir John Hoskyns, backed the open government cause. Mrs Thatcher opposed the idea of a 'right to know', and Michael Foot defended Cabinet secrecy and thought that FoI would make the work of government more difficult.

The traditions of 'closed' government were largely unquestioned in the 1940s and 1950s. 'No Government can be successful which cannot keep its secrets', Attlee minuted his ministerial colleagues in 1945. The Labour Prime Minister was content to keep most of the Cabinet, let alone Parliament and the public, in the dark about Britain's atomic weapons programme. Conservative ministers only reluctantly agreed to the opening of government files to researchers after a period of fifty years in 1958 (the Public Records Act), taking care to ensure that sensitive material could still be held back.

The Fulton Committee in 1968 was concerned that the administrative process was surrounded by too much secrecy and recommended a review of the Official Secrets Act. The Wilson government had introduced (in 1967) a thirty-year rule for access to public records, but in a 1969 White Paper it argued that secrecy was still necessary at the policy-making levels of government, that the Official Secrets Act was not in itself a barrier to greater openness, and that steps were being taken to expand the range of information released to MPs and the public. The Labour government also initiated the *Sunday Telegraph* secrets trial, concerning embarrassing information about its stance during the Nigerian civil war, which led (in 1971) to the acquittal of the defendants and the judge declaring that Section 2 should be 'pensioned off'.

The 1970 Conservative manifesto included a pledge to 'eliminate unnecessary secrecy' and Heath set up the Franks Committee to review the operation of the Official Secrets Act. In a hard-hitting report in 1972, Franks called Section 2 'a mess' and condemned its 'catch-all' character, proposing that criminal sanctions apply to narrower and defined categories of information. The Heath Cabinet announced in 1973 that it accepted Franks' essential recommendations but took no further action.

The events of 1974–9 showed the extent of insider resistance to open government reform and at the same time fuelled outside critics' demands for change. Labour's October 1974 manifesto included a commitment to 'replace the Official Secrets Act by a measure to put the burden on the public authorities to justify witholding information'. Most Labour ministers, though, were as unenthusiastic or hostile as their civil servants. In 1975 the government, arguing the need for Cabinet confidentiality, failed in its attempt to ban publication of the Crossman Diaries. Callaghan, stung by the *New Society*/child benefit scheme leak in 1976, decided he wanted more effective protection of government information. In a leaked memo he gave his view that disclosing any information about the Cabinet committee system 'would be more likely to whet appetites than to satisfy them'. Home Secretary Merlyn Rees talked, menacingly, of replacing the 'blunderbuss' of Section 2 with an 'Armalite rifle'; he loftily told a Labour back-bencher that probably only two or three people in his constituency were concerned about the open government issue.

A policy of more voluntary disclosure of background factual and analytical information used in policy-making was introduced in an attempt to head-off critics (the 1977 Croham Directive, which – ironically – only became public knowledge after it was leaked to the press), but the results were limited. The flow of documents from departments was uneven, the exercise simply becoming part of the normal public relations machine in some parts of Whitehall. It was 'a nine-days-wonder', said a former Home Office civil servant. A White Paper in 1978 pointed out the potential resource costs of freedom of information legislation and questioned the relevance of foreign experience for the British system. Put under pressure by the Labour Party NEC and other outside campaigners and by Liberal MP Clement Freud's private member's FoI bill, the government then published in 1979 further reviews of overseas practice and a Green Paper which talked about the desirability of an evolutionary approach, suggested a possible 'Code of Practice' on open government, and stuck to the line that voluntary disclosure rather than FoI legislation was the answer. Shortly afterwards Labour lost office.

The Thatcher government quickly abandoned monitoring of the Croham Directive, ostensibly as an economy measure, and in November 1979 introduced a Protection of Official Information Bill – a revealing title. This measure was abandoned, though, when it became clear that the book exposing Anthony Blunt as a KGB spy could not have been published had the bill become law. Open government was kept on the agenda by private members' bills, the Labour and Alliance parties support of FoI reform in their election manifestos in the 1980s, and by the launch in 1984 of a new Campaign for Freedom of Information. But the government's interest was clearly in tighter control over official information. Prosecutions under Section 2 of the Official Secrets Act increased in number. In 1984 a Foreign Office clerk, Sarah Tisdall, was sentenced to six months' imprisonment for handing over details of the arrival of US cruise missiles to the *Guardian* newspaper. The trial and acquittal (in 1985) of Clive Ponting, an Assistant Secretary at the Ministry of Defence, who had passed information about the government's cover-up over the sinking of the *Belgrano* during the Falklands War to the MP Tam Dalyell, greatly boosted the open government campaign and discredited the 1911 Act, as well as highlighting the issue of civil service ethics (see below). The humiliations the government experienced in its abortive attempts in British and Australian courts in 1986–7 to use the civil law of confidence to prevent publication of Peter Wright's *Spycatcher* memoirs – serving only to make the book a world-wide best-seller – also kept the secrecy issue on the boil.

While central government secrecy was being strenuously defended, the 1980s saw a number of measures reducing secrecy in other parts of the system of government as FoI campaigners steered through private members' bills on access to local government information, access to personal files (covering local councils' education, housing and social work records), access to medical records and to environmental and safety information.[20] But the unprecedented use of a government three-line whip to defeat a Conservative back-bencher's private member's bill in January 1988 (a whip defied by 100 Tory MPs) showed government determination to resist pressure for greater openness at the Whitehall level. A 1988 White Paper and the follow-up 1989 Official Secrets Act could be presented as a liberalizing measure of sorts – narrowing the scope of the criminal law to protect defined categories of information (defence, security and intelligence; international relations; law enforcement; interception of communications). But the rejection of a 'public interest' defence (the basis of Ponting's defence in 1985) and of the defence of 'prior publication' (central to the *Spycatcher* case) was criticized by open government supporters (including former Conservative Prime Minister Heath). Section 2 had gone but there was still nothing like a 'right to know'.

John Major's *Citizen's Charter* (1991) emphasized the importance of making information about the performance of public services available to the public, but this was still an exercise in 'openness' on the government's own terms. After the 1992 election Major made the symbolic gesture of publishing details of the Cabinet committee system, de-classifying *Questions of Procedure for Ministers*, the rule-book of Cabinet government, and announcing the names of the heads of MI5 and MI6. William Waldegrave, the minister responsible for the civil service, launched a review designed to reduce the number of statutory restrictions against disclosure.

Waldegrave's White Paper on Open Government was unveiled in July 1993. It proposed a code of practice (which came into effect in April 1994) on release of the background information used in policy decisions (a revival of the Croham Directive), but with a wide range of exemptions, including Whitehall's 'internal discussion and advice', commercial confidences, and information relating to defence and foreign policy and to the management of the economy. The parliamentary ombudsman (PCA) would monitor and police the code. There would be a right of access to health and safety information, and the right of access to personal information held by public authorities on computer files (set out in the 1984 Data Protection Act) would be extended to manual (paper) files.[21] Critics pointed to the limited resources of the PCA (currently taking over a year to deal with each case of his existing load), queried the disclosure code's 'get out' clauses, and argued that the plans fell a long way short of a proper FoI regime giving a genuine 'right to know'. It seems unlikely that the secrecy and openness issue will go away in the 1990s.

Civil Service Ethics

The Ponting affair did more than boost the open government cause in the 1980s, it also triggered-off a debate about the ethical dilemmas facing officials with crises of conscience about government actions or policies, involving questions about the loyalties of civil servants and the legitimacy of 'whistle-blowing' or 'leaking in the public interest'. Many observers believed that the greater ideological polarization of party politics in the eighties, and the high-handed attitude and actions of the Thatcher government towards the civil service, meant that old-style practices and assumptions in this area were increasingly redundant.[22]

The judge in Ponting's trial had equated the term 'interests of the state' in the 1911 Official Secrets Act with the policies of the government of the day, rejecting the idea of a 'public interest' defence in secrets cases. Sir Robert Armstrong's *Note of Guidance on the Duties and Responsibilities of Civil Servants in Relation to Ministers*, issued in February 1985, also defined the duty of civil servants as being solely to the government of the day. Armstrong spelt out the virtually absolute and unconditional duty placed on civil servants to serve ministers loyally. Civil servants, he conceded, should not be required to do anything unlawful. But the most he would allow for officials worried about possible improper orders or other conscience issues was that they could refer them 'up the line' to departmental Permanent Secretaries and – ultimately – to the Head of the Civil Service. There was an absolute obligation of confidence, Armstrong insisted: leaks were unacceptable and threatened the position of the civil service as a non-political body.

The Armstrong Memorandum stated that it was for ministers, not civil servants, to decide what information should be made available to Parliament, and how and when it should be released. Sir Robin Butler said in 1990 that it would be improper for ministers to instruct civil servants to mislead parliamentary committees but they could be ordered to withhold information – a fine distinction, to be sure. Sir Robert Armstrong would concede no more than that it was the duty of officials to 'remind' ministers of their responsibility to Parliament. There was no question, he thought, that a civil servant's duty of responsibility to ministers was in some way conditional upon ministers answering fully to Parliament (Clive Ponting had believed it was).

Armstrong's critics argued that his definition of the duty of civil servants was far too narrow. Many pointed to the USA, where a code of ethics enjoins officials to 'put loyalty to the highest moral principles and to country above loyalty to persons, party or government department'. The top civil servants' trade union, the First Division Association (FDA), produced its own version of a civil service code of ethics in 1984 with provision for officials to appeal to the PCA or the chairman of the relevant departmental select committee if they believed that ministers were misleading or lying to Parliament and the public. Sir Douglas Wass, former Joint Head (with Armstrong) of the

Civil Service, dreamt up the idea of an independent, quasi-judical 'Inspector-General' to hear civil servants' complaints and tackle these issues. That Sir Robin Butler could report in 1993 that he had had only one formal appeal to him he took as evidence that there is not that widespread dissatisfaction among officials that might justify an external appeals body; in contrast the FDA believes that it shows that the system is not working.

In an earlier time, unwritten rules and informal codes of conduct – the gentlemen's club approach – governed the application of professional and moral standards in the course of official work. Warren Fisher in the inter-war period had maintained there was no need for a detailed ethical code: 'the surest guide will . . . always be found in the nice and jealous honour of Civil Servants themselves'. At the time of Crichel Down, higher Whitehall opinion was against the promulgation of a formal code of conduct.[23] Whitehall's internal disciplinary code, dating from the 1940s – Estacode, later called the Civil Service Pay and Conditions of Service Code – said that the service's 'intangible and unwritten' code of conduct was enough. 'I am accountable to my own ideal of a civil servant', explained Sir William Armstrong in 1969.

The FDA had first looked at the question of standards of conduct and the loyalties of officials in the public service in the late 1960s, but the issue had soon fizzled out. The difference between that period and the mid-1980s could be seen in the absence of an outcry in 1970 when the Civil Service Department told the FDA that service to the Crown means in effect service to an official's departmental minister compared to the scorn heaped on Sir Robert Armstrong when he repeated that conventional constitutional formula in 1985. The breakdown of consensus politics made the old assumptions contentious. Concern over standards of conduct in government in the early 1990s kept the Whitehall ethics issue on the agenda. The 'good chap' theory of government was 'blown away' in the 1980s, according to Peter Hennessy. 'So much emphasis has been placed on "can do" civil servants, that few hesitate any more over ethical dilemmas', argued *The Guardian* during the arms to Iraq affair.[24] John Smith, the Labour leader 1992–4, put his weight behind calls for a new statement of ministers' and civil servants' roles and responsibilities. Nor was it just hard cases like Ponting and arms to Iraq which lay behind the calls for a rethink. Developments on the management front were also cited: 'Crown service is an old-fashioned concept which cannot be expected to transfer with the workload under contractorisation', argued Hennessy.

Back in 1972 Sir William Armstrong had pointed out that, constitutionally, the civil service was not and could not be neutral as between the government and the Opposition – it was on the side of the government. But what seemed to lie behind critics' reaction to the Armstrong Memorandum and the talk of a code of ethics was the assumption that, independent of its day-to-day work for ministers, the civil service has (or should have) a role as a safeguard of or watchdog over the democratic process – that it should in some circumstances be a check on government, not its accomplice or its tool. It must be said, though, that this view is constitutionally dubious and at odds with Whitehall's traditional executive-minded culture and ethos. If external (parliamentary) constraints on the executive are weak in Britain (and were arguably weaker in the 1980s, given Mrs Thatcher's massive Commons majorities), it is perhaps not surprising that some critics look to internal constraints instead. The idea of the civil service functioning as an effective constitutional check was, however, rejected by former 'insider' William Plowden, who doubted whether it would 'necessarily resist actions which the rest of us might regard as arbitrary, unconstitutional or threatening to the rights of individuals'.[25]

Civil service ethical dilemmas were not a creation of the 1980s. Suez in 1956 had been a testing and traumatic episode. The appeasement policies of the 1930s had also strained the loyalties of some officials – Winston Churchill's attacks on the Chamberlain government had indeed been based on secret information leaked to him by civil servants. But the Fisher / Bridges thinking on ethics and standards of behaviour held the line. In the 1980s and 1990s, party polarization and allegations of 'politicization', less deferential popular attitudes to government, and a succession of crises (including Ponting, Westland, and arms to Iraq) challenged the traditional approach – critics would say, undermined it and exposed it as inadequate.

Despite civil service minister William Waldegrave deriding in 1992 the idea of 'bits of paper' as a solution to the problem, and Sir Robin Butler insisting that reform was unnecessary, the government was forced to give way to pressure and introduce a new code of conduct for civil servants in January 1995. In 1994 the FDA had published a new draft code of ethics and proposed a civil service ethics tribunal, and in November 1994 the

Treasury and Civil Service Committee also called for a statutory code of ethics, with an independent appeals procedure involving a revamped Civil Service Commission.

The new code states that officials should act with 'integrity, honesty, impartiality and objectivity' in their dealings with ministers, and binds them not to act in a way that is 'illegal, improper, unethical or in breach of constitutional convention'. The code could be given a statutory basis, the government said, if agreement can be reached between the parties. An independent appeals route would be provided for civil servants faced with fundamental conscience issues – they would be able to refer complaints to the Civil Service Commissioners (in future, the First Civil Service Commissioner will no longer be a civil servant and will have a strengthened and more independent role).[26]

With the Nolan Committee on Standards in Public Life at work on the 'sleaze' issue, and with the Scott inquiry report due in mid-1995, the government's move was an attempt to respond to the flood of complaints that standards of conduct in government had been eroded over the last fifteen years and the neutrality of the civil service undermined. The FDA said that parts of the new code were rather weak and it was still concerned about the pressures that ministers may bring to bear on civil servants, as well as the broader issue of civil servants' duties to Parliament and the public. It may well be that the ethics issue has not been finally settled. To the extent that many ethical problems are bound up with the release of information (as in the Ponting case), further progress in the 1990s with open government or FoI may hold the key to its resolution.

Notes

1   Robert Pyper, 'Individual Ministerial Responsibility: Dissecting the Doctrine', *Politics Review*, 4 (1994), p. 12.

2   S. E. Finer, 'The individual responsibility of ministers', *Public Administration*, 34 (1956).

3   I. F. Nicolson, *The Mystery of Crichel Down* (Clarendon Press, Oxford, 1986); John Griffith, 'Crichel Down: the most famous farm in constitutional history', *Contemporary Record*, Spring 1987, pp. 35–40; D. N. Chester, 'The Crichel Down Case', *Public Administration*, 32 (1954), pp. 389–401.

4   Gavin Drewry and Tony Butcher, *The Civil Service Today*, 2nd edn (Basil Blackwell, Oxford, 1991), pp. 153–4.

5   R. Baker, 'The V and G Affair and ministerial responsibility', *Political Quarterly*, 43 (1972); Robert Pyper, 'Responsibility or Passing the Buck? The Strange Cases of Mr Baker, Mr Prior and the Disappearing Prisoners', *Teaching Public Administration*, 12 (1992).

6   Treasury and Civil Service Committee, *The Role of the Civil Service*, HC 27, 1993–4, report paras 120–34, and memorandum submitted by the Cabinet Office, pp. 188–91.

7   William Plowden, 'What Prospects for the Civil Service?', *Public Administration*, 63 (1985), p. 396; Robert Pyper, *The Evolving Civil Service* (Longman, Harlow, 1991), p. 69.

8   *Guardian*, 23 November 1992, 31 March 1994; *Independent*, 23 November 1992; Mark Phythian and Walter Little, 'Parliament and Arms Sales: Lessons of the Matrix Churchill Affair', *Parliamentary Affairs*, 46 (1993), pp. 293–308.

9   *Independent*, 10 February 1994 and 9 March 1994; Treasury and Civil Service Committee, *The Role of the Civil Service*, qs. 1832–41.

10 Select Committee on Parliamentary Questions, HC 393, 1972, qs. 133–225.

11 H. E. Dale, *The Higher Civil Service of Great Britain* (Oxford University Press, Oxford, 1941), p. 105.

12 Kevin Theakston, *Junior Ministers in British Government* (Basil Blackwell, Oxford, 1987), pp. 131–4; Roy Gregory and Jane Pearson, 'The Parliamentary Ombudsman after twenty-five years', *Public Administration*, 70 (1992), p. 474.

13 David Judge, 'The "effectiveness" of the post-1979 select committee system: the verdict of the 1990 Procedure Committee', *Political Quarterly*, 63 (1992).

14 John Delafons, 'Working in Whitehall: Changes in Public Administration 1952–1982', *Public Administration*, 60 (1982), p. 257; Chester, 'The Crichel Down Case', p. 397.

15 Gregory and Pearson, 'The Parliamentary Ombudsman after twenty-five years'.

16 *Guardian*, 30 April 1992; H. F. Rawlings, 'Judicial Review and the "Control of Government"', *Public Administration*, 64 (1986), pp. 142–3.

17 James Michael, *The Politics of Secrecy* (Penguin, Harmondsworth, 1982), p. 9; Peter Hennessy and Chris Westcott, *The Last Right? Open Government, Freedom of Information and and the Right to Know* (Strathclyde Analysis papers no. 12, Glasgow, 1992); Clive Ponting, *Secrecy in Britain* (Basil Blackwell, Oxford, 1990).

18 Robert Hazell, 'Freedom of Information in Australia, Canada and New Zealand', *Public Administration*, 67 (1989); Colin Bennett, 'From the Dark to the Light: The Open Government Debate in Britain', *Journal of Public Policy*, 5 (1985), pp. 194–5.

19 Quoted in: Kevin Theakston, *The Labour Party and Whitehall* (Routledge, London, 1992), p. 159.
20 A. P. Tant, 'The Campaign for Freedom of Information: a participatory challenge to elitist British government', *Public Administration*, 68 (1990).
21 *Open Government*, Cm 2290, 1993.
22 Barry O'Toole, 'T. H. Green and the ethics of senior officials in British central government', *Public Administration*, 68 (1990); *Politics, Ethics and Public Service* (Royal Institute of Public Administration, London, 1985).
23 Cmd 3037, 1928, p. 22; Richard Chapman, *Ethics in the British Civil Service* (Routledge, London, 1988), p. 283.
24 *FDA News*, January 1993; *Guardian*, 23 November 1992.
25 Select Committee on Parliamentary Questions, 1972, qs. 189–91; William Plowden, 'Whitehall and the Civil Service', in Richard Holme and Michael Elliott (eds), *1688–1988: Time for a New Constitution* (Macmillan, London, 1988), p. 191.
26 *The Civil Service: Taking Forward Continuity and Change* (HMSO, London, 1995); *Independent*, 27 January 1995; *Financial Times*, 27 January 1995.

7 Conclusion

Whitehall and Decline

The peculiar strengths and weaknesses of the civil service, and of the Treasury in particular, form a powerful contributory cause of our decline.

Sidney Pollard[1]

Identifying deficiencies in the institutions and personnel of the British state as key factors in economic and industrial under-achievement is not new. The pre First World War campaign for 'national efficiency', drawing in figures from across the political spectrum against a background of alarm over slipping national power relative to Germany, focused on themes that were to become the staple fare of later would-be modernizers: dissatisfaction with the machinery of government, the need for more technocratic officials and for a closer relation between government and science, the positive role that businessmen and business methods could play in government. In the inter-war period, too, its critics argued that Whitehall was an admirable instrument for a *laissez-faire* state but entirely unfitted for new tasks of economic planning.

Over the last decade or so, writers of different political persuasions have agreed that the nature and working of the British system of government must bear a large share of the responsibility for the shape of the British economy. Whitehall and Westminster, they assert, are part of the problem rather than part of the solution; their reform is a precondition for economic recovery.

Sir John Hoskyns, a former adviser to Mrs Thatcher, savagely attacked our 'failed system' in headline-grabbing lectures in the early 1980s. 'I do not think it is possible to look at our post-war national decline and argue that it happened in spite of high-quality policy-making . . . in the long-term the machine has a propensity to failure', he declared. 'The cure for the British disease must start with government itself.' Although he claimed not to be blaming the civil service for the country's decline, Hoskyns was scathing about Whitehall's culture and style: the absence of strategic thinking, the obsession with performance rather than results, the deep pessimism of officials ('few, if any, believe that the country can be saved'), the lack of dynamism (he rounded on the mandarins' 'passionless detachment' – 'as if the process they were engaged in were happening in a faraway country which they service only on a retainer basis'). The civil service was too closed and needed a large-scale influx of politically-committed business outsiders to generate the radical remedies the situation demanded.

But Hoskyns was clear that 'we have to look at our system of government *as a whole*. It is the effectiveness of the total "configuration" that matters, not the bits and pieces.' Also in his sights, therefore, were the small pool of governing talent provided by the parliamentary closed shop (producing both amateur and overloaded ministers); the electoral reform issue; and the need for open government ('not a fashionable option, but a precondition for any serious attempt to solve Britain's underlying problems'). Hoskyns was essentially a frustrated businessman – an outsider – railing against what he saw as the mediocrity and defeatism of an inbred Establishment.[2]

Positioned in the political centre, David Marquand took the argument onto the deeper issues of political culture and state tradition laying behind the absence of a 'developmental state' in Britain.[3] In two world wars, an entrepreneurial state apparatus had been created and the administrative machine had run the economy with great flair and success. The peace-time story was a dismal tale of irresolute, muddled and defensive interventions. Marquand's argument was that the institutions and conventions of the essentially Victorian 'Westminster Model' were incompatible with and had inhibited the evolution of a proactive and discretionary *dirigiste* state machine (the French or Japanese model) and stood in the way of more open and explicit power-sharing with organized producer groups (the Central European/ Scandinavian corporatist–consensual model).

Specifically in terms of Whitehall, Hennessy summarizes the argument thus: 'Postwar ministers and officials were attempting to run the modern state with the same bureaucratic instruments and administrative culture that had served Gladstone and Salisbury.' The civil service had been a central part of the post-war Keynesian social-democratic consensus, but the important point is that these ideas had not radically altered the character of the central state machine. The belief was that the economy could be fine-tuned and Keynesian economic ideas implemented without developing complex interventionist machinery and with the same breed of Treasury mandarins pulling the levers.[4]

In his passionate denunciation of the institutions that he believes have brought Britain down, *The State We're In*, Will Hutton also includes the civil service as among the 'guilty men'.[5] The British state, he argues, had not been designed actively to intervene in economic management at national or local level or to make industrial policies work effectively. 'The Civil Service tradition that officials should not engage in private sector activity remained strong and, unlike France or Germany, Britain had made no systematic attempt to train a class of officials competent in commerce and finance. The accent was still placed on administration rather than intervention; on high policy rather than commercial strategy.'

Hutton singles out the Treasury. Allied with the Bank of England, it is a lobbyist for the financial over the producer interest, benefiting the southern rentier and financial institutions over the northern manufacturer. Whitehall's 'rentier culture' blinds it to the social returns that can accrue from public investment. The 'embodiment of the book-keeping nightwatchman view of the state', and guardian of an over-centralized system of economic and budgetary decision-making, 'reform of the Treasury', argues Hutton, 'is one pivot on which national renewal hangs'.

The character of Britain's mandarin elite is, it is clear, a favourite target of 'declinist' critics. It is no accident, they suggest, that the civil service took on broadly its modern form at the same time – the end of the nineteenth century – as Britain's economic decline set in. The public school/Oxbridge anti-industrial culture was the breeding ground for the new corps of Northcote–Trevelyan administrators who were 'almost without exception lacking in scientific, mechanical, technological or commercial training or experience'. The mandarins were 'essay-writers rather than problem-solvers', in Correlli Barnett's dismissive phrase. 'The ethos of the British senior civil servant is that of the adviser-regulator, not of the original thinker-doer', according to Peter Hennessy. This meant that 'the British Civil Service in similar conditions could not have done what the Japanese or, particularly, the French bureaucracies did so brilliantly after the war on the economic and industrial fronts . . . because [it] was not designed for the purpose'.[6]

There is indeed a wide gulf of understanding between Whitehall and industry, arising from a difference in culture, outlook, training and experience. The mandarin who confessed that it had never occurred to him to visit a factory – 'what were they like?' – was not the fictional Sir Humphrey but a real-world senior official quoted in the *Financial Times* in early 1993! 'The civil servant is thinking of his public duty, his responsibility upwards to ministers, whereas the private sector person is thinking of how to get their company to survive in a competitive environment', a banker seconded for a spell into the DTI told Hennessy. 'Ruthless and single-minded maximisers of world market share or gross national product' are not the civil service ideal, Correlli Barnett complained, a view shared by Tony Benn in his 1960s technocratic phase: 'our present Civil Service is not interested in growth. It is geared to care and maintenance.'[7]

Attempts have been made via secondments and exchanges to give civil servants direct experience of industry and fill the skills gap in government by bringing in outside expertise. In 1993 the top one hundred Treasury mandarins were ordered to spend at least one day a year visiting industry – this was presented as a great step forward. The Whitehall exchange programmes are not large-scale, though, and seem to involve the financial sector and consultancy firms more than manufacturing companies. The Ministry of Defence accounts for the largest share of the two-way traffic; in the DTI secondments involve less than one per cent of personnel at any one time.[8]

The Treasury has long been a favourite bogey figure for those seeking to explain Whitehall's role in economic decline and deindustrialization. For Pollard, it institutionalizes a 'contempt for production'. Its responsibility for public expenditure control ensures that it will generally be hostile to increased state spending on programmes directed at industry (looking for cuts wherever it can find them, even if that means sacrificing productive investment). Its macroeconomic role, it is argued, together with its close links with the Bank of England and the City, invariably lead it to give priority to short-term and financial considerations (the exchange rate, the balance of payments, the rate of inflation), introducing measures (e.g. interest rate changes) which can affect industry more than any number of DTI 'supply-side' measures. It is said to be deeply-committed to a free-market approach and sceptical of anything like a positive and interventionist industrial policy. All this is in marked contrast to the position in other systems, such as France or Germany where the central economics ministries do not stand back from industrial policy questions, or Japan where the powerful Ministry of International Trade and Industry (MITI) has more clout than the Ministry of Finance.

The case against the Treasury should not be taken too far, however. Thain believes that there is only 'limited scope for blaming the Treasury for decline'. He argues that there is no monolithic 'Treasury line', that the Treasury's priorities have been determined by the political decisions of ministers, and that other Whitehall departments and outside interest groups limit its room for manouevre. The post-war consensus on foreign economic policy (the 'sterling lobby'), for instance, extended far beyond the Treasury. The long-term growth in the total of public spending is testimony to the limits of its power.[9]

In a broader sense, Peter Hall argued that 'The state is not primarily responsible for Britain's economic decline. However, it has not been an innocent bystander.' There may be plenty of blame to go round, but pinning down Whitehall's share with any certainty or objectivity is not straightforward. The economist David Henderson was sceptical about the idea that a country's economic success depended crucially on the quality of its civil service:

> I'm not sure that in the British case it's been a major influence on economic performance. Insofar as it has been, it has been to do with ideas that were held outside the Civil Service as well . . . The British Civil Service has something to answer for in its closed nature and the way it has not reacted to evidence. But it's very easy to overdo the extent to which you can blame economic performance on the administrators.

British decline is deep-rooted and a long-term phenomenon. Many important factors (e.g. national culture, world economic trends) are beyond the direct control of government. 'The economic policy machine of ministers and officials has given the impression of permanently trying to run up the downward escalator', as Keegan and Pennant-Rea put it.[10]

Correlli Barnett brackets the mandarins with other 'New Jerusalemers', who in the 1940s opted to build a welfare state rather than engineering a British economic miracle. But there is evidence of considerable civil service 'suspicion and distaste for increased welfare expenditure', and not just inside the Treasury, at the time that Beveridge was putting together his famous report on social insurance. And during the Second World War, Board of Trade officials had developed a clear (and pessimistic) analysis of Britain's industrial backwardness and its post-war competitive prospects, though ministers and Whitehall's powers-that-be then baulked at creating a full-blown 'Ministry of Industry' to push through some of the radical ideas being floated (e.g. for an Industrial Commission).[11]

David Edgerton has given the 'developmental state' debate a new twist by arguing that the British state *has* been 'committed to scientific, technological and industrial modernisation'. Its aims, however, have been primarily military and strategic ones – the British state has been a 'warfare state' – but there has also been a (related) commitment to the high-tech aircraft and nuclear sectors. Edgerton thus rejects the view of the British state as 'incapable of planning, of investing in science and technology, or of appreciating scientists and engineers'. But the result has been the development of a powerful 'military-industrial-scientific complex' (based on a defence-dominated R&D effort and high procurement expenditures), which has retained its strength as other parts of the British economy have fallen apart.[12]

In this context, it is significant that the Ministry of Defence employs 59 per cent of the scientific civil service, 80 per cent of the civil service's professional engineers, and spends over half of government's research and development funds.[13] Edgerton's analysis brings to light features of the British state apparatus previously neglected. For instance, the officials working in the service and military supply ministries, he says, 'differed radically from our image of the English civil servant: they were staffed by serving officers, scientific, technological and industrial experts, rather than generalist amateurs eschewing action for a quiet life'. These ministries (such as the war-time production departments and the post-war Ministry of Supply) also provided an alternative model for government relations with industry – embodying a more directive and interventionist rather than liberal or hands-off approach of the type traditionally favoured by the Treasury and the Board of Trade.[14] In this field, British government showed that it could successfully intervene in industry, discriminate between firms and sectors, and 'pick winners'. The problem is that it has failed to apply the methods and lessons of the state-sponsored high-tech military production sector to the civil sector (save possibly for a brief time in the 1960s with Labour's Ministry of Technology).

Britain cannot simply transplant a Japanese-style MITI or a French-style breed of technocratic officials. The traditions, constitutions and political environments of French and Japanese government are very different from those of Britain. But its own administrative history has lessons to teach if we were looking to reform the institutions and policy-making processes of government – the results of the war-time influx of 'temporaries' and the experience of the military/technological sector, as described by Edgerton, showing that Whitehall's task need not be just the 'orderly management of decline'.

Change in the Civil Service

'Thank God for the Civil Service', King George VI remarked to some of the new Labour Cabinet ministers in 1945. By the 1970s, judgements were more hostile: Lord Rothschild observed that 'disparaging the civil service has become a national pastime, rather like throwing beer bottles at football matches'. 'A decade later', noted the journalist Jeremy Paxman, 'beer bottles were banned from the football terraces, but the assault upon the traditions of the civil service had advanced beyond popular abuse to become an item of government policy.'[15]

'Britain's Ruling Class' was how Lord Crowther-Hunt and his co-author Peter Kellner described the higher civil service in the subtitle of their book *The Civil Servants*, published in 1980. The claim was rather overblown even then, but reading their account of a mandarinate confident in its power and secure in its role in the government of the country, one could see what they meant – here was a force to be reckoned with, a body whose acquiescence in their plans the politicians could not take for granted. 'We attempted to moderate the more extravagant demands of ministers', was how Lord Sherfield (Sir Roger Makins, deputy head of the Foreign Office and head of the Treasury in the 1950s) loftily recalled his time in Whitehall.

Things looked very different after 1979. The argument that the mandarins could always 'see off' troublesome ministers and resist change was proved to be false. There could be no doubt about the ability of the Conservative government elected in 1979 to impose its will upon Whitehall. Ministers, not mandarins, were in the driving seat.

Sir Alan Bailey, Permanent Secretary at the Department of Transport in the late 1980s described to the Treasury and Civil Service Committee in 1993 some of the key changes in Whitehall since he joined the Treasury in the mid-1950s:

> Then, senior officials had mostly worked with the National government in war-time. They had close relations with Ministers, who generally trusted them and co-operated with them. As a result many policy matters were negotiated and decided among officials, with at most a formal reference to Ministers ... Since then, Ministers (of both parties) have become more numerous and far more inclined to delve into minutiae of policy, casework and management ... There are now political advisers, and private-sector consultants are frequently brought in. There is less trust, and civil servants have less discretion. The management changes of the last decade can be seen as (in part) a formalisation of this process, with performance objectives set in advance, in a framework agreed by Ministers, and performance pay related to results.

This was not, he insisted, the same as 'politicization', though he went on to say that 'it would be surprising if, over a decade and a half, the senior civil service did not change in subtle ways to fit the image of a Conservative administration'.[16]

Although British public administration may have 'stood at the peak of reputation' in the late-1940s ('measured by the test of competition it was easily top of the league', one commentator argued),[17] its public standing was slipping from the 1960s onwards and its own self-confidence was badly dented even before Mrs Thatcher entered Downing Street. 'Compared to the pre-war period, or even to the 1950s, today's civil service is much younger, less stable and committed, and less motivated by an ethic of public service', observed one middle-ranking official in 1981. 'Many, if not most, civil servants are not particularly attached to their work or to the civil service as a career but see it just as a job . . . '[18] Motivation might have been high in the top mandarin grades, but there was a wide gap between the centre in Whitehall and the clerical/executive ranks in the large local office networks built up since 1945.

Many of the managerial reforms introduced since 1979 did tackle real weaknesses in the civil service and, in some cases, produced genuine improvements in performance, value for money and standards of service. But they have also had a destabilizing effect, driving morale down even lower. 'The managerial changes undertaken . . . during the past decade appear to be exactly what a management consultant might recommend to demotivate and alienate a public workforce', judged an American commentator.[19]

For a large part of the post-war period, the civil service was effectively a self-governing institution. The most senior civil servants like Bridges, Brook and William Armstrong, arguably had more influence on the development of the civil service than either politicians or outside inquiries, such as the Priestley Royal Commission or the Fulton Committee. Whitley negotiations with the civil service staff side unions helped ensure a consensual and incremental pattern of change.

It is notable that, among the outside critics and would-be reformers, the running was made in the first three decades of the post-1945 period by Fabians, with 'managerial' ideas becoming increasingly important in the 1960s. For a long time, Conservatives contributed little that was distinctive to this debate. In the late 1960s, under Heath, the Conservative Opposition undertook a great deal of work on 'business methods' and modern management techniques, but the political impetus to achieve much was lacking in government after 1970.[20]

Mrs Thatcher and Mr Major have broken with this pattern, forcing through increasingly radical reforms in public service management and in Whitehall, with the Conservatives seizing the high ground and setting the agenda on these issues. Ministers have been determined and single-minded in pushing forward with their plans, overcoming doubts and scepticism inside Whitehall (e.g. the Treasury's lukewarm attitude to Next Steps) and brushing aside the civil service unions.

Even up until about 1987, it could be argued that the civil service had not been changed in any far-reaching sense. Next Steps, agencies, contracting-out, market-testing and privatization are now fundamentally transforming the 'old civil service'. The time-honoured core values of civil service impartiality, integrity, objectivity, selection and promotion on merit, and accountability through ministers to Parliament are safe, the government and the Head of the Civil Service insist, but the fact that this guarantee has to be continually repeated and emphasized is in itself suggestive of wider doubts and uncertainties.

The Thatcher-Major 'revolution' is not finished. It could still get bogged down or diverted; a change of government could reverse important elements of it. But it is likely that the institution that was once called 'the one great political invention in nineteenth-century England'[21] will look very different at the end of the twentieth century, compared to 1945. Fifty years after the Second World War, the future of the civil service appears more uncertain than ever before.

Notes

1 Sidney Pollard, *The Wasting of the British Economy* (Croom Helm, London, 1982), p. 159.
2 Sir John Hoskyns: 'Whitehall and Westminster: An Outsider's View', *Parliamentary Affairs*, 36 (1983); 'Conservatism is Not Enough', *Political Quarterly*, 55 (1984).
3 David Marquand, *The Unprincipled Society* (Cape, London, 1988).
4 Peter Hennessy, *Whitehall* (Secker and Warburg, London, 1989), p. 722; Robert Skidelsky, 'The Decline of Keynesian Politics', in Colin Crouch (ed.), State and Economy in *Contemporary Capitalism* (Croom Helm, London, 1979); Colin Thain, 'The Treasury and Britain's Decline', *Political Studies*, 32 (1984), p. 588.
5 Will Hutton, *The State We're In* (Cape, London, 1995).
6 Macdonagh, quoted in Martin Wiener, *English Culture and the Decline of the Industrial Spirit 1850–1980* (Penguin, Harmondsworth, 1981), p. 24; Correlli Barnett, *The Audit of War* (Macmillan, London, 1986), p. 215; Hennessy, *Whitehall*, p. 717.
7 *Financial Times*, 21 January 1993; Hennessy, *Whitehall*, p. 523; Barnett, *The Audit of War*, p. 221; Tony Benn, *Out of the Wilderness: Diaries 1963–67* (Hutchison, London, 1987), p. 264.
8 Rosemary Gosling and Sandra Nutley, *Bridging the Gap: Secondments between Government and Business* (Royal Institute of Public Administration, London, 1990).
9 Thain, 'The Treasury and Britain's Decline'.

10   Peter A. Hall, *Governing the Economy* (Polity Press, Cambridge, 1986), p. 67; Hennessy, *Whitehall*, p. 688; William Keegan and Rupert Pennant-Rea, *Who Runs the Economy?* (Temple Smith, London, 1979), p. 9.

11   Rodney Lowe, 'The Second World War, Consensus and the Foundation of the Welfare State', *Twentieth Century British History*, 1 (1990), pp. 170–1; Keith Middlemas, *Power, Competition and the State, vol. 1 Britain in Search of Balance 1940–61* (Macmillan, London, 1986).

12   David Edgerton, *England and the Aeroplane* (Macmillan, London, 1991), pp. 82–3; David Edgerton, 'Liberal Militarism and the British State', *New Left Review*, 185 (1991).

13   Geoffrey Fry, *The Changing Civil Service* (Allen and Unwin, 1985), p. 49.

14   David Edgerton, 'Whatever happened to the British warfare state? The Ministry of Supply 1945–1951', in Helen Mercer et al. (eds), *Labour Governments and Private Industry* (Edinburgh University Press, Edinburgh, 1992), pp. 91–116.

15   Hennessy, *Whitehall*, p. 126; Jeremy Paxman, *Friends in High Places*, paperback edn (Penguin, Harmondsworth, 1991), p. 131.

16   Treasury and Civil Service Committee, *The Role of the Civil Service*, HC 27, 1993–94, vol. III, pp. 9–10.

17   W. J. M. Mackenzie, 'Does Our Administration Need Reform?', *The Listener*, 21 February 1963.

18   David Howells, 'Marks and Spencer and the Civil Service: A Comparison of Culture and Methods', *Public Administration*, 59 (1981), p. 348.

19   Quoted in: William Plowden, *Ministers and Mandarins* (Institute of Public Policy Research, London, 1994), p. 15.

20   Treasury and Civil Service Committee, *The Role of the Civil Service*, vol. III, p. 26 (G. Fry).

21   Graham Wallas, *Human Nature in Politics* (Constable, London, 1948 [first published 1908]), p. 263.

Index

Abel-Smith, Brian, 15
accountable management, 94, 105–6,
    107, 111, 114
Admiralty, 78
agency chief executives, 30, 133, 141,
    143, 149, 152, 153, 156, 168; *see*
    also executive agencies; Next
    Steps Initiative
Agriculture, Fisheries and Food,
    Ministry of, 18, 25, 26, 127,
    129
Anderson Committee, 60–1
Anderson, Sir John, 47, 60
Armstrong Memorandum, 16, 180,
    182
Armstrong, Sir Robert, 29, 35, 36,
    38, 42, 45, 51–3, 132, 170,
    180, 181
Armstrong, Sir William, 8, 17–18,
    20, 23, 27–8, 35, 45, 48, 50–1,
    87, 88, 90, 94, 96–7, 104, 105,
    109, 169–70, 181, 182, 194
Assheton Committee, 60, 62
Attlee, Clement, 3, 4, 12, 14, 21,
    40, 47, 48, 64–5, 66, 70, 164,
    165, 176

Bailey, Sir Alan, 193
Balogh, Thomas, 45, 85, 89
Bancroft, Sir Ian, 2, 9, 29, 40, 104
Barlow, Sir Alan, 60
Barnett, Joel, 6
Benefits Agency, 137, 139–40, 144

Benn, Tony, 2, 4, 7, 9, 25, 95, 171,
    176, 189
Berrill, Sir Kenneth, 112–13
Bevan, Aneurin, 4
Bevin, Ernest, 4, 13
Bourn, Sir John, 153
Boyd-Carpenter, John, 77
Boyle, Sir Edward, 17
Bridges, Sir Edward, 5, 18, 20, 21,
    28, 34, 44, 45–7, 48, 50, 53, 54,
    56, 65, 66–7, 70, 74, 77, 172,
    182, 194
Brittan, Leon, 166
Brook, Sir Norman, 5, 35, 44, 45,
    47–8, 49, 52, 65, 73, 74, 78–9,
    194
Brown, Sir Patrick, 40
Burns, Sir Terence, 24, 40
Butler, R. A., 22, 28, 49, 50, 77, 78
Butler, Sir Robin, 2, 10, 17, 34,
    38, 42, 53–4, 126, 132, 144,
    154, 156, 158, 167–8, 169, 180,
    181, 182

Cabinet Office, 1, 20, 21, 26–7, 41,
    49, 63, 68, 125, 132, 134, 138,
    145, 153, 155, 157
Cairncross, Sir Alec, 87
Callaghan, James, 6, 10, 24, 98, 105,
    109, 113, 175, 177
Cassels Report, 125
Central Economic Planning Staff, 69
Central Office of Information, 148

Central Policy Review Staff (CPRS),
    9, 34, 41, 53, 98, 110, 111–13
Central Statistical Office, 58
Centre for Administrative Studies,
    87, 93
Chamberlain, Neville, 27, 182
Cherwell, Lord (Professor
    Lindemann), 58, 78
Child Support Agency, 137
Churchill, Sir Winston, 4, 5, 7, 15,
    19, 22, 28, 47, 48, 57, 61, 73–4,
    78, 182
Citizen's Charter, 136, 145–8, 174,
    179
Civil Aviation Authority, 110
Civil and Public Servants'
    Association, 97
civil service, administrative class, 62,
    71, 72, 76, 89, 91–2, 98
    clerical class, 62, 71, 72, 76, 97, 98
    code of ethics, 10, 12, 179–83
    dispersal, 57, 72, 115, 126, 144
    and economic decline, 186–92
    elitism, 34, 36, 37–9, 42, 50, 84,
        92–3, 101–2, 156
    executive class, 62, 71, 72, 76, 92,
        97, 98, 101, 143
    generalists, 41, 90, 91, 92, 99–100,
        154
    industrial civil service, 70, 77, 78,
        80, 122
    industrial relations in, 104, 116–17,
        124, 126
    and management, 9, 42, 52, 53, 59,
        60, 62, 66, 72, 76, 83, 84–5,
        86, 90, 91, 94, 105–6, 128,
        129–30, 132, 133, 137, 143,
        154, 155, 193, 194
    morale in, 53, 114–15, 117, 123,
        193–4
    neutrality, 1–3, 4, 5, 6, 9–10,
        11–12, 16, 19–20, 53–4, 195
    and parliament, 59, 168–72, 180
    pay, 46, 74–5, 76–7, 115–16, 124,
        133, 142–3, 157
    politicization, 9, 10, 27–30, 193

    recruitment, 57, 59, 60, 62, 73,
        76, 87, 89, 91, 98, 101–2, 115,
        133, 143, 153–6, 158
    scientific civil service, 60, 72, 92,
        98, 191
    size of, 57, 70–1, 73, 77–80, 85,
        110, 111, 114, 122–3, 134, 157
    specialists, 62–3, 72, 73, 75–6, 85,
        92, 97, 99–100, 103
    training, 59, 60, 71, 73, 86, 87, 93,
        98, 102–3, 129–30
    unions (staff side), 60, 69, 72, 73,
        74, 76, 77, 92, 93, 94, 96, 97,
        103, 106, 110, 115–16, 122,
        124, 125, 128, 133, 140, 143,
        152, 194
    war-time 'temporaries', 6, 40, 57,
        58, 68, 192
    women in, 36–7, 73, 76–7, 115
Civil Service College, 59, 62, 65, 93,
    95, 102–3
Civil Service Commission, 60, 71, 83,
    143, 153–4, 158, 183
Civil Service Department, 44, 45, 50,
    52, 93–4, 95, 96, 98, 99, 100,
    103–5, 106, 107, 110, 114, 115,
    124–5, 181
Civil Service Selection Board, 71–2,
    101
Clarke, Kenneth, 155
Clarke, Sir Richard (Otto), 28, 86
Companies House, 134
contracting out, 126, 146, 147,
    148–53, 158, 195; *see also* market
    testing
Cook, Robin, 3
Cooper, Geoffrey, 66
Council of Civil Service Unions, 116
Cousins, Frank, 12
Crichel Down case, 116–17, 172, 181
Cripps, Sir Stafford, 4, 21, 49, 50,
    61, 69, 71
Crookshank Committee, 58, 60,
    61–2
Crossman, Richard, 7, 15, 49, 89, 91,
    95, 170, 177

Crowther-Hunt, Lord (Norman Hunt), 88, 90, 96, 101, 104
Customs and Excise, Board of, 25, 134, 147

Dale, H. E., 170,
Dalton, Hugh, 4, 21, 49
Davies Committee, 101
Davies, John, 12
Diplomatic Service, 26, 60, 87, 98, 113
Defence, Ministry of, 9, 29, 87, 128, 189, 191
Defence Procurement Executive, 111, 127
Dorrell, Stephen, 149
Dugdale, Sir Thomas, 166–7
Dunnett, Sir James, 36, 90

Ecole Nationale d'Administration, 71, 84, 93, 103
Economic Affairs, Department of, 21, 22–3, 89
Economic Section, 58, 68, 87
economists, 58, 68, 92
Eden, Sir Anthony, 5, 47, 78, 79
Education, Department for, 28, 39, 78, 87
efficiency strategy, 110, 127–8
Efficiency Unit, 127, 131, 132, 137, 138, 145, 151, 154, 157
Employment, Department of, 42, 111
Employment Services Agency, 111, 134, 137, 143
Energy, Department of, 109
Environment, Department of, 109, 111, 128, 169
Estacode, 69, 181
executive agencies, 42, 99, 107, 111, 133, 134, 136–45, 149, 151–2, 157; *see also* agency chief executives; hiving-off; Next Steps Initiative

Fabian Society, 64, 66, 85, 87, 88, 89, 109, 120, 175, 194

Fergusson, Sir Donald, 59
Financial Management Initiative (FMI), 103, 107, 126, 129–31, 132, 135
First Division Association (FDA), 85, 116, 151, 152, 180, 181, 182, 183
Fisher, Sir Warren, 27, 41, 44, 181, 182
Food, Ministry of, 78
Foot, Michael, 176
Foreign and Commonwealth Office, 4, 5, 18, 19, 25, 26, 98
Franks Committee, 175, 176
Franks, Oliver (Lord), 40, 66
Fraser, Sir Angus, 142
Fraser Report, 137–8, 144, 149
freedom of information (FoI), 142, 164, 174–9, 183, 187
Fuel and Power, Ministry of, 78
Fulton Committee, 7, 14, 39, 44, 50, 75, 85, 86, 88–108, 120, 121, 122, 129, 131, 133, 134, 140, 142, 194

Gaitskell, Hugh, 21, 50, 71
Gardiner, Sir Thomas, 59
Garlick, Sir John, 38
Garrett, John, 3–4, 90, 96, 100, 107, 116
Gater, Sir George, 40,
Government Communications Headquarters (GCHQ), 36, 52, 124
Gillmore, Sir David, 40
Gould, Bryan, 30
Griffith, James, 15

Haldane Committee, 61, 95, 109, 165
Hall, Robert, 22
Hamilton, Sir James, 39
Hankey, Lord, 72
Healey, Denis, 6, 23
Health, Department of, 4, 25, 138
Health and Social Security,

Department of, 18, 89, 124–5, 129, 170
Heath, Edward, 1, 7–8, 14, 15, 18, 20, 23, 28, 42, 48, 49, 50–1, 52, 53, 83, 97, 99, 104, 108–14, 116, 120, 121, 176, 178, 194
Heaton-Williams report, 102
Heiser, Sir Terence, 38, 126
Helsby, Sir Lawrence, 40, 85, 94
Henderson, Hubert, 68
Hennessy, Peter, 35
Heseltine, Michael, 128–9, 155
hiving-off, 94, 106, 108, 109, 110
HMSO, 134, 143, 148
Holland, Sir Geoffrey, 28
Home, Lord (Sir Alec Douglas-Home), 1, 48, 88
Home Office, 11, 18, 25, 28, 129, 138
Hopkins, Sir Richard, 63
Hoskyns, Sir John, 12, 29, 40, 154, 176, 186–7
Housing and Local Government, Ministry of, 5
Howard, Anthony, 35
Howard, Michael, 11
Hughes, Sir Trevor, 39
Hunt, Sir John, 49–50, 52, 105, 167
Hurd, Douglas, 8, 113, 155

Ibbs, Sir Robin, 107, 113, 127, 131, 132
Industry, Department of, 7, 19, 171
information technology (IT), 125–7, 140, 150, 152
Ingham, Bernard, 10
Inland Revenue, Board of, 123, 125–6, 134, 147, 173
Ismay, Lord, 47
Institution of Professional Civil Servants, 63, 92, 100

Jay, Douglas, 14, 21
Jellicoe, Lord, 99
Jenkins, Roy, 20, 23, 52, 95
Joseph, Sir Keith, 19
judical review, 173–4

Kaufman, Gerald, 142
Kemp, Sir Peter, 28, 135–6, 140, 144, 149, 155
Keynes, J. M., 68
Kinnock, Neil, 12, 29, 54

Labour, Ministry of, 62, 78
Labour Party, 1, 2–3, 5, 6, 7, 10, 12, 15, 21, 29–30, 64, 68, 89, 95, 98, 112, 122, 136, 140, 146, 156, 164–5, 173, 178
Lamont, Norman, 10
Land and Natural Resources, Ministry of, 89
Lang, Sir John, 38
Laski, Harold, 4, 36, 59, 63–4, 65, 94
Lawson, Nigel, 24, 140
Lee, Sir Frank, 19, 22
Levene, Sir Peter, 42, 149, 154
Lilley, Peter, 137
Lord Chancellor's Department, 39, 129

machinery of government, 60–1, 65, 68, 73, 74, 89, 90, 94, 97, 104, 109, 113
Macmillan, Harold, 5, 13, 14, 19, 22, 47, 48, 78, 79, 80, 86–7, 173
Major, John, 10, 11, 12, 37, 40, 120, 122, 125, 136, 140, 145, 146, 156, 179, 194, 195
Makins, Sir Roger, 5, 22, 193
Management Information System for Ministers (MINIS), 126, 128, 129
management by objectives, 94, 106
Management and Personnel Office, 125
Manpower Services Agency, 111
market testing, 136, 140, 145, 147, 148–53, 157, 195; *see also* contracting out
Mather, Graham, 147–8
Maud, Sir John, 39, 40
Middleton, Sir Peter, 24, 29, 40, 53
ministerial *cabinets*, 7, 14, 30

ministerial responsibility, 141–2, 165–8
ministers, 11, 12–14, 15, 17–18, 59, 187, 193
Morrison, Herbert, 4, 167
Mueller, Dame Anne, 144

National Audit office, 126, 172
National Economic Development Council, 87
National Insurance, Ministry of, 72
Neild, Robert, 92
Newsam, Sir Frank, 28
Newton, Tony, 137
Next Steps Initiative, 13, 30, 53, 94–5, 107, 131–45, 148–9, 153, 167, 170, 194; *see also* agency chief executives; executive agencies
Nichol, Sir Duncan, 11
Nott, Sir John, 16
Number 10 Policy Unit, 14, 112, 113, 140, 146

Office of the Minister for the Civil Service (OMCS), 125, 135
Office of Public Service and Science (OPSS), 28, 125, 135, 136, 138, 139, 157
Open Structure, 92, 98–9, 100, 154
Organization and Methods, 68
Osmotherley Rules, 166, 171
Overseas Development, Ministry of, 89, 171
Oughton Report, 154–5, 156

Parliamentary Commissioner for Administration (ombudsman), 164, 165, 166, 172–3, 179, 180
parliamentary questions, 141, 169–70
Part, Sir Antony, 20, 28
Passport Agency, 139
Patten, John, 28
Pay Research Unit, 75
Pirie, Madsen, 147
planning units, 95, 98, 106

Plowden Committee, 86, 95
Plowden, Lord, 22, 86, 87
poll tax, 9, 30
Ponting, Clive, 178, 179, 180, 183
Powell, Enoch, 88
Priestley Commission, 74–5, 115–16, 194
Prime Minister's Statistical Section, 15, 58
Prison Service Agency, 137
private offices, 41, 42
privatization, 140, 145, 146, 149, 195
Programme Analysis and Review (PAR), 109–10, 113
Property Services Agency, 111, 123, 148
Public Accounts Committee, 66, 139, 141, 152–3, 171–2

Radice, Giles, 136, 156
Rayner, Sir Derek, 105, 110, 111, 125, 127–8, 130, 131
Recruitment and Assessment Services agency, 153
Rees, Merlyn, 177
Ridley, Nicholas, 8, 133
Robbins, Lionel, 68
Robertson, Dennis, 68
Robinson, Sir Percival, 66
Rothschild, Lord, 111, 150, 192
Royal Ordnance Factories, 110, 123

Sandys, Duncan, 5
Scott Inquiry, 54, 169, 183
secrecy, 174–9
Senior Appointments Selection Committee (SASC), 46, 155
Sharp, Dame Evelyn, 5, 35, 36, 65
Sheldon, Robert, 99
Shinwell, Emanuel, 15
Shore, Peter, 95
Smieton, Dame Mary, 36
Smith, John, 10, 12, 136, 181
Social Security, Department of, 125, 126, 138, 173
Society of Civil Servants, 97

Sparrow, John, 113
special advisers, 14–15, 113
Spycatcher affair, 36, 51, 178
Stevas, Norman St John, 170
Strachan, Valerie, 36
Supply, Ministry of, 40, 78, 192

Tebbit, Norman, 18
Technology, Ministry of, 18, 28,
    89, 192
Thatcher, Margaret, 3, 8–10, 12,
    14, 18, 19, 24, 28–9, 40, 42, 44,
    47, 52–3, 89–90, 97, 99, 103–4,
    107–8, 110, 113, 114, 116, 117,
    120–5, 127, 129, 131, 132, 133,
    135, 138–9, 140, 146, 165, 176,
    179–80, 182, 193, 194, 195
Tisdall, Sarah, 178
Tomlin Commission, 74, 94
Trade and Industry, Department of,
    10, 12, 18–19, 25, 28, 109, 114,
    124, 138, 140, 148, 189, 190
Transport, Department of, 109, 138
Treasury, 4, 6, 9, 10, 17–18, 19,
    20–5, 29, 41, 44–5, 51, 59, 61,
    62, 63, 65, 68, 69–70, 71, 73,
    74, 77, 79, 85, 86, 87, 88, 89,
    92, 93–4, 95, 100, 104–5, 106,
    108–9, 110, 112, 114, 116, 123,
    125, 130, 132, 143, 147, 148,
    157, 186, 188, 189–90, 191,
    192, 194
Treasury and Civil Service
    Committee, 3, 42, 45, 129, 136,
    139, 141, 158, 167
Trend, Sir Burke, 6, 45–6, 48–50

Trosa Report, 138

UKREP, 26

Vandepeer, Sir Donald, 38
Vansittart, Lord, 6, 27, 35
Vehicle Inspectorate, 134, 139

Waldegrave, William, 28, 135–6, 145,
    148, 149, 151, 152, 169, 179, 182
Walker, Peter, 109
Walters, Alan, 24
Wass, Sir Douglas, 24, 29, 34–5, 44,
    52, 77, 180–1
Waterfield, Sir Percival, 59, 62
Way, Sir Richard, 38
Welsh Office, 89
Whitley Council, 69, 75, 77, 97, 116
Whitmore, Sir Clive, 11, 29, 40, 42
Wider Issues Review Team, 115
Wilding, Richard, 107
Williams, Marcia, 6
Williams, Shirley, 6, 18, 20
Wilson, Harold, 1, 2, 6–7, 13, 14, 22,
    42, 48, 49, 52, 53, 83, 85, 88, 89,
    90, 94, 95, 96, 97, 108, 109, 113,
    114, 121, 176
Wilson, Sir Horace, 27, 35, 48, 51,
    63
Wilson, Richard, 39
Woolton, Lord, 39
Working Patterns report, 144
Wyndham, John, 14

Young, Lord, 12